RACE, MULTICULTURE AND SOCIAL

GW01458437

Race, Multiculture and Social Policy

Alice Bloch

Sarah Neal

John Solomos

palgrave
macmillan

First published 2013 by
PALGRAVE MACMILLAN

Palgrave Macmillan in the UK is an imprint of Macmillan Publishers Limited, registered in England, company number 785998, of Houndmills, Basingstoke, Hampshire RG21 6XS.

Palgrave Macmillan in the US is a division of St Martin's Press LLC, 175 Fifth Avenue, New York, NY 10010.

Palgrave Macmillan is the global academic imprint of the above companies and has companies and representatives throughout the world.

Palgrave® and Macmillan® are registered trademarks in the United States, the United Kingdom, Europe and other countries

ISBN: 978–0–333–74972–2 paperback

This book is printed on paper suitable for recycling and made from fully managed and sustained forest sources. Logging, pulping and manufacturing processes are expected to conform to the environmental regulations of the country of origin.

A catalogue record for this book is available from the British Library.

A catalog record for this book is available from the Library of Congress.

10 9 8 7 6 5 4 3 2 1
22 21 20 19 18 17 16 15 14 13

Printed in China

For Brock, Nikolas, Daniel and Rachel

Contents

List of Illustrations

Tables

Figures

Preface

This book is a systematic effort to explore the evolution and impact of policies that address questions about race, ethnicity and multiculture in British society. All of these arenas have been the subject of much debate and controversy for a number of decades now, in terms of both public-media discourses as well as academic scholarship and research. Over the past decade, in particular, there has been a noticeable growth of interest in this broad area, often linked to studies of policy agendas about issues such as community cohesion, cultural and ethnic diversity, religious diversity and racial inequality. Much of the academic literature that has followed on this growth of interest has been framed around detailed empirical studies of specific policy arenas or on locally focused case studies. There has been a notable lack of systematic attempts to provide a critical synthesis of wider trends and processes, of the social and political transformations that have shaped social policies about multiculture and the impact of shifts in ideologies about multiculturalism.

In putting our efforts together to produce this volume we have sought to write a book that self-consciously aims to remedy this situation in two ways. The first way is through providing a theoretically informed but empirically focused analysis of the ways in which social policies about race and ethnicity emerged and helped to shape politics and social policy more broadly since the 1960s. The second focus of this volume is on the detailed and systematic analysis of core arenas of social policies in relation to increasingly complex questions of race, racism, ethnicity and difference in contemporary British society. By writing this book in the way that we have, we aim to provide a way of thinking about social policy interventions in this field that is both wide ranging and focused on specific policy arenas at the same time.

In writing a book such as this we have inevitably drawn on the support and advice of a wide range of friends and colleagues, including: Claire Alexander, Suki Ali, Leah Bassel, Annette Braun, Martin Bulmer, Kirsten Campbell, Milena Chimienti, Allan Cochrane, Patricia Hill Collins, John Clarke, Michael Keith, Marco Martiniello, Karim Murji, Kate Nash, Liza Schuster, Stephen Small, Carol Vincent, Satnam Virdee and Frank Webster. We are also grateful to Palgrave Macmillan for their long and patient wait for this volume, and in particular to Catherine Gray for starting us off and seeing the book through its final stages, and to Esther Croom and Anna Reeve who encouraged us along the way. To all of you we say a big thank you, and express the hope that they – and others – will find something of interest in this effort to provide a critical overview of the relationship between policy, race and multiculture in contemporary British society.

Acknowledgements

The authors and publisher wish to thank the following for permission to reproduce copyright material:

The Copyright Unit, Her Majesty's Stationary Office
  http://www.nationalarchives.gov.uk/doc/open-government-licence /open-government-licence.htm
  Adapted Table 8.1, from Rendall, M. and Salt, J. 'The Foreign-Born Population', in Chappell, R. (ed.) *Focus on People and Migration*, Basingstoke: Palgrave Macmillan, 2005.
  Zig Layton-Henry for Table 1.1, from Layton-Henry, Z. *The Politics of Immigration: Immigration, 'Race' and 'Race' Relations in Post-war Britain*, Oxford: Blackwell, 1992
  The Copyright Unit, Her Majesty's Stationary Office
  http://www.nationalarchives.gov.uk/doc/open-government-licence/open-government-licence.htm
  Adapted from Table 1.1, Summary Statistics, *Asylum Statistics 1999*, London: Home Office, 2000.
  Wiley Blackwell for an adpated version of Table 58.1, from Alcock, P., May, M., and Wright, S. (eds) *The Student's Companion to Social Policy*, Oxford: Wiley Blackwell, 2012.
  The Copyright Unit, Her Majesty's Stationary Office
  http://www.nationalarchives.gov.uk/doc/open-government-licence /open-government-licence.htm)
  Table 4.1 is adapted from Table S116: Tenure by ethnic group of household reference person 2008.
  Table 4.2 is adapted from Table S119: Trends in tenure 1984–2007: Ethnic group of household reference person 2008.
  Mark Johnson for Table 6.1, from Johnson, M. Johnson, M., Biggerstaff, D., Clay, D., Collins, G., Gumbar, A., Hamilton, M., Jones, K. and Szczepura, A. *'Racial' and Ethnic Inequalities in Health: A Critical Review of the Evidence* Draft Report to the Home Office, Coventry: University of Warwick, Centre for Evidence in Ethnicity Health and Diversity, 2004
  The Department for Education, Crown Copyright
  (http://www.nationalarchives.gov.uk/doc/open-government-licence /open-government-licence.htm)
  Table 7.1 is adapted from Statistical First Release 37–2010 Summary: Achievements at GCSE and equivalent for pupils at the end of Key Stage 4 by pupil characteristics

The Copyright Unit, Her Majesty's Stationary Office (http://www.nationalarchives.gov.uk/doc/open-government-licence)

Table 8.5; Table 8.6 and adapted versions of Table 8.3 and 8.4 from Heath, A. and Cheung, S.Y. *Ethnic Penalties in the Labour Market: Employers and Discrimination* London: Department for Work and Pensions, 2006

The Copyright Unit, Her Majesty's Stationary Office

http://www.nationalarchives.gov.uk/doc/open-government-licence/open-government-licence.htm

Table 6.10, from Bloch, A. *Refugees, Opportunities and Barriers in Training and Employment* Leeds: Department for Work and Pensions, Research Report Number 179, 2002

Part I
Politics and Policy

Chapter 1

Multiculture, Race and Social Change

At the beginning of the 21st century, as the UK becomes increasingly multicultural, ethnic difference, cultural diversity and ideas of race have become more complex, contested and uncertain. As the most recent census (Office of National Statistics 2012) data show, England and Wales have never been more multiethnically constituted. For example, data released by the Office of National Statistics (2011) reveal that while the white British population has not changed significantly the non-white British population has increased from 6.6 million in 2001 to 9.1 million in 2009. In the same period there have been significant increases in 'mixed ethnicity' populations and in the 'white other' populations that have developed as a result of new migrations, particularly from Eastern Europe.

Not only has the ethnic profile of the country been changing rapidly, so too have the geographies of ethnicity. The most recent data show that nowhere in England and Wales is the population a 100 per cent white British (Office of National Statistics 2012). These geographies are uneven with some areas being less ethnically mixed and others more ethnically mixed – for example, 96 per cent of the population of Powys, in Wales, are white British, while only 51 per cent of the populations of Haringey in London and Leicester are white British. But the overall pattern is of multicultural populations being widely dispersed across a broader geography of England in particular, but also in Scotland and Wales. In this book we refer only to the UK or Britain where it is possible to make general points across the whole territory, both because the devolved polity of the UK means that policy may vary between England, Northern Ireland, Scotland and Wales and also because the extent and nature of multiculture is highly varied across the geographies of urban settlement in Britain. Not only is the UK becoming an ever more multicultural society but the emergent forms of multiculture are more complex, contradictory and fluid than what seems to be imagined in the dominant policy and political language used in current debates about multiculture.

Over the past decade, a series of shifts has had a profound impact on the geographies and compositions of multiculture. Alongside social, economic, and generational diversification among established black and minority ethnic (BME) groups (McGarrigle and Kearns 2009), recent migration has generated a highly diverse social and cultural mix (Vertovec 2007; Cheong et al. 2007; Goulbourne et al. 2010; Perry 2008). The 1991, 2001 and 2011 censuses show that the dominant trend is the dispersal of BME populations (Finney and Simpson 2009; Simpson and Peach 2009). The socio-economic diversity that characterises both traditional BME *and* new migrant populations is mirrored in diverse geographies of settlement with some suburbanisation of established BME groups (Poulsen and Johnston 2008; Sabater 2008) and the settlement of new migrant populations in rural areas and smaller urban centres, as well as in areas associated with ethnic diversity (Neal et al. 2013).

What these social and spatial shifts in current multicultural formations mean – and how they manifest themselves in ongoing political discourses, patterns of social exclusion and inclusion, policy interventions and personal lives – are concerns which preoccupy academic debates (Lentin and Titley 2011; Hansen 2007; McGhee 2008; Mirza, Senthkumaran and Ja'far 2007). They also underpin many of the key themes that run through this book, which is framed around the need to explore the evolving policy and social debates around race and multiculture in contemporary British society.

While never straightforward as a set of concepts/identifications/practices/processes, multiculture and race demand an analytical frame that is multifactored, nuanced and multidimensional. This has become even more important for two key reasons: first, the 'super diversity' (Vertovec 2007) of emergent multicultural formations in many urban environments and second, the recent 'post-race' debates which have raised critical questions as to the continued use of the category race. So, before moving on to introduce the policy arenas that form the substantive basis of Part II of this book, we want to reflect, in this chapter, on aspects of the wider processes and patterns that have led to the current configurations of multiculture in the UK and take some time to examine the meanings of race and multiculture and clarify how the book engages with these.

Changing context of race in 21st century – a multicultural conjuncture?

The discourse of crisis

During the first part of the 21st century the questions outlined above have become more sharply focused through a series of traumatic and dramatic events in and beyond the UK. The first decade of the 21st century was framed by disorder and riots that had race and multiculture as central features, albeit in very different ways. This included unrest in Northern England in 2001, unrest across English cities and small towns in 2011, and terrorist attacks in London and in cities and places across the world. In England, the riots in England's Pennine towns in 2001 were the first of such events since

the 1980s. They came at a time when the murder of the South London teenager Stephen Lawrence and the subsequent Macpherson inquiry and report,
with its identification of 'institutional racism' as a core problem to be tack-
led within policing and criminal justice systems, seemed to mark something
of a turning point in the politics of race in the UK (see Chapter 2). In this
context, the intensity of the political, media and policy analysis as to why
the 2001 riots had taken place was significant as it tended, overwhelmingly,
to focus on notions of cultural difference and the cultural withdrawal of
members of these towns' Muslim communities as a core explanatory factor
(Amin 2002; Husband and Alam 2011; Phillips 2006b). While we return to
this in later chapters the point we wish to stress here is that the 2001 disorders saw an emphasis on ethnic polarisation rather than social division,
and the development of cohesion centred policy responses (see Cantle 2001;
Chapter 2).

A political and policy emphasis on cohesion

The policy and political move towards cohesion and culturalist agendas was
intensified as the events in the UK were engulfed in global events; the attacks
in New York and Washington in 2001; the bombings in Bali in 2003; the
Gulf War and the 'war on terror'; race riots in Paris in 2005 and the bombings in London in 2005. Although each of these events was politically distinct and born out of a particular set of dynamics, they could nevertheless
be connected and bundled together into a broad and rather imprecise, but
nonetheless potent, process that was seen as reflecting a 'crisis of multiculture' and the failure of populations to live with and 'easily' experience and
encounter cultural difference.

It is in this context that commentators, politicians and policymakers leant
towards culturalist models in which segregation and cultural division preoccupied public debate. For example, in 2005 Trevor Phillips, who was at
the time Chair of the Commission for Racial Equality, warned that Britain
was 'sleep walking its way to segregation' and that, 'we are becoming strangers to each other, and we are leaving communities to be marooned outside the mainstream' (Phillips 2005a). While he was later to retract this
comment, what is significant about the Phillips' 'sleepwalking speech' is the
degree of public attention it received and, the way in which the specific
worry of segregated populations as voiced by such commentators as Ted
Cantle, Herman Ouseley and Trevor Phillips appeared to offer such a per-
suasive sense-making architecture for social relations despite the emergence
of increasingly heterogeneous forms of multiculture.

Community cohesion and identification with British culture were heavily stressed in the aftermath of the London bombings in July 2005. Four
years earlier, in relation to his concerns about forms of thin cohesion and

'self-segregation', Cantle (2001: 18) had warned that 'Britain, like almost all countries, has been affected by globalisation and is now host to communities for whom concerns about their country of origin can be refreshed daily. In these circumstances, strategies for making them feel at home, rather than as reluctant exiles, need to be established.' As Ann-Marie Fortier (2007) notes, this reflected a new emphasis on binding black, minority ethnic and migrant populations to the national project in geographically local and culturally conditional ways. After the London bombings, increased anxiety about the 'outside' sympathies and the diasporic belongings of migrant communities referred to by Cantle, meant that the cohesion agenda, alongside increased security concerns, became further consolidated as the dominant social policy approach to diversity.

This was evidenced by the setting up of the Commission of Cohesion and Integration in 2006 which was tasked to conduct a 12-month examination and report on 'the issues that raise tensions between different groups in different areas [...] how local community and political leadership can push further against perceived barriers to cohesion and integration [...] how communities themselves can be empowered to tackle extremist ideologies [and] develop approaches that build local areas' own capacity to prevent problems and ensure they have the structures in place to recover from periods of tension' (Commission on Integration and Cohesion 2007: 17). While the story of the Commission and its final report *Our Shared Future* is discussed in Chapter 2, it is worth noting here that the Commission argued against a focus on residentially based 'self-segregation' and instead placed an emphasis on locality, social resiliance and the ethics of hospitality (Keith 2008). This is evident in the Foreword to *Our Shared Future*,

> A strong theme running through this report is that place matters and that all localities have unique qualities. This does mean that a one size fits all range of solutions cannot be prescribed from a national level. It also means that a new social contract between citizen and government needs to be developed at local, regional and national levels. The challenges facing different areas and therefore the solutions will be influenced by a range of factors, including histories of migration and settlement, levels of poverty and wealth, de-industrialisation and the current population profile. We strongly believe in tailored and bespoke local activity to build integration and cohesion.
>
> As a Commission we have been struck by the remarkable level of commitment that is focused on building stronger and better communities. From a spectrum of individual actions to those organised by the voluntary sector, faith organisations and Local Authorities the range of activity is impressive. The local focus of work moves forward in the context of a national government commitment to integration and cohesion. This is a welcome mosaic of activity and one that needs to be built upon, supported and enabled to make an even greater impact.

The most valuable contribution though comes from all of us as local citizens. Yes it is true that government – local and central – is essential to the mix of activity. It is also the case that the third sector is critical. However, it is through millions of small everyday actions that we can all either improve or harm our local communities. (Commission on Integration and Cohesion 2007b: 4–5)

What is striking about *Our Shared Future* is not only its careful attempt to manage the mainstream political demands for strategies for the effective governance of multiculture and address the complexities of multiscale (local, national, transnational, global) geographies and diverse neighbourhoods in the UK through locally based policy recommendations, but also the Report's sustained stress on the importance of the everyday interactions and processes of 'becoming'. As Michael Keith, a member of the Commission, argues, 'the complexity of local realisations of contemporary multiculture confounds attempts to characterise a singular understanding of British multiculturalism at the level of nation (2008: 197). He goes on to highlight the contradictions of urban multiculture in that it can deliver both entrenched conflict and transformative exchanges. For Keith, some of this tension gets diffused in the routine and day-to-day because 'we get by in the rub, in the everyday world, because the abstract contradictions of the communitarian and the liberal are subsumed in the everyday' (Keith 2008: 198).

The emphasis on cohesion and, more recently, on integration policy approaches is on community, locality, cultural interaction, participation and shared identity. But, as many commentators have pointed out, the responsibility for this agenda appears to be placed particularly on migrant and BME communities (see Chapter 2 for a full discussion). While the Commission for Integration and Cohesion (2007a: 27) rejected the arguments about increasing cultural withdrawal and the focus on segregation, describing this as a 'red herring', the discourse of segregation has continued to hold a tenacious place in public, policy and academic debates and is used as a frame and descriptor of the current state of multiculture in England and Wales despite the evidence that the dominant trend is towards the residential dispersal and diversity. Much of the segregation and crisis discourses focus, implicitly and explicitly, on Muslim populations, and the engagement of the media – local and national – with these issues have delivered mediated representations of 'ethnic conflict', segregation and extremism – for example Bradford being described as 'Britain's Islamabad' (Carling 2008: 553) and as 'Britain's unofficial racist capital' (*Observer* 15, 2002) – which work to disseminate the crisis and conflict discourse. As Chapters 4 and 5 on housing and education seek to demonstrate, ethnic segregation and cultural mixing continue to be a key feature in policy debates.

Arguments about evidence and multiculture

Academic research and writing has similarly provided a site of contestation around claims of crisis, cultural withdrawal and ethnic segregation. It is worth noting that Trevor Phillips' sleepwalking speech was made on the basis of the (mis)reading of academic data (Johnston, Poulsen and Forrest 2010), and in a long-running debate in the academic journal *Urban Studies* Bradford became a much argued-over city. While occurring in an academic environment, Alan Carling's(2008) paper and the response to it from Ludi Simpson, Charles Husband and Yunus Alam (2009) in *Urban Studies* evidence the highly charged political nature of segregation debates. Carling's controversial paper focuses on ethnic residential patterns in Bradford and describes the evidence of ethnic segregation as 'clear' and suggests that this segregation can be understood not only through structural factors but more provocatively through a choice process of 'self-segregation'. However, as. Poulsen and Johnston (2008) suggest, Census data for Bradford reveals rather contradictory and uneven residency and ethnicity patterns. For example, they note that the enumeration districts (EDs) of Bradford that were mixed rose from 152 in 1991 to 163 in 2001, predominantly white EDs fell from 617 in 1991 to 553 in 2001 and EDs that were exclusively South Asian were 0 in both 1991 and 2001.

However, Carling argues that those researchers who suggest that these shifts reflect a decline in monocultural segregation purposely overlook the statistics that show that in 1991 EDs that were predominantly South Asian rose from 29 to 77 by 2001 (Carling 2008: 558). For Carling, challenging the arguments made by quantitative and qualitative researchers that segregation and self-segregation are 'politically charged myths' is central. The paper is concerned not so much with residency patterns but, like Cantle and Ouseley, with the social separations rooted in (antagonistic) cultural differences. So while Carling argues that ethnic residential segregation can be identified in Bradford, he also proceeds to raise a series of questions about what dangers ethnic clustering present for Bradford's wider stability. The need for more research is regularly noted in Carling's paper and this does emphasise the speculative nature of some of his suggestions. For example, the paper discusses the possibility of white far-right politics *and* Islamic jihad fundamentalist politics increasingly thriving in the city, reinforcing volatile and entrenched ethnic polarisations.

In their response to Carling's article, Simpson, Husband and Alam argue that Carling's work 'fits within the wider discourse preoccupied with ethno-cultural conflict' (2009: 2000) and suggest that while 'some de-facto ethnic segregation' is to be expected this does not need to be viewed as apocalyptic, 'inherently problematic' or permanent in urban locations that are always engaged in processes of change. In addition, it seems important to acknowledge that such segregation patterns are likely to exist in relation to class and economic factors and to avoid over or even total ethnicisation. As Simpson, Husband and Alam note, 'to focus on ethnicity and faith and propose that they are somehow inherently dangerous and damaging, arguably says more about contemporary politics than it does about those who live within and across contemporary social spaces' (Simpson, Husband and Alam 2009: 2000).

The *Urban Studies* debate exemplifies the ways in which preoccupations with notions of segregation and crisis extend beyond public and policy spheres. The exchange also illustrates the contested segregation data and arguments in academic and research worlds. In this context segregation and notions of multicultural crisis have been challenged and countered by academics, researchers and some in the policy community, who have suggested that it is important to recognise that in contexts of super-diversity and increasing cultural difference there is much more interaction, dialogue and engagement between members of diverse populations in everyday environments – for example in work, in residential areas, in school, on public transport, in parks, at the doctor's surgeries, in the local shop – that are not always antagonistic and may even be amicable and unpanicked.

A focus on quotidian multiculture

Cultural geographer Ash Amin has suggested that the local and the 'prosaic' micro-social worlds in which people live need attention because 'much of the negotiation of difference occurs at the very local level through everyday experiences and encounters' (Amin 2002: 959). Amin's central argument is that by paying attention to everyday interactions and small routine encounters that take place when living with cultural difference, the socio-cultural divisions may be better understood and reconciled (See Gilroy 2004; Wessendorf 2012; Wise 2009). While Amin recognises the limitations of what may be no more than what he calls 'endless talk amongst adversaries', what his paper suggests is an alternate frame not only for encountering, describing and living intense cultural difference but also for transcending it. In other words, cultural difference and ethnic diversity do not always lead to conflict and ethnic polarisation. Rather ethnically mixed populations can become adept and skilled in negotiating and managing cultural difference and may potentially be changed by proximities and engagements with difference (Gilroy 2004).

As can be seen from our discussion of the *Our Shared Future* report, aspects of these arguments find echoes in the cohesion policy approaches. For example, in the London Borough of Hackney, the third most diverse borough in England and Wales, the Hackney Community Cohesion Review Report (2010) found little evidence of hostility and conflict based on

ethnicity. The cultural diversity of the borough was overwhelmingly posi-
tively commented on by residents surveyed in the review. Described as resilient and used to multiculture, the Hackney Cohesion Review worried less
about its ethnic diversity and more about the borough's social and economic polarisations (see Chapters 4 and 5 for further discussion). The raising of other structural lines of social division – social and economic status,
gender, education status, migration status, locality and so forth – and the
relational interaction of these with race, ethnicity and multiculture is very
much at the heart of this book.

What the arguments about the need to pay attention to what has been
called quotidian or 'everyday multiculture' (Neal et al. 2013; Wise 2009) do
is first, put place and geographies at the heart of debates about multiculture, ethnicity and racism. While these geographies tend to be overwhelmingly urban they also include newer and neglected spaces of multicultural
settlement – small cities and large towns, suburbs and rural spaces for
example. Second these perspectives stress the always negotiated and the
always 'becoming' nature of multicultural formations. Third, the focus on
the everyday means that majoritised ethnicities and other forms of difference and division become visible and addressed. In this way white, majority populations and other social stratifications can be incorporated within
the everyday multiculture focus (see for example Clayton 2009; Nayak
2008; Rogaly and Taylor 2009). The importance of recognising the relational nature of cultural difference, that is, cultural difference shapes and
is shaped by class, gender, migration status, length of residency, education
status, age and religion, is crucial.

As contemporary multicultural formations become more complex and
as more populations become more ethnically heterogenous the emphasis
on dialogue and encounter,also has to take into account the ways in which
other variables impact on social relationships. Making this point and drawing on his work in the multicultural city of Leicester, John Clayton (2009:
265) warns that 'knowledge of and physical co-presence with those seen as
different is no guarantee of progressive relations, particularly for those in
fragile economic and social positions who have not accrued the social and
cultural capital required to deal with such encounters. There is then a need
to address the terms on which such encounters take place, the power relations involved and the experiences brought into these situations.'

The importance of the relationality of ethnicity with other social axes and
their temporal nature is evidenced in Irina Kudenko and Deborah Phillips'
(2009) study of the changes in the Jewish population in Leeds. This study
shows first, the heterogeneity – social, economic, spatial and generational –
of the Jewish population in Leeds and second, the tendency for there to be
a direct correlation between the articulation of segregation discourses and
the extent of deprivation and poverty within the problematised population.

In other words, as the Jewish communities in the city have become more middle class, local cultural and religious anxieties have diminished.

Clayton (2009) and Kudenko and Phillips (2009) provide different reminders of why it is not possible to look at race and multiculture in isolation, as cut off from other sets of social relations. In many ways the riots that took place in England in 2011 illuminate some of the multidimensional relationships and shifting complexities of race and multiculture that we have been discussing (Murji and Neal 2011; Solomos 2011). While the 2001 disorders in Northern England were predominantly explained through culturalist factors and ethnic withdrawal, the explanatory discourses for the 2011 riots have been much more unstable – moving from and between themes of criminality, moral nihilism, social breakdown, gangs and lawlessness to themes of social exclusion, hopelessness and the anomic consequences of a consumerist and materialist society.

Race has been – and then not been – at the centre of post-riot political and policy responses. This race/not race couplet reflects older race discourses alongside some of the newer complexities of multiculture. Thus, the 2011 riots have been partially *racialised* because the events in North London most visibly involved young African-Caribbean men and the wider African-Caribbean community and because the unrest that was used as a reference point was the disorders of the 1980s rather than the disorders of 2001. For example, race was a topic that was present in David Starkey's BBC *Newsnight* interview, in which he made his widely criticised claim that it was African-Caribbean culture and, crucially, its appeal to a wider constituency of young people that was the root of the disorder.

But the 2011 riots have been harder to straightforwardly read as being about race. On one level, there was a process of *deracialisation* because of the mixed ethnic composition of the riots and the visible involvement of young white men. This deracialisation also had a spatial component in that the riots happened in unracialised or only selectively racialised geographies. So for example, the status of Ealing, a relatively affluent London suburb with a significant South Asian origin population, read 'differently' to the riotous 'gang culture' associated with those less-affluent areas of North London with significant African-Caribbean origin populations. On another level, the complexity of race as a narrative of the riots, and the super-diverse nature of urban England was apparent in the riots in London and Birmingham. The self-defense campaigns by shopkeepers such as the Turkish communities in Dalston and Green Lanes, in North London and in Southall, West London were, for example, viewed as heroic instances of community action and/or slightly suspicious vigilante action happening in a vacuum created by the police operating in full emergency response mode.

The disorders provided insight into the extent and depth of the super-diversity of England's urban spaces in which rioters, victims, bystanders, youth workers, commentators and residents were multicultural and heterogeneous. This was acknowledged by the Cameron administration which stated that 'these were not race riots. The perpetrators and victims of the disturbances were from a wide range of backgrounds, as were the local residents who came together afterwards to clean up their streets' (Department for Communities and Local Government 2012: 4). As Chapter 8 discusses, the 1981 disturbances in Toxteth, Liverpool and Brixton had also involved people from white and black local populations (Kettle and Hodges 1982). However, this ethnic mix was largely marginalised as race, read as black, became *the* coordinate through which that unrest was positioned and explained. Thirty years on, while the 2011 riots drew on the 1980s riots as their antecedent, the social and spatial complexity of cultural difference and ethnic diversity in England militated against those older and 'totalising' race discourses.

We have spent some time mapping the shifts and changing nature of race and multiculture at the beginning of the 21st century. Over-simplified, crisis-centred preoccupations with cultural difference and notions of segregation have in particular dominated public discourses and anxieties as the social and spatial formations of multiculture have become more intense, more diverse and more spatially dispersed. We have suggested that policy interventions have been part of this crisis process – responding to these anxieties but also contributing to them and we discuss this further in the next chapter. In this context we have argued that a focus on 'everyday' or quotidian multiculture is important because it problematises the claims that there is increasing ethnic segregation and highlights multidimensional social relations, social mixing and interaction across cultural difference.

This is an important story when official cohesion and integration policy discourse is formulated through an idea of bringing ethnoculturally 'separated' people together through locality and neighbourhood on the one hand and an insistence on a subscription to conditional, 'one nation' multiculturalism on the other. Such policy discourses do not emerge from political ether but from turbulent and heavily mediated political contexts which are shaped by high-profile crisis events such as riots and terrorism, or more 'creeping crisis' events such as the mainstream political pronouncements (e.g. Trevor Phillips' comments on segregation (Phillips 2005b) and David Cameron's declaration in 2011 (Cameron 2011) that 'under the doctrine of state multiculturalism we have encouraged different cultures to live separate lives, apart from each other and apart from the mainstream') and the electoral successes of the far right. Emphasising the importance of everyday multiculture is not about presenting 'warm glow' accounts of social mixing and cultural inclusivity. There are profound limitations as to what affective and informal processes of social interaction are able to deliver and counter. Such limitations are a reminder of the need to attend to relations of power and social division, processes of cultural defensiveness and the ways in which the formal policy agendas and interventions that are part of these.

But in this account of a multicultural conjuncture and a context of the changing and emergent formations of diverse multiculture, what do concepts of *multiculture* and *race* mean and why and how are we using them in this book?

Race, post-race and multiculture

We use the concept of multiculture to both capture and describe the complex diversity of social and spatial relations in the UK. This complex diversity has accumulated through the global, national and local migration of ethnically different populations during the latter-half of the 20th century and intensified in the early decade of the 21st century. The concept of multiculture describes environments and populations made up of multiple ethnicities but multiculture also emphasises hybrid and mixed cultural identities where *all* cultural boundaries are imprecise, unstable and blurred as people constantly move across and negotiate between cultures and ethnic identifications (Back 1996; Gidley 2013; Gilroy 2004; Hall 2012). Like the related concept of super-diversity, multiculture works as shorthand for the hetereogeneity that characterises contemporary urban populations. In this way the concept of multiculture is very different and distinct from the concept of multiculturalism. As Chapter 2 details, multiculturalism was primarily developed as a policy approach in which one or two different cultures associated with migration were seen as needing to be recognised and understood alongside the majority culture.

Given the increasing heterogeneity of current UK populations it is something of a paradox that it has been 'old' anxieties about ethnic segregation that have dominated public and policy discourses in England and Wales at the beginning of the 21st century. Closely associated with segregation, the concept of race also resonates with a past world. In the contexts of increasing multiculture and ethnic diversity that we have discussed above, how can race – as a social category – be understood and what is its role in continuing to shape social relationships and social policymaking processes?

The 19th-and 20th-century use of race as a biologically based and hierarchical categorisaton of humans has been discredited over the last five decades and is now generally and widely recognised as being without scientific basis although there is still some debate as to natural genetic profiles (Bernasconi and Lott 2000; Malik 2008). The physical differences that are visible and not so visible amongst the populations are made meaningful and significant not because they exist – which they do – but because their existence has become socially and politically inscribed and coded. Skin, in particular, but also hair texture, head shape, eye shape, faces and bodies, have been a fetishistic focus of traditional race thinking. It is this idea of race as a social and political construction that has meaning in specific environments and contexts that we tend to work with in the course of the arguments we develop in this book. Framed in this way, race can be seen as a set of ideas and institutional practices that help to shape wider sets of social, political and cultural relations (Goldberg 2008; 2010).

However, an absence of a conceptual consensus is very much part of the continuing power of race. Far from falling into disuse the late-20th century moral, political and, by and large, scientific rejection of race has not meant the disappearance of race just as it has not meant the end of racism or the processes of racialisation. Its continuing force relates to the cultural recoding of race and to its continuing influence as a political, social and cultural effect with a range of social, economic, cultural and political outcomes (Swanton 2008). By cultural recoding we refer to the ways in which the social and cultural identities and practices become hierarchically attached to ethnically different populations. In other words the old biological lexicon of categorising and hierarchically fixing populations has collapsed in sets of cultural ordering.

This has intensified as ethnicity has become a more widely used and preferred social category to race and as ethnic identifications have increased and diversified, globally and within the UK as the extended 2011 Census Ethnic classifications evidenced (Aspinall 2009). However, this has also meant that there are convergences between race and ethnicity and that they are used – and work – in interchangeable ways. Like race ethnicity can also be essentialised and imagined – and constructed – as primordial, fixed, inherited and bounded (Hall 2000). Ethnicity also has to be viewed with caution and with recognition of its social basis and 'made up-ness' (Fenton 2003; Jenkins 2008; Neal 2009). In this context assumptions and stereotypes about cultural and ethnic difference – some with historical and colonial imprints and others that are newer and emergent – shape and effect social relations in profound ways. Some of these processes were discussed in the previous section and will be discussed in the chapters to follow. Invariably – but to varying extents – these interact with other axes of social difference and social, economic, political and geographical contexts.

In this way race, as a social construct with social effects and outcomes, can be understood as a strange paradox of being both 'fictive' in that there is no such thing as race and 'real' in that race has systematic social impacts reflected in lines of social division; driving processes of discrimination and racialisation and shaping patterns of disadvantage and exclusion. In other words, race as a social category has adapted, mutated and developed from the colonial settings of the 19th and 20th centuries to the post-colonial, globalised and multicultural settings of the 21st century. It has old and new features and can be plural and singular. It works to inform and shape new racisms as ethnic difference gets differently racialised – in the context of the UK we can see these in the hostile and racialised responses to some white Eastern European migrants (Erel 2011; Hickman, Cowley and Mai 2008); in the rise of anti-asylum seeker and refugee discourses (Chapter 3); in the different responses to the 2001 (cultural withdrawal) and 2011 riots (criminality and gang culture) in England and to the emergence of what Husband and Alam (2011) have described as 'anti-Muslimism' as a way of capturing the systematic and structurally embedded vilification of Muslim populations (see Chapters 2 and 8).

With this in mind we have used race as a social category of analysis in our examination of the relationship between multiculture and social policy formations and interventions. We do this by explicitly tagging race as 'fictive', 'social', 'situational', 'relational' and 'fluid'. We are also aware of Anoop Nayak's (Nayak 2006: 414) observation, in an echo of Paul Gilroy's (2000) indictment of the continuing use of the concept of race in social theory, that there is an 'inherent paradigmatic tension in social constructionist approaches to race. This involves the tendency to view race as socially constituted on the one hand, yet to continually impart ontological value to it on the other, with the effect that race can take a reified status'.

Writing as part of an emergent debate about the possibilities, desirability and need of a post-race social world in which the idea of race is fully rejected and jettisoned, Nayak offers an anti-foundational reminder that 'race is a practice with no solid basis outside the discursive, material, structural and embodied configurations through which it is repetitively enacted, performed and, tenuously, secured' (Nayak 2006: 424). In other words, race is what we 'do' rather than who we 'are' (Dwyer and Bressey 2008: 7). In the context of a focus on social goods, social needs, social policies and social practices, it is the ways in which race gets 'done' that means we work with a race critical lens in the book by:

- Recognising its strange non-real/real status and its continuing 'force' in multicultural worlds
- Arguing that it is socially and culturally significant but in partial, uneven and unstable ways
- Demonstrating that race is situational and relational – it interacts with other social divisions, political discourses and crisis events and in this context
- Exploring the ways in which race, as a social category, has an ongoing social effect and continues to shape social outcomes

We return to these debates in our final chapter and reflect on how this approach, through each of the chapters to come, contributes to the post-race arguments. In Chapter 9 we review, in the context of this book, Gilroy's call for a 'planetary humanism' and the demise of race (Gilroy 2000: 2) along-side David Goldberg's (2002; 2008) argument that race continues to work as a social categorisation through which processes of discrimination, exclusion and subjugation operate. The the way in which the book is organised is set out and explained in the next, concluding section.

How the book is organised

So what do contemporary debates about race and multiculture mean in the material world of social policymaking and policy intentions and in terms of people's experiences of and access to social goods and social justice? In attempting to respond to these questions and challenges we have organised the book around the shifting and evolving policy arenas that have developed in this field at the end of the 20th century and the beginning of the 21st century. The book is organised in three interconnected parts.

Part I seeks to map some of the broader conceptual tussles and political knots that surround the shifting meanings of the categories race, ethnicity, identity, nation in the current period. In particular it examines the shifting deliberations and contestations that characterise theoretical, political and policy approaches to race and multiculture. In this chapter we have begun this process by exploring the connectivities between the changing social and spatial configurations of multiculture in the UK at the beginning of the 21st century; the crisis events and the nature of the political responses to these and the realignments is being made in terms of how the concept of race is approached and used in the current environment. In particular we have sought to provide an outline of the key questions and issues that constitute the broad contours of the racialisation of social policies in contemporary British society.

Chapter 2 further develops these concerns through an analysis of the relationship between the social world and social policy. We argue in this chapter that the relationships between policy making, race and multiculture in the UK can be effectively understood by exploring the various 'policy epochs', from assimilationist to integration, that have characterised policy responses to difference, diversity and inequalities in the UK context. This chapter draws on the notions of palimpsest and haunting to argue that successive policy approaches to race and multiculture are layered, one over the other, without completely disappearing. In this way, Chapter 2 suggests that policy approaches to diversity have been predominantly concerned with social order and the management of cultural difference. In this context it explores how the traces of older policies are apparent in current policy interventions even as the nature and formations of the social world and of multiculture shift and reconfigure.

Part II forms the bulk of the book and covers the key policy arenas in the field by providing thematic overviews and accounts of policy developments and changes over the past few decades. It is composed of six chapters that investigate what happens when a series of specific and key sites of social policy are examined through the lens of race and multiculture. Across the six chapters we examine:

- how specific policy interventions have, and have not, addressed ethnic diversity, difference, multiculture, racism and social division
- how policy interventions have they been a constitutive part of the racialisation of social goods and social relations
- the established and the emergent patterns of diverse experiences of social resources and interventions between and within different ethnic groups
- the relationship between ethnicity, race and multiculture and other categories of social differentiation such as class, gender, migration status, education status, age, location and religion.

In each chapter we provide a historically informed overview of the key concerns, events and politics that have influenced policy agendas and driven policy priorities, developments and interventions.

Chapter 3 looks at one of the most explicitly race-connected areas of policymaking, namely policy approaches to migration, settlement, asylum and refuge. This area of policymaking has dominated political and policy agendas since the early 1960s. It has been the site of intense debate and conflict and this chapter provides an exploration of the main policy frames around which governmental policies have been shaped over the ensuing decades. In particular it provides a working periodisation of policy shifts and changes in this field, including mapping the most recent changes and new migration patterns in the UK at the beginning of the 21st Century.

Chapter 4 is concerned with the relationship beween ethnicity, housing and residency patterns. The chapter suggests that despite an interest in the 1960s–1980s in the areas of race and housing, housing has since been somewhat marginalised in debates about ethnicity and multiculture. In an attempt to re-emphasise the importance of housing this chapter looks at how changing housing and residency geographies of BME and migrant populations both reflect and are a key dynamic of contemporary multicultural formations in England and Wales. The chapter examines these housing and residency changes and focuses on how they reflect the interactions between wider shifts in multiculture, choice, and structural constraints.

The relationship between race and ethnicity and housing policy is considered as is the role of housing and residency in cohesion and integration policy.

Chapter 5 is focused on the role of policing and the criminal justice system. This has been a high profile and highly emotive policy site since the 1970s, and has become even more so during the past two decades. Issues such as deaths in police custody, racism within the police, stop and search procedures and urban unrest have remained a recurrent theme in policy debates over the past few decades. This chapter works its way through the shifting criminalisations of black and minority ethnic groups and provides an account of the intense policing of particular populations and places as well as focussing on the emergence of security and anti-terrorism agendas in policing and criminal justice systems in the 21st century.

Chapter 6 focuses on the multidimesionality of the ethnicity–health relationship. It considers a number of connected although distinct concerns ranging from variations in ethnically differentiated patterns of physical well-being, access to quality health provision services, the employment and status of black and minority and migrant ethnic health care professionals within the NHS and health care services to mental health provision and the psychiatric systems in the UK. These concerns are themselves embedded in broader contexts of structural and socio-economic relations and compounded by a tendency within some medical models to either marginalise and neglect those illnesses that disproportionately affect particular ethnic populations or, conversely, ethnicise illness and culturally pathologise black, minority ethnic and migrant communities health needs.

Chapter 7 examines the relationship between education, race and multiculture. Education has been the site of some of the most bitter contestations over belonging, achievement, racism, exclusion and policymaking. The chapter examines this history and some of the often high-profile race and education battles. In the context of contemporary educational policy, how has this former turbulence been resolved and what are the issues that are of contemporary educational concern? The chapter reviews such issues as the changing and persistent patterns between ethnicity and educational outcomes and achievement; the relationship in an education context between ethnicity and class, gender, location and migration status; exclusions, education markets and school choice, faith schools and higher education. It addresses the extent to which these are qualitatively different education issues to those of the past and reflective of shifting ethnic and class relations or whether they present echoes of earlier tensions and troubles.

Employment and labour are the focus of *Chapter 8*. This has been a key area of debate from the earliest stages of post-1945 migration and it continues to occupy an important role in social policy discourses. In examining the forms in which ethnicity and labour intersect, this chapter looks at the ways in which contemporary employment markets in the UK heavily rely on both highly skilled and unskilled, documented and clandestine migratory labour. The chapter returns to themes explored in Chapter 3 and examines the relationship between migration policy and labour markets. It examines the relationship between shifting economic contexts and highlights the increasing differences between (and within) ethnic groupings and employment patterns.

Part III concludes the book by focusing on a critical analysis of possible race and policy futures and the related challenges, conflicts and dilemmas. At the beginning of *Chapter 9* the discussion returns to some of the themes and questions raised in this introductory chapter, particularly in relation to the current debates about post-race approaches and everyday multiculture and segregation. The chapter then reflects on the connections across the different policy sites. In particular it notes the contradictions between the emergence of more sophisticated policy approaches to multiculture, increasing differentiation between and within diverse populations and continuing ethnic inequalities.

Taken together the chapters of this book provide a synthesis of the key arenas of policy intervention on race and ethnic diversity. By bringing these key issues together in one volume we aim to capture the shifting and emergent social and spatial landscapes of race, multiculture and ethnicity; to explore the changing terms, contexts, intentions and nature of policy discourses; to describe the differential patterns, processes and practices of the delivery of key social goods and needs, and to consider how these relate to race, ethnicity and multiculture. While each of the chapters in Part II focuses on a particular site of social provision and policymaking – health, housing, education, migration, employment,, criminal justice systems – we would emphasise that these are themselves proximate and relational; in other words they are often entangled and connected with each other. Across these policy sites race and multiculture interact – in fluid, dynamic and context specific ways – with other lines of social division and will increasingly do so in the increasingly super-diverse UK.

Policy Approaches to Race and Multiculture

In the previous chapter we focused on the changing meanings of race and multiculture in the current conjuncture. In the course of the discussion we touched on some aspects of policymaking around race and multiculture. In this chapter we take this analysis a step further by exploring the reasons why race, ethnic diversity and cultural difference have become a site for policymaking and by unpacking the nature of the relationship between race and social policy.

A key concern in this context is the examination of the ways in which policymakers have responded to questions about race, ethnic diversity and cultural difference. In relation to the complex formations of multiculture that have defined the UK over the past few decades it is necessary to map the policy adaptations and interventions that have emerged in relation to minority communities and also in relation to the multicultural nation as a whole. However, we would suggest that alongside a focus on the responses that the policy world has made to race and multiculture, it is also important to pay attention to the ways in which policy has a constitutive role in relation to race and multiculture. In other words policy interventions can define, manage and racialise cultural difference; policymaking can very much be part of presenting multiculture as a set of problems, as a threat and/or as a set of possibilities and a desired future.

While each of the chapters in Part 2 look at particular policy domains and specific policies within these, the focus of this chapter is very much on the broader connections between policy worlds and the social worlds in which those policies operate. In this we follow the distinction made by the classic social administration theorist Richard Titmuss who argued:

> It is clear that the study of social policy cannot be isolated from the study of society as a whole in all its varied social, economic and political aspects [...] To understand policy [...] we have to see it in the context of a particular set of circumstances, a given society and culture, and a more or less specified period of historic time. In other words, social policy cannot be discussed, or even conceptualised in a social vacuum. (Titmuss 1974: 15–16)

The iterative nature of the relationship between policy and the society is particularly evident in interventions concerning race and multiculture where political contexts directly shape race-policy approaches but at the same time race-policy approaches inflect and shape wider politics of difference and diversity.

There is an emphasis in this chapter, via its documentation of race-policy tropes, on the extent to which the race-policy landscape is and has been characterised by turbulence and contestation. Some of this turbulence is reflected in the ways in which multiculture emerges onto policymaking agendas as well as to changes in the policy approaches to multiculture, and the chapter addresses the very mobile and shifting nature of both the agenda and the policy responses to and management of race and multiculture. While it is the shifts in the configurations of race-policy approaches that are notable it is important to acknowledge the relationality of previous policy approaches in seemingly new policy approaches. We refer to these imprints of former approaches in current approaches as a form of palimpsest or 'policy hauntings' and although race and multiculture are not unique policy domains it is certainly a particular feature of this field. For example, we will suggest that there are lines of policy connection between assimilation and cohesion and integration and between multiculturalism and celebrating diversity.

The turbulence of the race-policy field needs to be related to the highly politicised nature of race-policy approaches. Race and multiculture are among the most politicised areas of policymaking and race policymaking approaches can perhaps be most accurately described as reactive and crisis-driven. It has been crisis events – most often in the form of urban disorder but also individual violence – that have been the catalysts for bringing about changes in particular policy approaches. The number and range of public reports that have emerged from such crisis events and thus provided the framing of policy thinking demonstrate this tendency in race interventions. There is an extended discussion on these reports within this chapter.

The intense political nature of race-policy approaches is also reflected in the levels of media interest and engagement that they receive. This chapter suggests that the media relationship with race and race policymaking is not simply one of reporting. The media relationship is far more animated and interactive. The chapter suggests that media can be understood as having a constitutive influence in deciding not only what makes-up race-policy agendas but also the future of race initiatives.

Just as the media are entangled in race politics and race policymaking, this chapter argues that people are too. Race policymaking is a field in which wider community networks, organisations, 'grass roots' and family-based campaigning and lobbying has been particularly marked and influential. The chapter will evidence the ways in which the processes of policymaking around race and multiculture are not simply 'top-down' but tend to be partial, complex and non-linear.

The chapter is organised around each of these areas of concern. The first part of the chapter addresses the question 'what is policy' and examines the policy relationship to the social world in which policies intervene and contribute to. With this discussion in mind, the second part of the chapter examines the changing formations of policy approaches to race and multiculture. In particular the chapter considers how they shift and reconfigure – and yet remain similar. Exemplifying the chapter's argument that policy can only be understood in relation to the social and political environment in which they emerge and to which they contribute, the chapter highlights the role played by public inquiries and their reports in policy development related to race and multiculture and provides an overview of these while embedding them within their political and policy contexts.

What is policy?

While the question 'what is policy' seems fairly self-evident on the one hand, on the other policy has a set of multiple and inconsistent meanings and understandings. As Bochel and Bochel (2004: 9) note, policy can range from being a reference to a field of activity to a specific set of proposals and intentions, to decisions of government, to a programme, and to a process of decisions and implementation. This book and in particular this chapter discusses the differences between policy meanings and the difficulty of defining policy. We emphasise the notion of policy as an unstable and argued-over set of *processes* that occur in particular *contexts*. This echoes the arguments of Lindblom and Woodhouse which state that, 'deliberate, orderly steps [...] are not an accurate portrayal of how the policy process actually works. Policy-making is, instead, a complex inter-active process without beginning or end' (Lindblom and Woodhouse 1993: 11).

In contrast to perspectives which idealise policymaking as being *rational*, logical and about distinct and planned policy changes, policy theorists such as Lindblom and Woodhouse (1993) and Burch and Wood (1990) have stressed on the 'muddling through' and *incremental* nature of policymaking. In the incremental model, policymaking happens within the status quo and stays within familiar territory. This means that policies tend to be restricted to being reactive, fragmented and ongoing as policymakers recognise that social problems and issues change over time and involve different organisations and institutions (Bochel and Bochel 2004: 34–35). While the rationalist approach emphasises the possibility of policy change, the incrementalist approach emphasises the limitations of policy in the realities of complex, restrictive and negotiated policy worlds.

From the forthcoming chapters, it will be clear that it is possible to map aspects of both policy models onto race and multiculture related policymaking and to wider policy making agendas which have had particular impacts on race and multiculture. For example, the sale of council houses (Chapter 4) and the Education Reform Act (Chapter 7) sit within a rationalist policy model while Academies and Free Schools (Chapter 7) and the 'big' approaches to cultural difference – assimilation, multiculturalism, cohesion and race relations legislation (discussed below) – are examples of policy formed within a much more incremental model. We thus see something of the development or change policy dilemma summed up by Robert Drake (2001: 16) when he identified 'the crucial question' as being, 'how far are social policies really the products of principle and to what extent are they merely reactions to on-going events?' Also, Drake goes on to ask 'Do social policies accord the values, beliefs and intentions of their instigators, or do they arise from more immediate reposes to the immanent pressures of the everyday world?'

These are questions that are particularly visible in race-policy landscapes. There is 'top-down' governmental policy decision-making (e.g. immigration legislation) and at the same time 'bottom-up' policy influencing organisations and events which can range from community and pressure group lobbying to large-scale urban unrest. This can produce a convergence between rationalist and incrementalist approaches, as the crisis events and public inquiry reports that shape race-policy (see discussion below) demonstrate.

The rationalist and incremental and the top-down and bottom-up mix in race-policymaking processes reflects the pluralist character of the policy world more broadly and the race-policy world in particular. Describing this world as pluralist – i.e. that power in policy decision making is unevenly and complexly distributed in multiple locations and not simply with any one government institution or organisation – does not mean that all affected and/or interested groups have equal influence or participatory access to shaping policy agendas and interventions. At certain times, policy influence may be more clustered around government and government organisations and at other times around the media, families or community organisations. While poor and disadvantaged populations have generally not found – or been allowed – routes into influence and policy participation, the policy narrative for BME populations has always been more complex as is evident in this and other chapters of this book. What is important to note is that race policy-making happens in an intensely unstable and contested landscape and to emphasise that power and influence moves through it in contradictory and unexpected ways.

It is in this context that this chapter's focus on policy processes, policy contexts and the wider social and political world follows some of the more recent developments in thinking about how to most effectively understand policy and policymaking. In particular we suggest that the attention paid to notions of policy communities and policy networks in these 'models' capture the multiple constituencies orbiting around a policy field with greater and lesser degrees of connection, interest, power and influence. This provides a helpful map for understanding how social phenomena become social problems, which then become the focus of policy argument, policy development, policy intervention and re-intervention.

The chapter now turns from these somewhat abstract discussions of policymaking to apply them to cultural difference and ethnic diversity. Approached historically, the chapter explores how these mostly incremental, but sometimes radical, policy interventions reflect and contribute to the wider social world from which policies emerge and shape.

Shifting worlds of policy approaches to race and multiculture

It is possible to identify a series of policy epochs in the ways in which governments in the UK have responded to race and multiculture (Kesten 2011). We suggest that these 'epochs' cannot be understood as straightforwardly chronological or bounded. They connect and disconnect and have a temporal nature. Older policy ideas haunt and reappear in emergent and new policy thinking and approaches (Phillimore 2011).

Responding to difference: assimilationism

Although, as it has been widely noted, the UK has a long history of diverse migration and a multicultural presence, it was the shift to large-scale migration and settlement patterns in the post-colonial arrangements of the second half of the 20th century that produced the initial official social-policy responses to the widespread emergence of the UK – particularly its large urban and industrial centres – as multicultural and ethnically diverse. Race and colonial thinking directly informed these initial policy formations. The need to 'manage' the new migratory populations was a key premise for the emergence of race and diversity as a field of policymaking. Not only did the spectre of the US race situation of ghettoes, segregation and social tension feed into policy imaginations but, despite the citizenship status of migrants, there was also a pervasive sense of the temporary nature of the migrants being in Britain.

In this context UK policy approaches to ethnic difference were shaped by the US race-policy approaches and in particular were dominated by notions of assimilation and integration. Assimilation was seen as a strategy that would help avoid the development of geographies of settlement and place a demand on migrants to 'behave' according to British cultures and ways of life. Assimilation worked on the basis of treating the migrants' destination countries as being 'host societies' and migrants as 'guests'. This host–guest relationship reflected the race and colonial based thinking of policymakers at this time. The emphasis was on the need for migrants to not only 'fit in' with the society in which they had settled but that the 'host society' acceptance of difference could only be achieved if migrants became culturally indistinct. Assimilation placed the weight of social responsibility on the migrant populations with 'no inter-cultural dialogue between the centre and the periphery' (Kivisto 2010: 267).

The concrete manifestations of assimilation are reflected first, in the development of immigration-control legislation and race-relations legislation and second, in housing and education policy initiatives (see Chapters 4 and 7) during the 1960s. All of these legislative measures need to be understood as developing in response to wider social and political discourses (Solomos 2003). They represent the formal attempt to control the number of migrants coming to the UK with an endeavour to manage and stabilise multicultural social relations (see Chapter 3). The very proximity of the 1965 and 1968 Race Relations legislation reflects the degree of governmental concern to establish 'good race relations' and hence avoid social conflict. While the early race-relations acts did outlaw discrimination on the grounds of race, the central focus of both the 1965 and 1968 Acts was on the setting up of special bodies such as the Race Relations Board and the Community Relations Commission which had not only the responsibility to address racism but also to manage the 'adjustment' and 'welfare' of migrants and to educate and familiarise the wider population with the concept of cultural difference.

The assimilationist preoccupation with social instability and the need for social adjustment extended to policy interventions in housing and school place allocations (see Troyna and Williams 1986; Chapters 4 and 7). While these were phased out by the late 1960s and early 1970s, a more lasting assimilation policy was the provision of the central government allocated resources to those local authorities with significant migrant populations who had lobbied for recognition of their 'extra' social demands because of this. This funding primarily went into education for teaching English and providing additional teaching support. Under the 1966 Local Government Act this additional resource policy became formalised as Section 11 funding. The identification of cultural difference as the cause of social disadvantage of BME migrants was at the heart of Section 11's approach. That Section 11 funding was to survive well into the 1990s reveals the tenacity of this policy thinking. Section 11 funding was overwhelmingly allocated to language and education support initiatives in schools and colleges, in-service training for teachers and home-school liaison projects that supported families from minority ethnic communities.

In many ways Section 11 is a prime example of policy incrementalism and policy argument. It's 'burden of migrants' premise was problematic as was its 'assimilation of migrants' remit and the inability to use Section 11 funding for explicitly anti-racist and race-equality projects reflected the culturalist focus of the projects and services that it did fund. However, its widespread acceptance by policy and service providers and its longevity – it finally ended in 1999 – demonstrated both the need for resources and an apparent policy receptiveness to such resources when filtered through a 'fitting-in' cultural approach.

While it is assumed that assimilation approaches to multiculture were rather quickly discredited and jettisoned by the late 1960s the Section 11 story disrupts this narrative. The attempts at direct assimilationism in the forms of bussing BME children to white schools and housing allocation ratios for BME tenants have become notorious but traces of assimilation thinking are recognisable in the dispersal of asylum seekers in the late 1990's immigration policy (Chapter 3) and in the cohesion agenda of the 2000s (see below). The shift in the 1970s from demands for minority migrant groups to effectively 'disappear' within the majority culture to an emphasis on accepting (some) cultural difference was not a policy approach that represented a distinct break with assimilation thinking but was more, we suggest, of a new iteration and development, a shift in policy emphasis, of what had happened before.

Recognising difference: multiculturalism

By the late 1960s and early 1970s it was becoming clear that the demography of the UK had shifted permanently and Britain had become an ethnically and culturally diverse society and would remain so. The recognition of this population shift by politicians, policy networks and government institutions was amplified by a number of other factors for example, the racialisation of mainstream politics, an active far right, violent racism, the emergence of evidence of systematic disadvantage and discrimination in access to and experiences of social goods and by the organisation and lobbying of BME communities. In this new context the need for a policy approach that was more than migrants having to 'fit in' and 'culturally adjust' was increasingly apparent. The then Home Secretary Roy Jenkins expressed the political shift in what is now a well-known speech when he argued for an integrative approach to cultural difference defining integration as 'not a flattening process of assimilation but an equal opportunity, accompanied by cultural diversity, in an atmosphere of mutual tolerance' (Solomos 1988: 65).

In legislative terms, the worries about widespread discrimination, the lack of equal opportunity and wider social stability were expressed through the development of the race-relations law. The 1976 Race Relations Act reorganised the 1966 and 1968 race-relations architecture and replaced the Race Relations Board and the Community Relations Commission with the supposedly more powerful Commission for Racial Equality (CRE). The 1976 Act also attempted to recognise the complexities of racism and discrimination and offered a refined definition of discrimination to account for both direct and indirect discrimination. While the 1976 Race Relations Act can be seen as part of a symbolic policy willingness to recognise the need to address racial inequalities and widespread discrimination it was not effective in addressing and countering either of these patterns as numerous studies by the CRE demonstrated. The limits of what the 1976 Act achieved were not only because of the remit and content of the Act itself but it also reflected the limitations of what legislation can do as part of a technique of governance in a wider political and cultural environment in which cultural difference continued to be a ready short-hand for social problems and hierarchical differentiation.

In political terms the formal acknowledgement of the UK as a multicultural nation has always been resisted. Unlike the declarations of multicultural national identity established in Canada and Australia, in the UK political recognition of its multicultural status has remained informal (Cohen 1994; Parekh 2000). Instead, political discourses during the 1970s and 1980s focused on the cultural differences and the need to be open and tolerant to these. In this way a political settlement could be made around cultural difference – privately populations could choose/retain some of their ethnic and cultural identities but in the public and civil sphere there was a requirement to support and be part of the cultural centre. But this was an uneasy and defensive recognition. For example, during the 1970s and 1980s high-profile political figures were publically worried about Britain becoming 'culturally swamped' and the national allegiances of migrant populations. The acknowledgement of difference was heavily conditional and regulated through a notion of cultural hierarchies in which white-Western-Global North cultures were the centre and other cultural forms exist, as always, outside of and distinct from this civilised core. In this 'us/them' binary version of multiculturalism, ethnicity and identity were treated as fixed and bounded with little fluidity and interaction. Intercultural dialogue, exchanges and practices had to either transcend this polarisation or operate within it, and multiculturalism as a policy approach reflected this with its tendency to focus on ethnic and cultural otherness. As Chapter 7 argues, education became a key site in which multiculturalism as a social policy was played out. Cultural pluralism, tolerance and learning about other cultures dominated multicultural education (Ball and Troyna 1989) and, as with assimilation, language was a policy concern. But rather than a demand for learning English there was widespread provision made, in social goods related services, for other languages. Local government services began to provide information in multiple languages with interpreters in key resources such as health centres and front-line social services. Cultural sensitivity was also part of this approach. For example, it became legitimate for Sikh employees to wear turbans in the workplace. Celebrations of key dates in different faith calendars were encouraged in schools and community centres. In-housing multiculturalism was articulated around an awareness of the role of extended families and larger family sizes and responding to this need.

While these initiatives were not wrong or misplaced – and some changes were a reflection of minority group campaigns and lobbying – their integral problem was the wider frame in which culture and ethnicity were over-emphasised in a context where majority culture was the norm, and wider issues of social and economic constraints and particular issues of ethnic inequalities, racism and discrimination were at worst ignored or marginalised and at best not directly or effectively addressed. The political and social cost of this was seen in the extensive urban unrest that took place in cities across the UK in the early and mid-1980s (see Chapter 5).

Although media and conservative political responses to the unrest tended to criminalise and demonise those involved, it was nevertheless clear that the seriousness of the events demanded a political response. The disturbances in Brixton in South London led to a public inquiry chaired by Lord Scarman whose report suggested that the conflict was the result of a combination of exclusion, racism, racist policing and structural factors. The sociological framing of the Scarman Inquiry is reflected in the report's argument that the disorders 'cannot be fully understood unless they are seen in the context of complex political, social and economic factors' (Scarman 1981: para 2.34). This approach fed directly into the policy recommendations made by Scarman – not only was reform of police and policing practice proposed but the Report stressed the need for urgent wider policy interventions to be made in housing and education and racial discrimination.

The Report had an ambivalent media and political reception. There was some public recognition of racism and disadvantage but this was consistently linked to criminality and social breakdown. For example, the *Sun* newspaper (26th November 1981) reported that 'Scarman claims that all were to blame in some way for the savage outburst of rioting that stunned Britain [but] the police were faced with a still unresolved problem of how to cope with a rising level of crime'. Taking an apocalyptic tone the *Mirror* newspaper (26th November 1981) stated that Scarman was the 'final warning' explaining that 'it is the nation's choice. Either act on Scarman or put it on the shelf with countless other. But if we decide on the shelf it will not be dust that this report gathers. It will be blood.'

For black communities the Report's failure to identify the police as intuitionally racist and its problematic use of cultural deficit model – i.e. the pathologisation of African–Caribbean families – meant that there was little confidence in what the Report could deliver and change. The Thatcher government's response was able to navigate between limited reform of the police and developing police techniques for dealing with public disorder and generally denying the social and economic context while making limited policy gestures to addressing social and economic disadvantage in the worst affected areas such as Liverpool and London (Benyon and Solomos 1988).

More profoundly though, what the 1980–1981 unrest and the Scarman Inquiry contributed to were wider policy and political debates, campaigns and arguments to recognise structural disadvantage, cultural hierarchies, racism and institutional racist practices. It was these that began to gain ground in the more progressive and radical left-led urban local authorities during the 1980s.

Challenging division: anti-racism

While the recognition of cultural differences defined the parameters of multiculturalism, the focus for what became known as anti-racism was the concept of racism and processes of discrimination. Race equality rather than cultural awareness lay at the heart of anti-racism as a policy approach and political aim. In the political environment of the 1980s, in which the Thatcher administration was redefining Conservative and national politics, those national and local politicians, policymakers and service providers in the Labour Party and on the political left relocated political opposition to local government (Boddy and Fudge 1984; Lansley, Goss and Wolmar 1989; Solomos 2003). This converged with an emergence of identity politics in which the older-class based politics gave way to a vocal, active, high-profile social movement driven by agenda based issues of gender, sexuality and race and became known as the New Left. Labour local authorities in diverse urban areas of the UK especially in a number of Labour London boroughs, such as Hackney, Brent, Haringey, Lambeth, Islington, Camden, the Labour-led Greater London Council (GLC), the Inner London Education Authority (ILEA) and also councils in Manchester, Sheffield, Leicester, Coventry, West Midlands and Bradford became identified to various extents with New Left political commitments and policy initiatives. But it was the London boroughs, the ILEA and the GLC and perhaps Manchester that became most associated with anti-racism as a policy approach. The growing evidence of racism and the activism and lobbying of community based groups meant that exclusion from and discrimination in key services and resources such as housing, education, health and employment (see Chapters 4, 6, 7 and 8) was reaching a critical point. This was compounded by the problematic relationship with policing – highlighted by the urban unrest and – and in terms of local politics by a chronic under-representation of BME councillors and employees in local government structures.

Under the policy umbrella of anti-racism those local authorities, political, community and third-sector organisations most committed to it developed a raft of initiatives specifically aimed at delivering equal opportunities and outcomes in relation to race and ethnicity. The other chapters in this volume discuss specific policies in detail but it is worth noting some examples here as they are illustrative of the extent to which anti-racism shaped policy approaches and political thinking during the 1980s. Some of the initiatives took their inspiration from policies in the US although positive discrimination and quota systems remained illegal in the UK. However, positive-action initiatives and target commitments for BME recruitment and representation were commonly adopted by organisations and radical local authorities. The need to have ethnic monitoring procedures in terms of access to and allocation of social goods became a widely accepted norm and the collection of data relating to ethnicity, gender and sexuality gradually became a standard aspect of routine activities such as applying for jobs, employee profiling, health service provision and experience, housing and policing services and so forth. While efforts went into the technical collection of these forms of data what happened to it in terms of using it to interpret the fairness, success or otherwise of policies was more uncertain. But monitoring did emphasise the visibility of race equality issues in social policy.

Monitoring and surveys which revealed BME under-representation in local-authority employment led to a series of policy interventions such as specialist advisors, the review of job specifications, job selection and promotion criteria, to posts being advertised in BME media and widespread race awareness training for employees and particularly for those involved in recruitment. The London Borough of Lambeth – an early pioneer in anti-racist policy intervention – saw these strategies yield results. As Lansley, Goss and Wolmar note in 1978 the Borough employed only about 8 per cent black workers but this had increased to 25 per cent of its staff identified as BME in 1985 (Lansley, Goss and Wolmar 1989).

Many organisations and local authorities sympathetic to anti-racism appointed race advisors, established race units and race committees, declared themselves 'equal opportunities employers', and made discrimination and racism disciplinary offences in the workplace. Race hatred and racist violence became a focus of concern in housing departments particularly in authorities with significant South Asian populations. Local authorities pressured police to tackle racial harassment. Racial harassment policies became part of tenancy agreements which meant that tenants could now be evicted for race-hate behaviour (Hesse et al. 1992). Consultation with and the participation of local BME communities became a key activity for organisations with an anti-racist approach. This commitment saw black activists co-opted onto a range of committees in education, health, housing, leisure, policing and the establishment of consultative forums across a range of issues from young people and the arts to health and the elderly. Tender compliance, a practice borrowed from the US, was also introduced by authorities such as the GLC, ILEA and Lambeth. This meant that suppliers or companies employed or bidding to be employed by councils had to demonstrate their own commitment to race equality and equal opportunities policies. Failure to do so disqualified them from consideration for council employment. The material reach of anti-racism extended to local geographies as streets, squares, public buildings and estates were renamed in efforts to reflect Britain's multicultural and colonial past and present.

Some organisations adopted all of these strategies, others were more partial but what is notable is the visibility of these initiatives within the public sphere. Some of this visibility was in the everyday environment. Organisations like the GLC and ILEA publically advertised and exposed their anti-racism work and policies. For example as part of its 'London Against Racism and London as an Anti-Racist Zone' campaign the GLC issued a series of billboard adverts which carried strap lines such as 'if you're not part of the solution you're part of the problem' and 'when racism stops you being efficient are you doing your job?' (see Gilroy 1987: 142, 147).

Anti-racism was created and caught up in an intensely mediated and political environment as the acrimonious battlegrounds between local and national politics were struggled over and national identity and access to social goods and equal service delivery were campaigned and fought for. The achievements of anti-racism as a set of policy interventions are difficult to straightforwardly assess. What is clear, with a 30-year hindsight, is that it constituted an extraordinary policy moment in which politics, dissent, race, social justice, anxiety, social change and formal processes and community based campaigns and interventions converged and became deeply entangled. Anti-racism as a policy trope, unlike multiculturalism, tapped directly into the 'big questions' of disadvantage, discrimination, exclusion, marginalisation and racism and did so by mobilising uncomfortable and challenging sets of issues relating to power and subordination. This meant that anti-racism was not going to ever have an easy passage or affectionate place in the public domain. Some of this is reflected in the media relationship with anti-racism and the deeply acrimonious nature of this and in the nature of the opposition from the political right to the anti-racist policy interventions made by some municipal policymakers.

The then anti-racist policy interventions did have an impact in terms of redistribution of social goods, equal access to services and the opening up of processes and procedures. In this context it is possible to see that anti-racist initiatives put race onto the policy agenda and it did so in a new and very different language compared to previous policy approaches to race and multiculture. It ushered in new policy procedures for fair and equal access, delivery, allocation, recruitment, selection and promotion. It established new policy architectures such as race committees, advisors, units and led to increased numbers of BME local-authority employees in areas that had previously been exclusively white and established lines of consultation with BME groups, communities and organisations. So for example, writing at the end of the 1980s Lansley, Goss and Wolmar conclude that because of the anti-racist policy initiatives:

> The number of black staff has increased, black people enjoy better access to services and there is greater awareness about the problems of racism. Race policies are now firmly on the political agenda and have gained growing acceptance. Race monitoring, one of the first initiatives, and other policies, have been adopted by some nationalised industries, Whitehall departments and even some large private firms. (Lansley, Goss and Wolmar 1989: 141)

But clearly anti-racism as a policy approach was often contradictory and uneven in terms of its successes. In a well-known critique of municipal anti-racism, Paul Gilroy has highlighted the crude essentialism in which race and the social relations that it shapes are overwhelmingly conceived of as 'victim and perpetrator' and racism as a process that comes into being when 'prejudice + power' come together. He goes on to argue:

> 'Race' is, after all, not the property of powerful, prejudiced individuals but an effect of complex relationships between dominant and subordinate social groups [...] Even within a single social formation at particular phase of its development racism will not be an unbroken continuous presence. It will be unevenly developed. Even where it is diffuse it will never be uniform. The different forces which form 'races' in concrete political antagonisms will operate at differing tempos and in contrasting ways according to immediate circumstances. Racial attacks may be higher in one area than the next. (Gilroy 1987: 149)

For Gilroy the efforts to counter racism and deliver a different approach to multiculture are too essentially and bureaucratically formed and framed to be able to effectively cope with the highly contingent, always in flux and intensely complex formations that racism inhabits. While this is an important point and one with which we agree we would also suggest that the efforts to create an agenda and a set of interventions that confront and address racism were significant. Looking back at these policy epochs it is remarkable that anti-racism happened at all. It went beyond the incremental policy development model and burst with a peculiar energy and intensity onto formal and informal local – and national – politics. This intensity, along with its conceptual limits, meant that anti-racism as a policy moment was not likely to endure. It came about through a temporal but creative constellation of migrant communities reaching a tipping point, of a new right government and a new set of political agendas for the left.

More prosaically anti-racism prioritised race and raised expectations beyond what anti-racist policy interventions were able to achieve or resource. Anti-racism was then unable to successfully manage the fall out. Its essentialised approach to race meant that some groups and populations were not encouraged to buy into the intentions of anti-racism – in this way anti-racism was perceived as favouring particular sections of populations and not others. Promising more than it could actually deliver in terms of countering discrimination, an over-focus on individuals and the personal, lacking broader hearts and minds appeal, a limited over-simplified con-ceptualisation of race and social relations, structural constraints, a hostile media, a series of badly managed rows and events all of which meant that municipal anti-racism has been viewed in predominantly negative terms.

By the end of the 1980s explicit commitment to anti-racism had waned and most local authorities, experiencing various restructuring and reorgan-isation of key services away from local-authority control, retreated from anti-racist influenced policy interventions. But this retreat did not signal a straightforward return to multiculturalism. It is a rather strange para-dox that the antagonisms and divisiveness that appeared to characterise anti-racism managed to nevertheless still deliver a form of policy consensus. This consensus was sanitised in that the more radical, social-justice think-ing of anti-racism was marginalised. Nevertheless the notion of racism as anti-egalitarian and socially unjust became part of an acceptable mainstream discourse (Bonnett 2000). An element of this was the positive recognition of multiculture and nation formation. In short, the 1990s saw a public dis-course emerging in which British national identity was acknowledged and *valued* for its cultural diversity. It is this that we now consider.

Celebrating difference: cultural diversity and conditionalism

While the 1990s did not have the high-profile local and national based political and highly politicised debates that defined the 1980s, it marks an important decade for policy approaches to race and multiculture. While the 1990s did not have a clearly delineated policy agenda it was a decade marked by a distinctive 'policy mood'. Some of this mood was inflected by and reflective of the failures and achievements of both anti-racism and multi-culturalism. Some of this mood was created by the policy changes that had taken place through the restructuring of local authorities, the relocation of some key local authority services and education policy reforms. Apart from these legacies two very different events shaped and influenced the bigger policy mood and drove policy approaches and policy language surrounding race and multiculture in the 1990s. The first was the racist murder of the African–Caribbean teenager Stephen Lawrence in London in 1993. The second was the election of the New Labour government in 1997.

The death of Stephen Lawrence and the subsequent failure of the Metropolitan police to properly investigate and respond to the event have been subject to extensive commentary and scrutiny (see Chapter 5). What we want to note in the context of our discussions here is the way in which Stephen Lawrence's murder and the campaign led by the Lawrence family –with support by the *Daily Mail* newspaper – to have his death properly investigated had a profound impact on national politics and the national 'structure of feeling' in relation to race and multiculture. The media engagement with Stephen Lawrence was qualitatively different to other racist murders and violence. Not only was there media coverage but this coverage was overwhelmingly empathetic. In part this shift could be explained by the particular circumstances of and individuals involved in Stephen Lawrence's murder but the response was indicative of a bigger social awareness of and cultural shift in race thinking in the UK. This was obviously exemplified in the high-profile involvement of the *Daily Mail* – a deeply conservative newspaper – in calling for a full inquiry into why the police investigation of Stephen Lawrence's murder had failed.

Whether the struggles and contestations of the 1980s contributed to this greater receptiveness to issues of racism is impossible to definitively know but what is clear is that the murder of Stephen Lawrence had a profound effect on race politics in the UK. At the core of this change was a more inclusionary receptiveness to notions of racism, multiculture and social justice. This effect connected directly into the second key event of the decade – the election of New Labour in 1997. Not only did this mark the end of a 17-year Conservative administration it also appeared to offer the beginning of a new political approach across social, economic and cultural spheres. This can be understood as a moment of possibility and optimism in mainstream thinking and progressive approaches to British national identity. For example, in the early days of New Labour the government signed up to the 1998 Human Rights Act and signalled its desire to 'modernise' all things British: 'Cool Britannia' would replace 'Rule Britannia'. Headline grabbing initiatives were launched to shake the country free from the former Conservative Prime Minister John Major's 'warm beer' and 'cricket greens' image of 'old Britain' and to emphasise instead the creative, urban-based, culturally diverse 'New Britain'. This new mood was symbolically amplified by the death of Enoch Powell (a figure who had had a key impact on the racialisation of British politics in the 1960s) and seemed to be reflected in the receptiveness of the political mainstream towards a new national narrative – the then new Conservative Party leader, William Hague, made a widely publicised attendance at the Notting Hill Carnival and described

Conservative Party members, who made anti-multicultural statements, as 'dinosaurs' (see McLaughlin and Neal 2004; 2007).

More specifically, in this context of the celebration of diversity and 'national renewal' governmental policy shifts on issues of racial justice were anticipated. These were concretised when then Home Secretary Jack Straw agreed to set up an official government inquiry into the murder of Stephen Lawrence and police investigation of this. Chaired by QC Lord William Macpherson and widely referred to as the Macpherson Inquiry the investigation sat for 12 months and its full report on the murder and Metropolitan police practice was published at the beginning of 1999 (Macpherson 1999a).

With its main finding that 'institutional racism' had played a central part in the failure of the London Metropolitan Police to prosecute the killers of Stephen Lawrence the Macpherson Report (discussed in detail below) is significant in three ways. First, its public reception fed into the seemingly receptive new 'race mood'. The widespread sense of sorrow expressed in relation to the Lawrence murder extended into a sense of 'shame' as Macpherson shed light on the failures in investigation – for example the *Daily Mail* headlined the Report's publication with 'The Legacy of Stephen: Judges Damning Report Will Change Britain' (25 February 1999) and the *Times* led with 'Campaign to Banish Racism: Reform of Law to Bring a New Era' (25 February 1999). Second, the Macpherson Report brought the marginalised concept of 'institutional racism' onto mainstream political and policy agendas. This was a concept, in the UK, that had previously only belonged to the political left and influenced the anti-racism approaches discussed earlier. But in the wake of the Macpherson Report, the *Daily Mail* commented that 'the most resounding finding of the Report is that not only the Metropolitan police but all the main organs of the state are infected with institutional racism and must be radically reformed' (25 February 1999). Third, the Macpherson Report directly contributed to policy development through its recommendation for an amendment of the existing 1976 Race Relations Act so as to put a mandatory responsibility on all public organisations (with the exception of prisons) to achieve race equality. This recommendation was to become the Race Relations Amendment Act (2000).

Butler (2001) outlines the following main requirements of the Act:

- Public bodies are mandated with a general duty to promote race equality and must promote equality of opportunity and 'good relations' between people of different racial groups.
- The general duty to promote race equality requires public authorities to actively avoid unlawful discrimination.
- Organisations covered by the Act must monitor their workforce and take steps to ensure that ethnic minorities are treated fairly and make that data publicly available.

- Public bodies must review how policies and programmes can affect ethnic minorities, and take remedial action where any potential for 'adverse differential impact' on ethnic minority communities is identified.
- Public organisations must have a stated policy on race equality.

In many ways the central provisions of this new legislation would not have looked out of place in the anti-racist approaches that had been so vilified in the 1980s.

The Macpherson Inquiry and the public response to its findings extended public anxieties about racism, institutional practices and the meaning of multiculture at the turn of the century. Two examples particularly highlight this. In the first example, the strange exclusion of prisons as the one public body not subjected to the requirements of the new race relations legislation was highlighted by the racist murder of Zahid Mubarek by his white cell-mate at Feltham Young Offenders Institute in 2000. Raising questions on the institutional procedures, institutional racism and the failure of the prison service the parents and supporters of Zahid Mubarek campaigned for a public inquiry. That this four-year campaign was eventually successful – the then Home Secretary David Blunkett agreed to a public inquiry into what had happened which reported in 2006 – can again be seen as indicative of the particular race mood of the 1990s. However, the longevity of the Mubarek campaign and the involvement of the legal system in compelling the New Labour government to establish an inquiry also testifies to a wider ambivalence towards racism in the post-Macpherson period.

This ambivalence was again to become apparent in our second example – the Commission of the Future of Multi-Ethnic Britain (Parekh 2000). The Commission, established in 1998, with high-profile political support, by the think-tank Runnymede Trust, was to sit for two years and produce a report that could work as a template for future policy thinking and approaches to race and multiculture. While we return to the Commission and its report below, the Commission is noteworthy here because its existence appeared to further evidence the willingness to reflect on Britain's national identity and celebrate its cultural diversity.

However, for all the apparent 'new receptiveness' and new race consensus in the 1990s, the New Labour government was extending immigration legislation with the containment of refugees and asylum seekers as a core focus of this policy development (see Chapter 3). This mix of developing immigration legislation and race-relations legislation represents an older policy dualism that Labour governments had adhered to since the introduction of both types of legislation since 1962. The rigorous pursuit of immigration legislation at the same time as seeming to encourage and support an enlightened race and multiculture policy approach gives a hint of the inherently fragile nature of the 'new mood' and the consensus of celebrating diversity.

The negative public reception of the report of the Commission on the Future of Multi-Ethnic Britain in 2000 can also be understood as indicative of this fragility as the report's authors were widely condemned for being 'out of touch' and 'anti-British' in their call for a new inclusive narrative of national identity. In a context of hostile media responses to the report, the report – intended as a policy guide for future interventions for achieving multicultural inclusion – became immediately marginalised in policy terms (Fortier 2007; McLaughlin and Neal 2004; 2007). These signs of a political and policy backlash to a culturally diverse and at-ease-with-itself UK were consolidated by the beginning of the 21st century, as a profound shift in policy thinking was to become dramatically apparent.

Worrying about difference: disorder, community cohesion and integration

As Chapter 1 noted, the outbreaks of urban unrest and violent conflict between South Asian communities (predominantly young men), white racists and far-right activists and the police that took place in Burnley, Oldham, Bradford and other socially deprived towns in Northern England in 2001 led to various panicky pronouncements about the 'end of multiculture' and the 'death of multiculturalism'. These responses marked a distinctive shift away from what can be seen as more open and reflexive race thinking discussed above. The return to a defensive race mood was consolidated by the explanations offered by the public inquires set up to look into them. The cluster of reports that published the findings of a series of investigations into the towns and areas affected by the unrest – the Community Cohesion Review Team (Cantle 2001), John Denham (2001) and the Bradford Race Review Team (Ouseley 2001) – appeared to tell a shared story of residentially based ethnic segregation, social separation and a more general milieu of ethnic tension and suspicion. For example, one of the best known and most widely cited findings of the report of the Community Cohesion Review Team, chaired by Ted Cantle, investigating the disturbances in Oldham and Burnley begins by noting:

> Whilst the physical segregation of housing estates and inner city areas came as no surprise the team was particularly struck by the depth of polarization of our towns and cities. The extent to which these physical divisions were compounded by so many other aspects of our daily lives was very evident. Separate educational arrangements, community and voluntary bodies, employment, places of worship, language, social and cultural networks, means that many

communities operate on the basis of a series of parallel lives. These lives often do not seem to touch at any point, let alone overlap and promote any meaningful interchanges. (Cantle 2001: 9)

The phrase 'parallel lives' had become a short-hand term for multicultural troubles and segregation anxieties in the UK and dominated the responses made to the Cantle Inquiry. The apparent finding of separate, isolated and concentrated enclaves of Muslim populations was threaded through in public discourses not only of a 'cultural otherness' but also that these were communities that were 'self-segregating' and chose to be away from mainstream British society and culture. As Deborah Phillips observes:

People from the Pakistani and Bangladeshi communities of the northern textile towns were represented as poor, backward (especially compared with what was represented as a more cosmopolitan south) and socially isolated. These British Muslim families were frequently pathologised as inward looking, reluctant to learn English, and clinging to unacceptable traditions such as forced marriages and the ritual slaughter of animals [...] The young men involved in the rioting were readily criminalised and their grievances were given little voice. (Phillips 2006b: 28)

These 'demonising' worries, which socially and spatially problematise British Muslim populations, resonate with earlier racialised anxieties about other BME communities. This is a moment of incremental policy (and political) haunting in both the return to the idea of spatial and cultural segregation as the issue of concern and in the policy suggestions as to how to manage this. Again, in an echo of the assimilationist approaches of the 1960s these suggestions tended to focus on the need to foster more contact and understanding between culturally different populations. For example, the Review Team suggested that given the tendencies towards segregation:

Programmes therefore need to be devised to counter, on the one hand, enforced choices and to ensure equality of opportunity in practical terms and, on the other, to counter the ignorance, which may be associated with completely divided or segregated communities. We would emphasise that such programmes should be devised to inform the different black, Asian and other ethnic minority communities about each other, as well as about the majority white community and vice versa. (Cantle 2008: 29)

The emphasis on problematising and managing cultural difference was a clear departure from the valuing of diversity approaches of the late 1990s. By the 2000s the overwhelming political and policy emphasis was placed on common values, common civic understanding and behaviour and 'cross cultural contact' and community cohesion.

Borrowed from North American policy thinking, community cohesion attempts to bring together social exclusion and inclusion on the one hand and community and social capital on the other. This drawing together is often contradictory. Community and social capital are identified as both the problem – i.e. too much community can result in spatial separation, cultural insularity and social exclusion – *and* the solution – i.e. the social capital of shared identities and resources can deliver civic care, trust, social order and senses of belonging (Mooney and Neal 2009). For Robert Putnam, a key proponent of social capital theory, there is a need to achieve a good balance between what he terms 'bonding' – the processes, practices and shared civic values which bind similar populations together and provide a sense of shared identity and what he terms 'bridging' – the processes, practices and shared civic values by which diverse populations can come together, interact and cooperate. An imbalance in which there is more bonding and insufficient bridging is the precursor of defensive and polarised communities (Putnam 2000; 2007).

How to identify a balanced bridging–bonding in cohesive communities and neighbourhoods is not defined. Citing Forest and Kearns (2000) the Cantle Report settled on the argument that the simplest observable measure of community cohesion 'would be of groups who live in a local area getting together to promote or defend some common local interest' (Forrest and Kearns 2001: 8). But this definition hints at the challenges for community cohesion namely its avoidance of structural constraints, racialised inequalities and exclusions and racism. In this way 'the ideology of community cohesion is grounded in the somewhat simplistic notion that social integration can be promoted by greater residential mixing, which will in turn foster common values and a sense of common identity' (Phillips 2006b: 38).

As with previous policy approaches education was a particular focus of cohesion policy (see Chapter 7). Community bridging and the facilitation of 'contact, awareness and inter-community activities' defined cohesion interventions within and outside the frame of the Cantle Report (Cantle 2008).

The cohesion agenda, along with the anxieties about cultural differences and how to effectively manage these continued to dominate policy thinking and circulated in the wider public sphere of race and multiculture debates in the 2000s (see Chapter 1). In terms of the impact of the events of July 2005 on policy, community cohesion not only remained at the centre of governmental policy thinking but was also extended and developed. In 2007 the then New Labour government set up the Commission on Integration and Cohesion (COIC) for one year to investigate not the bombings but to more broadly review the success and efficacy of cohesion practices that had been implemented following the Cantle Report and to make further recommendations for improving the cohesion approach. In an evidence based investigation the Commission conducted a series of nation-wide, regionally based consultations with various stakeholders, policymakers and service deliverers and in their final report – *Our Shared Future* – made a total of 57 recommendations across a range of areas for refining and extending the cohesion and integration agenda.

Like the Cantle Report, COIC Report also focused on the rights and responsibilities of citizens but COIC also moved the cohesion policy debate along in a number of key ways. It stressed the importance of locality and bespoke the policy approaches, it refined the definitions of cohesion and integration by highlighting interdependency, it recognised the changing geographies of multiculture in England and the existence of highly diverse and globalised populations; it addressed the relationship between cohesive communities and deprivation and suggested that this was more complicated than some of the supposed deprived communities showing high levels of cohesion around ethnic diversity; it placed particular value on social capital and the capacity and need to build hospitable communities which would be resilient to economic, social and/or cultural change and strain. Translated into policy-applied recommendations this 'refined' cohesion approach iden-tified four key spheres for policy work – schools; workplaces; sports, culture and leisure; shared public spaces and residential areas – and set out a raft of mostly 'light touch, locally driven' social bridging and community building suggestions that could be implemented in each of these communities, for example a Community Week, school twinning, employers giving time off for employees to take part in community based activities and volunteer-ing. Alongside community building strategies cohesion policy has driven a mainstreaming of race and other discrimination and equalities agendas and organisations. This emphasis can be seen in the establishment of the Equality and Human Rights Commission (EHRC) in 2006. Coming into being the following year, the EHRC replaced the Commission for Racial Equality (set up by the 1976 Race Relations Act), the Equal Opportunities Commission and the Disability Rights Commission. Mainstreaming is also evident in legislative developments such as the Equalities Act (2010). This 'umbrella' anti-discrimination act replaced a range of existing equality laws in relation to race (the 1976 Race Relations Act for example), gender and disability and also extended to the categories of protection from dis-crimination to include sexuality, religion and age (Equalities and Human Rights Commission 2012). These institutional and legislative convergences represent a policy approach that seeks to address a broader conception of discrimination which works across rather than within categories of diffe-rence in efforts to most effectively enforce anti-discrimination and equalities strategies in contexts of social diversity.

We have spent some time discussing cohesion as a policy approach. One reason for this is because cohesion represents the most recent and sustained policy manifestation as to how to make social interventions in – and manage – ethnically diverse and culturally different societies. The current Conservative government's focus on and use of integration as its leitmotif for race policymaking represents a broadening and modification but not departure from cohesion strategies. For example, while it has ended the requirement of schools to engage in cohesion activities (see Chapter 7) and emphasises social mobility, the integration approach continues to rely on cohesion-framed demands of common values, rights and responsibilities alongside community interaction and participation. As with cohesion, current integration approaches put localities and neighbourhoods at the centre of policy initiatives, as this extract from the Department of Communities and Local Government explains:

> Integration means creating the conditions for everyone to play a full part in national and local life. Our country is stronger by far when each of us, whatever our background, has a chance to contribute. And our communities are stronger when different people not only treat each other with respect, but contribute together. Integration is achieved when neighbourhoods, families and individuals come together on issues which matter to them, and so we are committed to rebalancing activity from centrally-led to locally-led action and from the public to the voluntary and private sectors. (Department for Communities and Local Government 2012: 2)

Another reason for looking at cohesion agenda is its strange mix of inclusions and elisions in policy thinking. It recognises complex social and spatial relations and the importance of 'everyday life'. The cohesion policy in the Cantle Report, and more so in COIC, does speak to the issues of deprivation, social justice and racial equality and argues that there is not necessarily a straightforward correlation between deprivation and conflict. Deprived areas can be cohesive ones. But in this way the community cohesion agenda actually marginalises the impact of structural constraints and the cohesion approach stops short of direct interventions on structural and organisational contexts – for example neither the Cantle nor COIC reports make specific policing related recommendations despite the proximity of both reports to civil disturbance and violence.

Related to these absences is cohesion's neglect of how racism and the uneven flows of cultural power affect social relations (Amin 2002; Kundnani 2001). For example, the implicit responsibility is on the need for 'other' or problematised minority populations to interact and mix rather than on majority populations – who are the most segregated population group. This is a point made by Deborah Phillips when she argues that although Cantle stresses the need to widen housing choices for all populations, the 'onus would seem to be on black and minority ethnic mobility and change' (Phillips 2006b: 38). The cohesion focus on residential patterns is also simplistically conceived in cohesion thinking as both Chapter 7 on education and Chapter 4 on housing evidence some of the ways in which high levels of residential mixing do not necessarily deliver high levels of social mixing.

But perhaps the inherent contradictions of cohesion approaches are most starkly apparent in their connections to counter-terrorism policy initiatives such as the Prevention of Violent Extremism (PVE). The Prevention of Violent Extremism programme was developed to:

> Stop people becoming or supporting terrorists or violent extremists' not only through security and intelligence measures but also through a 'hearts and minds' approach to develop local community resilience to violent extremism, communities must be at the centre of the response to violent extremism. We need to foster community cohesion [...] a solely security based response will not be sufficient to counter the current threat. We remain committed to a response that gives equal precedence to countering ideas as well as the activities of violent extremists. (Department for Communities and Local Government 2008: 12)

While nominally aimed at all forms of violent extremism PVE has focused in particular and most publicly on Muslim communities and a notion of a Muslim threat. What PVE and subsequent counter-terrorism policing strategies such as PREVENT – the Conservative government's recent revision of PVE (Home Office 2011) – have done is to both intersect with, and contradict the broader cohesion approach of developing common understanding by maintaining and reinforcing notions of the dangers of cultural difference and threatening populations (see Chapter 5). As Husband and Alam observe the policy dualism of community cohesion and prevention of terrorism reflect a convergence of governmental anxiety about 'how Muslim communities might be brought more into acceptable participation in British life' with 'a parallel agenda: namely, their subjection to appropriate measures which respond to their status as a security threat' (Husband and Alam 2011: 2). Indeed the House of Commons Communities and Local Government Committee reported to the House of Commons that PREVENT's focus on Muslims 'has been unhelpful [...] stigmatizing, potentially alienating and fails to address the fact that no section of a population exists in isolation from others. The need to address extremism of all kinds on a cross-community basis, dependent on assessed local risk, is paramount' (House of Commons Communities and Local Government Committee 2010).

This policy paradox has a long history – the blend of race relations legislation to manage multiculture with immigration legislation to control (and vilify) migrants has been a consistent feature of the relationship between race, multiculture and social policy in the UK. The historical familiarity of cohesion and integration as policy approaches are apparent in their reliance on many of the same policy arenas and concepts that have been features of previous assimilation, multicultural, anti-racist and valuing diversity agendas. Similarly policing, education and housing and the concepts of community and locality are consistent features of race and diversity policymaking and policy debates. This underlines the haunted nature of policy development in relation to multiculture and difference and also highlights the extent to which social order – and increasingly security – sits at the heart of the race-policy relation and the reactive, defensive, crisis-driven character of race policymaking in this area.

Conclusion

In this chapter we have mapped the shifting configurations of policy approaches to race and multiculture. These policies are not simply responsive and adaptive to issues of race and diverse populations. Rather, policy is constitutive in that it also animates, defines and then manages race and multiculture in the social world. While we have suggested that the race-policy relationship can be viewed as series of epochs we have emphasised that these are not straightforwardly chronological and/or linear. In doing this genealogy of race policymaking we have shown how emergent policies are haunted by and rehabilitate traces of past policies. In this context we have sought to highlight four key defining features of the race-policy relationship.

First, is the extent to which specialist reports and public inquiries have driven and consolidated the development of race policy. Table 2.1 provides an overview of the key race reports that this chapter has discussed and which have been published in over three decades.

What is striking in this table is simply the number of reports and the way in which nearly all of them emerge from high-profile crisis events. Table 2.1 does not include a number of other crisis inquiries and reports that have taken place in education (e.g. the Swann Report, the Burnage Report) and health (e.g. the Ritchie Report, the Bennett Report). These are discussed in Chapters 6 and 7. That there is an ongoing context of crisis in which race policy is generated and made is reflected in the public inquiry genesis that the majority of these reports have. This also means that 'big' race policy tends to be made in an intense and highly mediated environment. This makes for an unstable and partial policymaking environment as reports are subject to particular, prejudiced, unpredictable and wilful readings and interpretations. Reports can be reduced to, and defined by, one or two small paragraphs. For example, the Cantle Inquiry's opening paragraph about ethnic polarisation and parallel lives reintroduced ethnic segregation as the frame for the cohesion agenda.

Second, we have argued that a defining feature of the race-policy relationship is that it is constantly evolving and subject to change, in an incremental fashion. This 'policy shifting' reflects the extent of the profound

Table 2.1 **Summary of key race-focused public inquiries and their reports**

Date	Report	Status	Focus	Key Feature
1982	*Scarman Report*	Public Inquiry	Riots and Policing	BME social and economic disadvantage. Police 'unwittingly racist' but not institutionally racist.
1999	*Macpherson Report*	Public Inquiry	Policing	Metropolitan police institutionally racist.
2000	*Parekh Report*	Independent	Social citizenship	The need to redefine national identity.
2001	*Cantle Report*	Public Inquiry	Riots	Ethnic separation and polarization and need to ensure interaction.
2006	*Mubarek Report*	Public Inquiry	Prisons	Institutional failure to protect and care for inmates. Racism treated casually by staff.
2007	*Our Shared Future*	Public Inquiry	Cohesion	Refine and extend cohesion strategy.

entanglements between race-policy interventions and wider political and social worlds. In this context it is possible to track the chaging policy agendas in this filed with the increasingly complex, multicultural UK and the changing and differently problematised diverse populations.

Third, we have pinpointed the profound entanglements between policy worlds and social worlds which can also be seen present in the way in which some race policies have been shaped through activities 'from below' and multidirectional pressures. For example, the lobbying and campaigning work of individuals, families and communities has been a significant impact on policy processes and, at times, been key to policy development. Most obviously the Macpherson report emerged as the result of the high-profile attention given to the Lawrence family's campaign. In a number of the chapters to follow there will be more detailed accounts of how the 'from below' mobilisations for changed and revised policy has brought about different policy delivery and service.

But alongside, and surrounding, these 'from below' processes of policy formation is the extent to which race-policy displays an anxious over-preoccupation with maintaining social order and securing and affirming national identity. This is our *fourth* defining feature of race policy. We suggest that in a context of crisis and reactive policymaking it is techniques of governance – the management, control, containment and securitisation – of cultural difference and ethnic diversity which continue to inform and concern policymaking in relation to race and multiculture. It is possible to see in the policy trajectories examined in this chapter that the forms of social order concerns have changed and developed but social order remains core whether in the assimilationist initiatives of the newly multicultural 1960s or securitisation–cohesion agenda of the super-diverse 2000s.

The chapters that follow return to and variously explore and examine these themes and features of race policymaking in relation to specific policy sites.

Part II
Policy Arenas

Chapter 3

Migration

The period since the 1950s has seen an intense debate, both in civil society and the state, about the question of migration in British society. This debate has taken a variety of forms over the decades and has evolved in a number of directions. Through the period from the 1950s to the present day we have seen a wide range of political controversies about immigration, resulting in both restrictions on the entry of new migrants and in the measures aimed at the integration of migrant communities. We have also seen localised and often contentious debates about migration in cities and towns all over the country. But it remains clear that even at the beginning of the 21st century migration and its social, cultural and political consequences remains at the heart of many of the changing facets of race and multiculture in contemporary Britain. Indeed, it is impossible to discuss race and multiculture in contemporary Britain without confronting issues linked to immigration, whether in the form of the increasing diversity of UK populations, economic migration or asylum and refuge.

The centrality of immigration to any rounded analysis of questions about race and multiculture is something that we have touched upon already in the overview of policy debates that we have provided in Chapters 1 and 2. In this chapter we want to take the analysis of this issue a step further by providing a historically informed account of the impact of immigration on British society. We begin by discussing the broader historical background to this issue and we then move on to cover the evolution of political and policy agendas during the 20th century and the beginning of the 21st century. This part of the chapter examines the ways in which social policy has responded to – and impacted on – different and changing migration flows and the incremental affects of immigration policy in terms of restricting entry into Britain for migrants and asylum seekers and curtailing their social and economic rights and their access to citizenship. The second part of the chapter then explores the relationship between migration and politics, focusing on the changing terms of political and social discourses about immigration. The final part of the chapter focuses more directly on the impact that changing discourses about immigration have on policies about race relations, equality, multiculturalism and cohesion and integration. In this sense the analysis in this chapter provides an overview of how the contentious politics of immigration links up to the specific policy arenas that we cover in the substantive policy arenas covered in the rest of this part of the book.

Historical and emergent migration trends

Britain has a long history of immigration and of providing asylum to those fleeing persecution. The profile of migrant groups has changed over time, partly as a consequence of technological advancements that facilitate longer journeys and also in response to factors that include post-colonial struggles, civil wars and internal conflicts, poverty, uneven development and economic and educational opportunities and shifting political agreements such as the expansion of the European Union. The contemporary UK is ethnically very diverse and the foreign-born population residing in the UK rose steadily over the course of the 20th century and rapidly during the beginning of the 21st century.

In 1901 there were 619,678 people who were born overseas, of which the large majority (69 per cent) were born in Ireland. Most of the foreign-born population living in Britain at the start of the 20th century had been born in Europe with Germany, Russia, Poland and France being the main countries of birth (Panayi 1994). During the second half of the 20th century, the foreign-born population continued to grow, increasing as a percentage of the total population of the United Kingdom, as Table 3.1 shows.

During the latter half of the 20th century, continental Europe continued to be the main sending region with more than half (50.9 per cent) of the foreign-born population, in 1971, coming from Europe and nearly a quarter (23.8 per cent) coming from Ireland. However, by 2001 there was a change in the profile of the foreign-born population, most notably a reduction in the proportion of immigrants from other European countries, which included Ireland. In total, a third was born in Europe, with Ireland accounting for only 11 per cent of the European total. The change at the start of the 21st century was the increasing proportion of migrants from South Asia and Africa. The 2001 census found that 21.1 per cent of the foreign-born population was from South Asia and 17 per cent were

Table 3.1 Foreign-born population, 1951–2001

Year	Total foreign born (thousands)	Percentage of total population
1951	2118.6	4.2
1961	2573.5	4.9
1971	3190.3	5.8
1981	3429.1	6.2
1991	3835.4	6.7
2001	4896.6	8.3

Source: Rendall and Salt (2005), table 8.1.

from Africa (Rendall and Salt 2005). It is estimated that since 1800 there have been 8,570,000 migrants to Britain with nearly three quarters (73 per cent) arriving since 1945 (Panayi 2010). The main characteristic of the post-1945 migration compared to the period of 1800–1944 is the longer journeys made by migrants that were made possible by technological developments and globalisation. The most significant example is migration from Africa where 10,000 Africans came to Britain before 1945 and 1,000,000 have arrived since 1945. However, migration is also influenced by social networks, transnational ties, as well as demographic, economic and political factors (Panayi 2010).

Linked to the changing profile of overseas born migrants was the proportion of the population who described themselves as coming from an ethnic group other than white: 5.5 per cent of the population described themselves as coming from a non-white minority ethnic group in 1991 which increased to 7.9 per cent of the population a decade later. In 2001, half of the ethnic-minority population described themselves as Asian or Asian British, a quarter as black or black British, 15 per cent as mixed, 5 per cent as Chinese and 5 per cent as another ethnic group. At the beginning of the 21st century the diversity of Britain's population continued to significantly increase as new migrants entered the UK through a range of routes – workers, students, family members, asylum applicants – and settled, predominantly in England, either with or without gaining residency status (see Chapters 1, 4 and 7).

It is important to note the extent of the shift in the migration. The University of Oxford's Migration Observatory collation of available data shows that between 1993 and 2011 the foreign-born population in the UK almost doubled from 3.8 million to around 7 million with 12.3 per cent of the UK's population being foreign born in 2011 compared to 7 per cent in 1993 (Migration Observatory 2012a). In relation to employment, migration from Eastern Europe has been particularly significant to these rises. So while India is the most common country of birth among foreign born populations, the highest numbers of foreign citizens are from Poland. It is within this context that migration, and more specifically the control and management of migration, which has long been a persistent policy, political and electoral agenda item, has become increasingly high profile in both public and policy debate and also within the changing agendas of race and multiculture.

Immigration and asylum policies: changing agendas and shifting concerns

Immigration and asylum policies in Britain can be divided into four main phases. Between 1905 and 1945 policies were mostly concerned with

Jewish aliens from Europe; the post–Second World War period through to the 1980s saw the racialised control of immigration from commonwealth countries; from the late 1980s to the end of the 20th century the policy focus was on the control and reduction of the numbers of asylum seekers entering Britain and from 2000 onwards, the agenda has been managing migration, both labour migration and asylum, and the social cohesion agenda (Sales 2007).

Britain has a long history of migration though prior to the 20th century the majority of migrants came from Europe. The largest minority group in Britain during the 19th century was the Irish. Germans remained the second largest migrant population, second only to the Irish community, until the latter part of the 19th century when Russian Poles, most of whom were Jews, formed the second largest group. Jewish migrants from Russian Poland migrated to Britain in increasing numbers from the 1880s as a consequence of Tsarist persecution (Panayi 1993) with the largest community settling in the Whitechapel area of London's east end. Between 1870 and 1914 it is estimated that 120,000 Jewish people had settled in Britain and by 1914 the Jewish population had reached around 300,000 (Miles and Solomos 1987).

There were a number of other migrant communities present in Britain during this period from Europe and elsewhere. Europeans included Lithuanians and Italians, the former migrating due to the competition for land in rural areas and because of persecution as a consequence of 'Russification' policies in the late-19th century (Holmes 1988). Italians came to Britain largely as a result of economic problems in Italy. From outside of Europe there were, by this time, small but established Chinese communities who came as seafarers to the port towns of London, Liverpool and Cardiff and then set up laundries (Holmes 1991). At the start of the 20th century Britain was already multiethnic. In addition to Europeans and Chinese people, there were also people from Africa living in Britain as students and seafarers, people from the Indian subcontinent were present as seafarers, performers, students and businessmen and people from the Caribbean were students. Non-Europeans formed a tiny proportion of the total population – much less than 1 per cent – until settlement patterns changed in the 1950s (Spencer 1997). It was migratory patterns that influenced legislative responses and thus it was in response to the increased migration of Jews fleeing pogroms in Eastern Europe and the resultant 1905 Aliens Act that the nature of the public debate on immigration changed and began what Panayi describes as the 'template for the history of British immigration control' (Panayi 2010: 62). The following section will explore the evolution and development of immigration controls and the ways in which they have responded to different migration flows and political agendas.

Control of aliens from Europe: 1905–1945

The 1905 Aliens Act excluded what were seen as undesirable aliens from Britain's territorial borders. These were in fact poor and sick Jews from Eastern Europe who were fleeing persecution. The 1905 Act was the first piece of legislation to make the links between immigration and welfare, a link that has been consistently made in subsequent pieces of legislation. Under the 1905 Act, migrants could be deported if they were in receipt of poor relief within one year of entering Britain. To mitigate this, a number of voluntary organisations helped the Jewish poor including the Jewish Board of Guardians, the Poor Jews Temporary Shelter and the Jewish Soup Kitchen. The Act was significant not only because of its exclusionary focus, but also because it reflected the emerging Darwinian ideology of a scientific hierarchy of race where Britons were seen as superior and the limited welfare, 'is for our own' (Hayes 2002: 38).

One of the reasons why Jewish immigration resulted in legislative measures was the visible difference of these migrants from the majority population. Jewish migrants were spatially clustered in densely populated areas of the east end of London and responses among the general population, to these migrants, are not dissimilar from the racialised responses to later migrant groups where the association between migration and competition for resources including housing and employment are replicated. In the case of Jewish migrants, the prevalent narratives were of them taking over geographical areas, and in so doing forcing 'English' people out, being prepared to accept undercut wages and in so doing jeopardising the chances of the working classes by taking scarce employment away from indigenous people. The following quotes from parliamentary debates from the late-19th and early 20th centuries illustrate the perception of Jewish migrants at this time:

> 'There are some streets you may go through and hardly know you are in England'. (Hansard, 11 February 1893, as cited in Jones 1977)
>
> 'if you desire to improve the condition of the working classes of this country...we must...do something to prevent this country from becoming the dust heap of Europe'. (Hansard 1890, as cited in Jones 1977)
>
> 'the inhabitants of whole streets in some cases have been turned out to make room for the foreigners...you can scarcely find a street in which the alien has not penetrated'. (HM Government 1902–1903, as cited in Jones 1977)

While the 1905 Aliens Act set out to limit the arrival of what were seen as undesirable Jewish aliens from Eastern Europe, other migrants were arriving in Britain during this period and this migration also resulted in legislative measures. The main cohorts of migrants during this period were refugees of a number of European countries including Belgium (1914–1918), Germany,

Czechoslovakia, Austria (to escape Nazi persecution) and Spain (Kushner and Knox 1999). In addition to refugees, workers came from the West Indies to fill labour market gaps due to conscription during the First World War.

The legislation that was enacted in the early part of the 20th century showed a consensus across political parties on issues of immigration (Sales 2007) and reflected the social, economic and political climate of that time. In Britain, the Aliens Restriction Act of 1914, the Aliens Restriction (Amendment) Act of 1919, the Aliens Order of 1920 and Special Restrictions (Coloured Alien Seaman) Order of 1925 had the cumulative effect of increasing controls over the entry, employment and the deportation of aliens. Under the Aliens Order of 1920, for example, all immigrants had to obtain work permits and entry to Britain would be refused to anyone who could not support themselves. Powers of deportation were also increased so that the Home Secretary could deport anyone who was not 'conducive to the public good' (Solomos 2003) though in reality deportation was rarely used outside of wartime (Bloch and Schuster 2005).

Parliamentary debates and legislation in this early period was overtly racialised focusing first on Jews from Eastern Europe, then on Germans due to the hostility towards them as a consequence of their enemy status during the First World War and then on black and Asian seafarers who had settled and were working in dock areas around Britain and were seen as a threat to the majority population during a period of high unemployment (Panayi 2010; Spencer 1997). The debates that took place during the first part of the 20th century set the precedent for the nature of the political debates in the post-war period (Solomos 2003).

Racialised control of immigration: 1945–1980

The second phase of immigration control began in the post–Second World War period (post-1945) because Britain needed migrants to rebuild Britain due to the labour shortages as a consequence of the war. Initially workers from Europe were favoured and the government actively recruited Irish workers and Eastern Europeans who were living in displaced persons camps. The workers recruited from the displaced persons camps came under a number of schemes, the largest being Balt Cygnet, Westward Ho! and the European Voluntary Worker Scheme. These displaced persons and refugees arrived in Britain under restrictive conditions that affected both their employment and settlement rights and they were recruited purely on the basis of their economic utility (Kay and Miles 1988; 1992). The government favoured these European workers over workers from colonial countries and former colonies because of the control they had over their employment and residency, and also because they were white and European and this brought the idea that they could be easily assimilated in a way that commonwealth migrants from the Caribbean, South Asia and Africa could not (Layton-Henry 1992). The following quote from the Royal Commission on Population (1949) demonstrates the above

> Immigration on a large scale into a fully established society like ours could only be welcomed without reserve if the immigrants were of good human stock [presumably European] and were not prevented by their religion or race from intermarrying with the host population and becoming merged with it. (cited in Layton-Henry 1992: 28)

Although the government had reservations about immigration from Commonwealth countries, the 1948 British Nationality Act ensured that all citizens of British colonies and the Commonwealth had rights of entry and British citizenship. The arrival of 492 Jamaicans on the *Empire Windrush* in 1948 was a symbolic demonstration of this 1948 Act. It wasn't until the 1950s that immigration from the West Indies became more significant. Between 1945 and 1959 around 126,000 workers form the Caribbean came to Britain attracted by factors that included recruitment by large employers including London transport.

The increase in immigration from the Caribbean and the Indian subcontinent in the 1950s were especially significant because between 1944 and 1948 legislation was passed that formed the basis for the welfare state. The new welfare state operationalised in 1948 provided for Britain's population from the 'cradle to the grave', and the provision of these new and precious services, including the National Health Service, corresponded with the arrival of migrants from the Commonwealth (Jones 1977). It is no surprise that issues of rights and ownership entered into the discussion of immigration and that welfare became and continues to be an important aspect of immigration control.

Immigration in the post-war period can be divided into two parts: immigration prior to the 1962 Commonwealth Immigrants Act which comprised mostly of migration from the Caribbean and immigration after the Act which comprised mainly of migrants from the Indian subcontinent (Jones 1977). Immigration correlated strongly with the demand for labour until 1960 when restrictive legislation was debated in Parliament, amid public concern about migration, and came into force in 1962 (Peach 1986). Table 3.2 shows the increase in immigration in 1961 in a 'rush to beat the ban' which paradoxically distorted the relationship between immigration and the needs of the economy.

The 1962 Act marked a watershed in immigration policy because for the first time restrictions were placed on the entry and settlement of UK Commonwealth citizens born outside of the UK. The Act basically set up a system to control immigration to Britain by black Commonwealth citizens

Table 3.2 Estimated net immigration from the New Commonwealth, 1953–1962

Year	West Indies	India	Pakistan	Others	Total
1953	2,000				2,000
1954	11,000				11,000
1955	27,500	5,900	1,850	7,500	42,650
1956	29,800	5,600	2,050	9,350	46,800
1957	23,000	6,600	5,200	7,600	42,400
1958	15,000	6,200	4,700	3,850	29,850
1959	16,400	2,950	850	1,400	21,600
1960	49,650	5,900	2,500	–350	57,700
1961	66,300	23,750	25,100	21,250	136,400
1962*	31,800	19,050	25,080	18,970	94,900

* First six months up to the introduction of the 1962 Commonwealth Immigrants Act.
Source: Layton-Henry (1992: 13).

by distinguishing between citizens of Britain and its colonies and those of independent Commonwealth countries (Solomos 2003). Under the Act immigration controls were placed on Commonwealth passport holders, unless they had been born in Britain, held a British passport issued by the British government or were included in the passport of someone who was born in Britain. In short, under this Act for the first time there was a distinction made between the rights of British subjects whose passports were issued in Britain and those whose passports were issued in Commonwealth countries (Spencer 1997). The Act therefore racialised rights by targeting people of black and Asian origin, not those of white descent from Australia, New Zealand and Canada (Sales 2007). The Act also introduced different categories of work vouchers for Commonwealth citizens. Category C was for unskilled workers and this category of voucher was capped and expected to be for black and Asian Commonwealth citizens (Sales 2007: 140). Though the 1962 Act was introduced by a Conservative government, the Labour government elected in 1964 continued the restrictive and discriminatory direction of policy, in light of the obvious popularity among the electorate for curbing black and Asian migration (Spencer 1997).

The second Commonwealth Immigration Act 1968 introduced by a Labour government was rushed through Parliament in only three days amidst fears that East African-Asians would exercise their rights as UK passport holders to come to the UK as a consequence of post-independence Africanisation policies in Kenya, Uganda and Malawi. Under the Act, any citizen of Britain or her colonies, holding a British passport would be subjected to immigration controls unless they had a parent or grandparent who had been born, adopted or registered in Britain as a British citizen or a citizen of its colonies (Solomos 2003). Sales notes that the Act, 'involved a racialised division between Commonwealth citizens' (2007: 142) which meant that those white Commonwealth citizens from Australia, New Zealand and South Africa were likely to be able to establish a patrial link while non-white citizens from Asia, Africa and the Caribbean were unlikely to be able to establish such a link which excluded them from entering the UK freely. Like previous legislation, the 1968 Act coincided with an economic downturn, in this instance brought about by the onset of deindustrialisation.

While governments were bringing in racialised immigration controls, there was also an awareness of racism and inequality, so alongside increasingly draconian immigration controls came a formalised race relations strategy. The conflation of good race relations, articulated as an end to discrimination through integration, and strict immigration controls to promote better community relations has been a key tenet of the immigration policy since the 1960s. Schuster and Solomos note that the approach 'was based on the idea that the few immigrants, particularly ones that were visibly different in some manner, there were, the easier it would be to integrate them into the "British way of life" and its social as well as cultural values' (Schuster and Solomos 2004: 268).

Therefore, linked to immigration controls from the 1960s was the idea that immigration control is a prerequisite for 'good race relations'. It is not surprising that, during this same period, the Race Relations Acts were introduced. There were four Race Relations Acts in quick succession: 1965, 1967, 1968 and 1976. The introduction of Race Relations legislation was significant because, as Goulbourne argues, 'it was a political recognition that racism was an undesirable aspect of British life, and demonstrated a willingness to use the law in the fight against racial discrimination' (Goulbourne 1998: 101). The cumulative aim of the Acts was to reduce discrimination in public places, on public transport and in other areas of public and economic life including employment, provision of public goods, advertising and housing. The 1976 legislation included racial disadvantage brought about by systematic racism making it illegal to discriminate on basis of 'colour, race, nationality or ethnic or national origin' or to segregate people on racial grounds and the promotion of equal opportunities. In order to deal with cases of discrimination, the 1965 Act set up the Race Relations Board while the Community Relations Commission was set up under the 1968 Act to promote harmonious race relations at the grassroot level. Both the Race Relations Board and the Community Relations Commission were replaced under the 1976 Act by the Commission for Racial Equality which existed until 2004 when it was merged with the Equality and Human Rights Commission (see also Chapter 2).

Legislation in 1971, 1981 and 1988 brought about new and even more restrictive immigration controls. The 1971 Immigration Act superseded the 1968 Act and further restricted the entry criteria by allowing the right to entry for only those who had been born or had a parent born in the UK, which excluded virtually all non-white commonwealth citizens. The Act also changed the status of employment vouchers to work permits that did not carry with them rights to permanent residency or family reunion. In short, the legislation was, 'another major milestone in the process of erecting racist immigration controls' (Layton-Henry 1992: 85).

The 1981 British Nationality Act removed the automatic right of citizenship to those born in the UK; only those satisfying the partial rule were entitled to citizenship. The cumulative effect of the legislation was that nearly all non-white commonwealth citizens were excluded from entry to Britain and the right to abode. This divided British subjects by perceptions of their 'real' Britishness (Paul 1997). The final piece of immigration legislation during this period was the 1988 Immigration Act and this act again made a clear link between welfare and immigration. Under this legalisation all British and Commonwealth citizens who wanted relatives to join them had to sponsor them and prove that this could be done without recourse to public funds.

The period between 1962 and 1988 was significant because it brought to a close virtually all migration from Commonwealth countries. Part of the argument used to justify legislation was the necessity to ensure good race relations. In short, successive governments argued that the only way to ensure good race relations was to limit the number of migrants entering Britain and so immigration control was linked with integration strategies and race relations (Solomos 2003).

Migration from Commonwealth countries was not the only form of migration during this period. Refugees and asylum seekers came to Britain from all over the world including East Africa, Chile, Vietnam, Sri Lanka, Kurds from Turkey and Somalia. Until the 1970s, the majority of refugees in Europe were from other European countries and so the changing origins of refugee and asylum-seeker arrivals as well as the increase in numbers resulted in legislation aimed at curtailing these flows including the imposition of visas to restrict migration from refugee producing countries such as Sri Lanka and Turkey. Visa restrictions also coincided with the introduction, in 1987, of the Immigration (Carriers Liability) Act. Under this Act, fines of £1000 were imposed on carrier companies that transported passengers with incorrect documentation. This in effect added airline companies to the arsenal of immigration controls already in place. Because the legislation up until 1988 had bought virtually all primary migration from Commonwealth countries to an end, asylum seekers became the main category of primary migrants in the

Table 3.3   Asylum applications, 1988–2000

Year	Number	% Change from previous year
1988	3998	−6
1989	11640	+191
1990	26205	+125
1991	44840	+71
1992	24605	−45
1993	22370	−9
1994	32830	+47
1995	43965	+34
1996	29640	−33
1997	32500	+10
1998	46015	+42
1999	71160	+55
2000	80315	+6.5

Source: adapted from Home Office (2000).

1990s. The consequence of this change was that successive governments began to focus on restricting asylum migration which was less controllable, increasing and brought to the UK asylum seekers from all over the world. Table 3.3 shows the numbers of asylum seekers coming to the UK from 1988–2000.

The focus on asylum: late 1980s onwards

The changing numbers of asylum applicants, year on year, were a reflection of refugee producing conflicts. During the 1990s the largest single country of origin of asylum applicants was the former Yugoslavia reflecting the Bosnian and Kosovo crises. There were continuous flows of asylum seekers from Sri Lanka and Somalia during the 1990s. The consequence of increasing numbers of asylum seekers and its notable rise from 1989 onwards is that successive governments attempted to curb the numbers of asylum seekers arriving spontaneously in Britain through restrictive legislation. There were three pieces of immigration and asylum legislation in quick succession during the 1990s: 1993 Asylum and Immigration Appeals Act, 1996 Asylum and Immigration Act and 1999 Immigration and Asylum Act. The political discourse during this period once again conflated the need for immigration controls with good race relations. Moreover, successive pieces of legalisation incrementally curtailed access to welfare and employment for asylum seekers arriving in Britain.

Part of the reason for curtailment of welfare rights was the adoption, by the Conservative Thatcher government elected in 1979, of a neoliberal approach to welfare. Such an approach extends market principles to the welfare state and these reforms were to have a large affect on both asylum seekers and ethnic minorities more generally. Under the changes asylum seekers were excluded from mainstream welfare provision and a separate agency was set up to administer support for eligible asylum seekers. At the same time minority ethnic groups were disproportionately affected by changes in entitlements to unemployment benefits and pensions as well as the introduction of new sponsorship rules and residency tests that limited eligibility (Bloch 2000b). In short, British society was becoming increasingly stratified in terms of access to social goods and welfare creating different categories of migrants with different rights within Britain (Cohen 1994; Morris 2007).

The links between the asylum legislation of the 1990s and welfare, or more explicitly notions of 'bogus' asylum seekers abusing the British welfare system, being a burden or a drain on limited resources became entrenched in political debates and within the media reportage of asylum (Sales 2007). Competition for scarce resources once again influenced the nature of the discussions around immigration and asylum legislations and this was located within the race relations rhetoric (Bloch 2000a). The first piece of asylum focused legislation was the 1993 Asylum and Immigration Appeals Act. This Act ended the statutory duty of local authorities to house asylum seekers if they had access to any accommodation however temporary, while under the Act the welfare benefits for asylum seekers were set at 70 per cent of the income support level, which is a subsistence level benefit. The second piece of legislation, the Asylum and Immigration Act 1996, took asylum seekers outside of the mainstream benefits system following the parliamentary debates that once again conflated asylum with welfare and employment but also with the notion of illegality. Michael Howard, who was the Home Secretary from 1993 to 1997 and presided over the introduction of the 1996 Act, maintained that 'firm but fair immigration controls' (House of Commons, 20 November 1995: 335) was a prerequisite for good race relations. He justified the introduction of the Bill by linking immigration with welfare provision and employment opportunities when he stated that the UK

> is far too attractive a destination for bogus asylum seekers and other illegal immigrants. The reason is simple: it is far easier to obtain access to jobs and benefits here than almost anywhere else. (House of Commons, 20 November 1995: 338)

Under the 1996 Act two categories of welfare entitlement for asylum seekers were created. Those who applied for asylum at the port of entry were entitled to 90 per cent of income support while those who applied in-country and those appealing against a Home Office decision on their case were excluded from benefits; the implication being that genuine asylum seekers would apply at the port of entry. This ignores the reasons why asylum seekers do not always declare themselves as such at the port of entry. Instead in-country applicants and those appealing were given in-kind support by local authorities, in the form of vouchers to be spent at designated supermarkets and housing, under the 1948 National Assistance Act. Families with children were supported under the Children Act 1989 and the consequence was that asylum seekers were being increasingly moved out of the mainstream benefits system and into local authority in-kind non-cash support (Sales 2007). Moreover, asylum seekers were visible in their localities because of the vouchers and became increasingly targeted for verbal and sometimes physical abuse.

In 1996, the right of asylum seekers to seek permission to work on arrival was withdrawn and employers found to have hired someone without the correct documentation were fined which deterred employers from hiring refugees and asylum seekers because of the extra bureaucracy of checking documentation (Bloch 2000a; Refugee Council 1999). This was a precursor to the 1999 Immigration and Asylum Act introduced by the Labour government that had been elected in 1997. Under the Act, a completely separate system for asylum seekers and a new organisation to administer the system called the National Asylum Support System (NASS) was created. The 1999 Act also continued the dual strategy of restricting entry to the UK and curtailing welfare provisions for asylum seekers (Bloch 2002a). A number of pre-entry controls were either introduced or strengthened including the extension of carriers' liability to trucking companies to target asylum seekers being smuggled over land. Welfare provision once again was central to the debates which, agues Sales, created the dichotomy of 'deserving' and 'undeserving' with asylum seekers 'cast as "undeserving", while denied the means (employment) to join the "deserving"' (Sales 2002: 459). Such a policy was in keeping with New Labour's emphasis on social obligations rather than social rights, social inclusion or equality (Lister 1998). In short, the welfare state exists to benefit citizens and so asylum seekers, as non-citizens, were not to be included either in mainstream welfare provisions or in the labour market (Sales 2002). Destitute asylum seekers, that are those without any other means of support from family or friends, were entitled to £10 in cash and vouchers with a combined total value of 70 per cent income support. The primary aim of the policy as Hynes and Sales (2010) note was to control entry and ensure that there were no incentives for economic migration.

The 1999 Act also introduced the compulsory dispersal of asylum seekers administered by the central agency (NASS). Asylum seekers were to be dispersed on a no-choice basis to regional consortia around the United

Kingdom. Dispersal itself was not a new policy; it had been used with cohorts of refugees, notably Ugandan Asians and Vietnamese refugees in the 1970s and 1980s and Bosnians and Kosovars in the 1990s. Dispersal was a settlement strategy adopted to deal with the arrival of relatively large numbers of refugees in response to a crisis (Boswell 2001) so as to prevent the spatial clustering of refugees in a few areas though there has been a pattern of secondary migration to areas with established communities (see Chapter 2). Dispersal has been described as 'spreading the burden' of asylum from concentrated areas in London to the country as a whole (Robinson, Andersson and Musterd 2003) though the language of the asylum seekers and the compulsory nature of the scheme clearly impacted on and reinforced negative public attitudes towards asylum seekers and served to exclude them within the dispersal locations (Hynes and Sales 2010). Moreover, as Flynn notes, in the press dispersal it was reported 'as a disaster for race relations' (Flynn 2005: 474). Not all asylum seekers were dispersed, instead some opted for subsistence-only support from NASS and stayed with family members or friends, often in the Greater London area.

The key difference in dispersal policy prior to 1999 and from 1999 onwards was that prior to 1999 if refugees chose to move from their dispersal area there were no punitive consequences in terms of eligibility for welfare support. However, the 1999 Act changed the conditions of welfare entitlements for asylum seekers, linking housing benefit directly to dispersal. Those who chose not to be dispersed were ineligible for financial support with their housing costs and relied, instead, on family members or friends for accommodation.

In theory, under dispersal, asylum seekers were to be sent to cluster zones in ethnically diverse localities, to ensure that appropriate language and other support was available (Mynott 2002). In reality though, dispersal locations were often selected based on the availability of short-term housing, and so asylum seekers found themselves in areas with high levels of deprivation (Hynes and Sales 2010). Such a policy reinforced the social and economic exclusion of asylum seekers and was part of the 'arsenal of control' aimed at managing migration and reducing the numbers of asylum seekers (Bloch and Schuster 2005: 508). The consequence was that asylum seekers were left isolated and vulnerable and without the support of social, cultural and community networks that are so important in the early stages of settlement (Bloch 2002a; Zetter and Pearl 2000).

Managing migration: 2000s

Since the new millennium the focus of immigration and asylum legislation and policy has been on managing migration, fostering integration, community cohesion and national identity. During this recent period, migration policy has become attached to economic priorities in terms of the needs of the labour market for both unskilled temporary workers and skilled workers through a points based system (Somerville 2007). Sales (2007) notes that the publication of the White Paper *Secure Borders: Safe Havens* in 2002 as the precursor to the 2002 Nationality, Immigration and Asylum Act was the beginning of an explicit 'managed migration' approach.

In the last decade there have been five separate pieces of legislation, as Table 3.4 shows. These have been accompanied by a number of policy interventions relating to entry into the UK, citizenship, social cohesion and integration. The key elements of the legislation relate to the support of asylum seekers, pathways to citizenship, control through detention, tagging and biometric documents.

In the period since 2010, the Conservative–Liberal Democratic Coalition has continued to emphasise the links between welfare and immigration, the need to curb migration and to highlight the links between immigration and negative impacts on social cohesion by clearly placing the blame on migrants. One of the main policy interventions has been to impose a cap on the number of skilled migrants allowed into the UK from non-EU countries. In a speech on immigration, the Prime Minister David Cameron stated that immigration

> has placed real pressures on communities up and down the country. Not just pressures on schools, housing and healthcare – though those have been serious…but social pressures too. Real communities are bound by common experiences…forged by friendship and conversation…knitted together by all the rituals of the neighbourhood, from the school run to the chat down the pub. And these bonds can take time. So real integration takes time. That's why, when there have been significant numbers of new people arriving in neighbourhoods…perhaps not able to speak the same language as those living there…on occasions not really wanting or even willing to integrate…that has created a kind of discomfort and disjointedness in some neighbourhoods. (14 April 2011 reprinted in http://www.bbc.co.uk/news/uk-politics-13083781 on 16 May 2011)

This integration argument has its roots in the early 2000's community cohesion response to criticisms of multiculturalism brought on in part by urban unrest in 2001 in Bradford, Burnley and Oldham (see Chapters 1, 2 and 5). The Cantle Report commissioned as a consequence of urban unrest highlighted polarised towns with segregated communities living 'parallel lives' (Cantle 2001: 9). The consequence of the shift towards community cohesion and increasing integration has been the critique of multiculturalism as a policy that encourages separateness between ethnic groups (McGhee 2008). Significantly these polarised communities were not communities

Table 3.4 Key legislation on immigration, nationality and asylum

Date	Legislation	Key elements
2002	Nationality, Immigration and Asylum Act	Introduced Section 55 which allowed the Home Office to withdraw access to NASS support from those who do not apply for asylum 'as soon as reasonably practicable' leaving asylum seekers without financial assistance. The very unpopular and contested voucher system was phased out.
2004	Asylum and Immigration Act	A failed asylum seeker with a family can have their support withdrawn if the person has failed without 'reasonable excuse' to leave the UK voluntarily. Local Authorities have a duty to provide for children under 18 under the Children Act 1989 and if necessary children will be separated from their family.
2006	Immigration, Asylum and Nationality Act	People granted refugee status given five years leave to remain in the UK after which time their case is reviewed. Asylum seekers who are unable to travel back to their home countries due to medical situations or there being no safe route home is given board, lodgings and vouchers instead of any cash. Electronic tagging, without consent introduced for those not detained.
2007	UK Borders Act	Increases power of immigration officers to detain, to enter and search homes for documentation and to search and arrest in relation to illegal working. Provides for biometric immigration documents and allows the Border and Immigration Agency (BIA) to require anyone granted limited leave to enter and remain to report to the BIA or stipulate address of residence.
2009	Borders, Citizenship and Immigration Act	The Act increased the residence period required prior to naturalisation from 5 to 8 years though it can be reduced to 6 through voluntary work known as 'active citizenship'. Refugees will have to meet the language proficiency requirements and/or Knowledge of Life in the UK test before being granted citizenship. The welfare of children in the UK to be safeguarded and promoted by immigration officers.

Source: adapted from Bloch (2012: 417).

of new migrants but of established black and minority ethnic populations born and educated in Britain. However this did not prevent others making the links between migration and urban unrest such as David Blunkett former Home Secretary who argued that, 'Unless properly managed, however, migration can be perceived as a threat to community stability and good race relations' (Blunkett 2002: 65). Since the early 2000s these areas have been among those affected by new migration flows including those from the expansion of the European Union. The settlement of new migrants in those areas associated with established black and minority ethnic populations have disrupted older residential patterns and contributed to emergent and super-diverse formations of multiculture. For example, as we discuss in more detail in Chapter 4, Deborah Phillips' (2010b) research in the city of Leeds in Northern England found ambivalent social interactions – both hospitable and hostile – between established, predominantly Muslim local populations and more recent migrants from Eastern Europe living in the same neighbourhood (see also Hickman, Cowley and Mai 2008).

The impact of new migration on existing and emergent forms of multiculture was recognised and commented on by the Commission of Integration and Cohesion (see also Chapter 2). In its report, *Our Shared Future* (2007), the Commission identified discrimination as a barrier to community cohesion though the report emphasised that this was not always the case but depended on a number of interacting local factors. The report noted that globalisation and the resultant population diversity added an additional layer as 'settled communities are worried about the fair allocation of public services – with some thinking immigrants and minorities are getting special treatment' (Commission on Integration and Cohesion 2007: 33). In a direct echo of this, the coalition government also emphasised its concerns about migration in its integration strategy document (Department for Communities and Local Government 2012). It states that although 'immigration has brought benefits [...] the last decade has brought fresh challenges [...] with substantial and sustained increases in migration into the UK from both within and outside of the EU. The resulting pace of change in our local communities is unprecedented. Most places have accommodated the changes but there is no room for complacency.' The integration strategy proceeds to suggest that there is a need for 'greater control' of immigration in order to make it a 'source of national strength rather than a concern'.

These current policy and political discourses linking migration with social cohesion and social order reflect and resonate with much older debates established in the 20th century, most notably the continued conflation of different categories of migrants and the mobilisation of often highly mediated, problematising and contradictory narratives of migrants as being unwilling to integrate, exploiting the British welfare system or of migrants having preferential access to limited labour market opportunities and public resources such as health care and social housing and so forth (see Chapters 4 and 6). These discourses are effective. Negative public opinion in relation to migration is widespread in the UK although as the Migration Observatory noted while around three quarters of British people favour reducing immigration there is a more positive response to skilled migrants, and in something of a paradox 'while vast majorities view migration as harmful to Britain, few claim that their own neighbour is having problems due to migrants' (Migration Observatory 2012b). In other words the negative responses to migration are often in the abstract. But to some extent this reflects the potency of the problematisation of migrants discourse. This potency is particularly effective in relation to the issue of migrants – particularly asylum applicants and refugees – and welfare entitlement.

Migration, ethnicity and welfare

While economic and labour market factors have been key drivers of migration dynamics there has, as noted earlier, been a long standing conflation of immigration, deprivation and welfare policy. This has its origins in the 1905 Aliens Act and has been very much a part of the asylum regime in the UK. Legislation and social policy in the areas of welfare and employment have contributed to a stratified system, not only for asylum seekers but for migrants and people from minority populations more generally. Asylum legislation means that asylum applicants are unable to legally work and are therefore locked into the welfare system and dependent on reduced levels of benefits. Asylum applicants and their dependents – usually children – live in conditions far below the poverty line for extended periods of time (Children's Society 2012). Welfare therefore acts as a mechanism for reducing stratification but also for increasing it (Esping-Andersen 1990). Sometimes stratification is obvious, as is the case for asylum seekers who receive only a proportion (between 55% and 70%) of the subsistence level benefits such as Income Support and Job Seekers Allowance.

Such differentiation began in the mid-1990s, and was exemplified by the then Home Secretary Michael Howard when he stated in 1995 that Britain must be 'a haven, not a honey pot' for genuine refugees. In short, genuine refugees would be grateful for a safe destination and would not seek out the UK for its generous provision. In the 1990s, as Sales notes

> Official thinking was that 'genuine refugees' would be prepared to undergo a period of hardship since the process would weed out 'bogus' claimants. (Sales 2002: 466)

In reality though, decisions about asylum destinations are more complex and often asylum seekers know little about asylum provision in the destination before arrival. The choice of destination can often be in the hands of the agent who organises the journey and destinations are also shaped by social networks where there is a choice, not by perceptions of benefits and eligibility to work, which was removed for most asylum seekers in July 2002 (Bloch 2002a; b; Gilbert and Koser 2006; Robinson and Segrott 2002).

However, it is not only asylum seekers who have been targeted by welfare stratification. Morissens and Sainsbury (2005) found that both immigration status and ethnicity are associated with a greater risk of poverty and that among citizen households benefits are much more likely to help people out of poverty than migrant households. They conclude that benefits have a differential impact on households and part of the rationale is the view that

> perceptions that foreigners rely heavily on social assistance have prompted restrictions of their eligibility to benefits and fragmented support for the welfare state. (Morissens and Sainsbury 2005: 641)

One of the ways in which differential access to welfare is analysed is through stratified rights which are a continuum of rights, including social citizenship rights, with citizens at one end and undocumented migrants and rejected asylum seekers at the other end (Morris 2007). Social citizenship includes access to welfare rights and services and the interplay of these rights with immigration policy affects migrants (Corden and Sainsbury 2006). However, though disproportionately affected, it's not only migrants who experience differential access and greater welfare poverty; a number of poorer BME groups are more likely to be excluded or have no access to benefits compared to others. We explore some of these issues and concerns in relation to housing and health in Chapters 4 and 6. These patterns of migrants' highly differential access to and experience of social goods is partly a consequence of welfare reforms affecting eligibility and/or the amount of benefit entitlement and also due to institutional and cultural actors. There are a number of reasons for this including low pay, greater periods of unemployment, fewer National Insurance contributions over the working life course, residency criteria, periods aboard and interrupted contributions, all of which have an impact on benefits, including pensions, and disproportionately affect ethnic minorities regardless of immigration or citizenship status. Structurally and culturally research has identified that some ethnic-minority customers are less knowledgeable about benefit entitlement criteria which affect not only the access to benefits but also claim making (Jones and Tracy 2010) while others are treated differently due to their ethnicity by DWP staff when applying for benefits which in turn affects access (Kirkwood 2005). The myth of migrant-benefit dependency is therefore challenged by the cultural variations in benefit claiming which in some instances emphasises family responsibility over and above the welfare state (Chan 2006).

Conclusion

This chapter has outlined the changing periods of migration and shown the similarity of responses to the different migrant groups. Legislation has been increasingly restrictive and new migrants, including asylum seekers, have become increasingly marginalised from the rest of the population. The contentious nature of immigration in the period since 1945 has done much to shape the policy agendas and interventions we have seen in relation to race and multiculture in British society. This has been evident both in the specific policy responses to immigration as well as in other policy trends on wider issues concerned with race and multiculture. Although successive governments have attempted to reach a consensus on questions linked to immigration and asylum this has not proved to be possible for most of the period since the 1950s. Indeed the period since the 2000s has highlighted the tendency for migration to remain a deeply contested issue, particularly in the context of the increasingly globalised and complex patterns of migration that have characterised this period and have contributed directly to the new geographies of multiculture and the emergence of super-diversity in urban England (see Chapters 1 and 4). As we have argued in the course of this chapter the focus of migration policies has, if anything, become even more intimately tied up with questions about the management of cultural diversity and social cohesion.

In this early period of the 21st century the shifting dynamics of immigration and asylum are likely to bear heavily on the policy agendas of the UK and other societies in the Global North. The economic and social dislocations that we have seen in both the Global South and the Global North in the past decade make it likely that the issue of immigration will remain deeply contested and the focus of intense political and social mobilisation. With rising unemployment, economic crisis and global restructuring very much a part of the emerging situation in Europe and other geopolitical environments the likelihood is that restrictive immigration policies will continue. When combined with hostility to migrants and the espousal of anti-immigrant attitudes, such policies are likely to have a direct impact on the position of migrant and black and minority ethnic communities as well as on the future of multicultural policies and initiatives.

Chapter 4

Housing

Houses, housing and where people live are central to individual, collective and social well-being. As Robinson and Reeve note,

> Housing experiences are significant because housing is a critical determinant of health, well-being, quality of life and settlement experience. In most cultures, and for most people, housing provides the realm within which the ontological security and safety of home is nurtured and, as such, can represent a sanctuary from hostility and exclusion that many new immigrants encounter in wider society. (Robinson and Reeve 2006: 25–26)

Housing can be understood as a social good and integral to the delivery of social stability. Changes in houses and housing reflect wider social changes. The homes in which people live combine a mix of personal lives and social and contextual factors. Houses are also about places and the geographies of where people live – streets, estates, neighbourhoods, towns, cities, villages, regions. In other words housing is always about a combination of the social and the spatial and has long been associated with political debate and is a key site of social policy interventions. This has been especially marked when housing and residence are considered in relation to race and ethnicity. Housing and patterns of residential settlement have centrally and very directly shaped what was previously thought of as 'race relations' and continue to underpin current political, policy and academic debates about ethnically based segregation, integration, multiculture and cohesion (see Chapter 2).

However, unlike education, policing and health, housing has become somewhat marginal to more recent race and ethnicity agendas. As Ratcliffe (2004: 59) observes, 'spatial segregation and its implications are currently very much at the top of the policy agenda in the UK; housing inequalities, curiously are less so'. He notes that *The Future of Multi-Ethnic Britain* report (Parekh 2000) made no reference to housing and while housing is included in the Commission for Integration and Cohesion's final report *Our Shared Future* (2007) it is not a major area of substantive commentary despite community and neighbourhood being a key focus for the Commission. As Ratcliffe argues, 'housing is absolutely pivotal both to the 'future of multi-ethnic Britain' [...] and to the prospects of greater inclusivity' (Ratcliffe 2004: 59).

This chapter, continuing this argument, is divided into four broad parts. The first part examines the new geographies of contemporary multiculture and reviews evidence about the relationship between ethnic identification and the forms, types and qualities of housing in which majority and minority populations live. In the second part of the chapter we examine the housing-race-residency research, moving from the place focused work on early 'race relations' studies in the UK (for example Rex and Moore 1967) to more recent studies (Kudenko and Phillips 2009; McGarrigle and Kearns 2009; Ratcliffe 2009; Sarre 1986). In part three the challenges of identifying relationships between ethnicity and residential space are examined alongside the ways in which housing and residential settlement patterns can be analysed through the various, changing interactions of structural constraint and agency based choice. The role of housing policy is also crucial in understanding the relationship between choice and constraint and it is the broad directions in housing policy that are the focus of part four of the chapter. Alongside a reflection on evidence the chapter will consider key urban policy interventions – dispersal, regeneration and community cohesion – made in relation to race and ethnicity. Reference will also be made to urban policy in non-UK contexts – namely the Hope VI project in the US.

What threads through this chapter is the shifting nature of ethnicity and residency patterns. Most obviously these patterns have been associated with urban settings but established race-urban geographies are being disrupted by new migratory movements and by established BME relocations and residential mobilities. It is clear that recognition of the extending geographies of multiculture – into smaller cities and towns, suburbs and rural areas – is necessary for understanding the relationship between race, ethnicity and residency.

Identifying changing patterns of multicultural residency

As we noted in Chapter 1 census data and releases from the Office of National Statistics (ONS) (2011; 2012) show that a great number of areas in the UK are becoming more ethnically mixed. This dispersal of multiculture is likely to continue as the proportion of the England and Wales populations that is minority ethnic increases (Wohland et al. 2010). However, there are significant regional and local authority variations in the levels and forms of multicultural settlement. For example it is the big urban environment of London and the South East of England and to a lesser extent the West Midlands, in which multicultural residency concentrations are most evident. In the London Boroughs of Brent, Newham and Haringey the overall minority ethnic population is larger than the overall white British population. ONS data show that 50 per cent of the total Caribbean, African and Bangladeshi population live in the Greater London area compared to only one in ten of the white British population. While these super-diverse concentrations exist it is equally important to recognise the complexity within this diversity, the continuation of ethnic residential change and the absence of any areas where populations identify as completely white British. Three different places in England illustrate each of these.

The first example is the city of Birmingham that has a long-established multiethnic population. Drawing on ONS population estimates for 2008–2009 Birmingham City Council's demographic profiling of its residents showed that the city was ranked 17th in terms of ethnic diversity. Within this there were some significant trends. The Pakistani population group is the largest minority group in Birmingham followed by Indian, Black Caribbean and White Other. However, there were decreases in all of these groups with the exception of White Other. The White Other category is increasing, and projected to replace Bangladeshis as the fourth largest minority group in the city. There has been a significant growth in the Black African population between 2001 and 2009, making it the most rapidly growing ethnic group in Birmingham (Birmingham City Council 2011).

The changing ethnicity profile of residential settlement can be seen outside of those urban environments, like Birmingham, which have long associations with multicultural residents. While the London boroughs are areas with the highest concentrations of super-diversity, what is significant are the ways in which small cities and large towns are becoming increasingly multiethnic. Both the South East of England and the large towns and surrounding areas of Slough and Luton are examples of this. Slough was 9th in the ONS projections of the 20 most diverse local authorities in England, with Leicester 10th and Luton 18th (Birmingham City Council 2011). This was confirmed in the 2011 Census in which Slough was identified as the borough outside London with the lowest percentage of white British in its population (ONS 2012).

Outside of the ONS top 20 most multicultural places there are other cities and more remote towns that testify to the extent of diverse residential settlement. Milton Keynes in South-East England and the market town of Thetford in East Anglia are two further examples worth briefly reviewing so as to illuminate some of the shifts in migrant residential settlement. School census data from Milton Keynes show that the ethnicity profile of those attending schools in the city is both significant and changing (Milton Keynes Intelligence Observatory 2010). Overall black and minority ethnic groups represent 31.0 per cent of school pupils compared with the 20.7 per cent figure recorded in 2005. Milton Keynes Schools Census shows that of those children of primary school age 33.2 per cent come from minority ethnic groups and 26.7 per cent of those children of secondary school age come from minority ethnic groups. There are emergent but rapidly establishing Ghanaian and Somali communities in Milton Keynes and this reflects the schools census finding that it is the Black African group that accounts for being the largest minority ethnic group in the city's schools survey (Kesten et al. 2011).

While very different in terms of settlement types and geography East Anglia, which was until recently overwhelmingly monocultural, also demonstrates patterns of culturally diverse in-migration and population change as its agricultural and tourism/leisure industries attract large number of migrants from European Union countries as the case of Thetford shows. In the 2001 census, 95.27 per cent of residents in Breckland (the local authority in which Thetford is based) classed themselves as White British. The largest other minority ethnic group identified in the census was the Other White group at 2.67 per cent with all other minority ethnic groups recorded as being well-below 1 per cent. However, in an echo of the Birmingham story, estimates from ONS suggested an increase in population in Breckland with the share of the population who are White British decreasing to 92.1 per cent and the Other White population increasing to 4.1 per cent (Office for National Statistics 2006). These increases are mainly Eastern European (but also Portuguese) migrants (see Taylor and Rogaly 2004).

The examples of Birmingham, Milton Keynes and Thetford demonstrate the extent to which current geographies of England are reconfiguring: changes can be seen on the one hand in those geographical areas which have recently become more ethnically diverse through BME social mobility, through migrants from new EU countries and through refugee and asylum arrival and dispersal *and* on the other hand changes can be seen in those areas where new migrants present a far greater mix of nationalities and these feed into a well-established and much older tradition of multicultural settlement.

John Perry (2008) notes that not only has migration become a much bigger factor in population growth in the last ten years but also 'new migrant communities often have few social or cultural similarities to longer established BME groups'. These established BME groups are themselves highly diverse and part of structural shifts as some BME populations become economically prosperous and middle class (Harries, Richardson and Soteri-Proctor 2008; Moore 2008; Vincent et al. 2011) and generational differences begin to disrupt older patterns of cultural identification and aspiration (Kudenko and Phillips 2009).

It is clear that residential geographies of multiculture are evolving. The next section will explore the patterns of different ethnic groups and housing tenure.

Ethnicity and housing tenure

As with where people live, understanding *what* housing different populations live in also requires a multifactor approach. The relationship between

ethnicity, housing conditions and *forms* of housing tenure – owner occupied, private rented sector, social rented sector (housing association and
local authority) – is a process which involves a range of other contextual
factors which interact with ethnicity and race. Examples of these other
factors are most obviously social and economic but local and generational
factors are also key variables that need to be taken into account as are
migratory histories, changing household formations, social capacities and
aspirations and housing policies. How then to make sense of the intensely
complicated and multifactored housing landscapes? One obvious place to
start is with the available data. We have used the Labour Force Surveys
(LFS) (2008) for the ONS as a baseline of the national picture of housing type and ethnic categorisation in England (see also Department for
Communities and Local Government 2010: 23).

Both Table 4.1 which details the ethnicity-housing tenure relationship
in 2008 and Table 4.2 which reveals the broader trends in this relationship over time can be understood as documenting of the most basic key
categories of the housing-ethnicity relationship. Some of the important

Table 4.1 Housing tenure by ethnic group

Ethnic group by household reference person	Owner occupied			All social renters	All private renters	Total
	Owned outright	Mortgage	All owner occupiers			
White British	34	38	72	17	11	100
White Other	22	27	49	14	37	100
All white groups	33	37	70	17	13	100
Black Caribbean	14	35	49	41	11	100
Black African	4	24	28	44	28	100
Indian	28	45	74	7	20	100
Pakistani	29	40	68	16	16	100
Bangladeshi	9	29	38	47	15	100
Chinese	15	37	52	13	35	100
Mixed	11	29	39	33	28	100
Other	9	28	37	28	35	100
All minority ethnic groups	16	34	30	26	24	100

Source: Adapted from ONS LFS 2008, S116. All figures are in percentages.

Table 4.2   Trends in housing tenure by ethnic group, 1984–2007

Year and ethnic group	Owner occupied			All social rented	All private rented	Total
	Owned outright	Mortgage	All			
White						
1984	26	36	62	28	11	100
1994	26	42	68	22	10	100
2004–2005	31	40	72	18	10	100
2006–2007	31	39	70	18	11	100
Black Caribbean						
1984	5	30	35	57	8	100
1994	10	37	47	44	9	100
2004–2005	12	34	46	41	12	100
2006–2007	20	34	54	38	8	100
Indian						
1984	24	53	76	13	10	100
1994	23	60	83	8	9	100
2004–2005	32	43	74	10	16	100
2006–2007	29	43	72	8	20	100
Pakistani						
1984	27	50	78	13	9	100
1994	18	50	68	18	14	100
2004–2005	23	47	70	20	11	100
2006–2007	27	45	72	14	14	100
Bangladeshi						
1984	7	36	43	50	7	100
1994	8	31	38	54	8	100
2004–2005	9	28	37	56	7	100
2006–2007	5	33	38	53	9	100

Source: Adapted from ONS LFS 2008, S119. All figures are in percentages.

patterns it reveals relate to the differences between ethnic groups as well as the diversity in housing type and it is these that we now highlight:

- There is a strong correlation between owner-occupied housing (with and without mortgages) and Indian and Pakistani origin populations. Owner occupation was highest for Indian origin groups, followed relatively closely by those populations defined in the Pakistani and the White British category. Correspondingly the percentage of the Indian and Pakistani population in the social rented sector is relatively low.

- Local authority social rented housing is high among Bangladeshi, Black Caribbean and Black African populations.
- Although the Labour Force Survey for 2008 does not break down the social rented sector its earlier surveys did. LFS data for 2006 show the important role that 'Third Sector' social rented housing (e.g. housing associations) played for some ethnic groups. In particular, those populations in the Black Caribbean and Black African and Bangladeshi categories have comparatively high percentages in this form of housing tenure – 19 per cent, 16 per cent and 14 per cent respectively. Only 7 per cent of the White British category was represented in this form of housing tenure.
- In terms of the private rented sector Table 4.1 shows that Other White groups as disproportionately high. The private renting experience is also significant for populations in the Other Minority and Chinese categories.
- The data in Table 4.2 are particularly significant in the long-term ethnicity-housing trends they reveal. A key trend is the dominance of owner occupation (with and without mortgage/loan) as the main form of housing tenure for *all* ethnic groups. However there are complex variations between ethnic categories within this overall trend. The rise in owner occupation for the Black Caribbean group is particularly marked, as is the decline of this group in social housing. Although the owner occupation trend is upwards for Bangladeshi category so too are the social housing rates. The private rented sector shows an increase in all ethnic categories.

While there is much value in having census and ONS LFS data for mapping macro patterns and trends these data sets struggle to capture some of the more nuanced diversities between and within ethnic groups and emergent dynamisms of the ethnicity and housing relationship. It is in this context that we now examine two examples of the more nuanced and dynamic aspects of that relationship. The first example is the movement of established BME groups away from more traditionally associated inner city urban settlement areas to smaller urban and particularly to suburban areas of or just outside major cities (Sabater 2008; Tyler 2006). This is not to suggest that greater residential dispersal and economic affluence is common to all established BME groups. As Perry (2008: 6) notes in his review of research findings for the Joseph Rowntree Trust, both Moss Side in Manchester and Tottenham in North London remain among the most deprived wards in England and have long-established BME communities. However, the extent of the move away from inner urban areas is significant. The second example is the impact of new migration patterns and the tendency for newer migrants to live in poor quality, private rented housing. These are both considered in more detail below.

A suburban BME population?

This shift in ethnic residency patterns is a result of the wider changes in the labour market and education (see Chapters 4 and 7) reflected in the increasing economic advancement of some BME populations over the last decade. Generational differences have also been significant in shaping housing aspirations. For example, in their research with young adult South Asian and white women Harries et al. (2008) noted that South Asian participants tend to favour living in ethnically mixed neighbourhoods and do not necessarily want culturally sensitive housing design or culturally specific services (e.g. in relation to mortgage and lending arrangements). Social, economic and generational shifts have been most pronounced among Indian origin population groups but it is not confined to this group. In their research in Glasgow McGarrigle and Kearns (2009) compared 1991 and 2001 census data for ethnicity and residency in the city and found a marked increase in South Asian (Indian and Pakistani) populations away from established areas of settlement and into neighbouring suburbs.

McGarrigle and Kearns (2009) also conducted 40 in-depth interviews with suburban South Asian households which explored questions about ethnically mixed living and suburban residential motivations. Not only did interview responses indicate a general readiness and desire to live in more mixed areas, but for the Indian respondents the move to suburban areas of the city represented a 'motivating factor' for greater social and spatial integration. The findings from the interview data revealed a complex, uneven and intersecting mix between lifestyle aspiration, social prestige and distinction, related environmental pulls such as quality and size of houses and improved social resources such as perceptions of better schools and a desire to create social, personal and cultural distance from traditional areas of settlement. For some of the younger participants (aged 20–45) social and cultural distance was more marked as a motivation although this was often inflected by a commitment to 'not living too far away' from localities where they grew up and where their families still lived. Ultimately, what the Glasgow research shows is that it is not helpful to explain ethnic settlement patterns only through the lens of ethnicity. Moreover, the study demonstrates the fluid and changing residential trends within minority ethnic populations, as well as the heterogeneous and dynamic nature of the processes involved in residential choice.

The significance of residential mobility is echoed in the empirical findings of Finney and Simpson who state that minority ethnic groups are leaving their traditional places of residence. Analysing census data they note that, 'Indians are leaving Leicester, Caribbeans are leaving Lambeth, Bangladeshis are leaving Tower Hamlets and Pakistanis are leaving Bradford' (Finney and Simpson 2009: 127).

In Bradford and Leeds in West Yorkshire, Deborah Phillips' research findings demonstrated a willingness among Muslim respondents to live in more mixed areas and an openness to new migrants who have settled in established BME areas (Phillips 2006a; 2010b). Kudenko and Phillips' (2009) research on the changes within Jewish settlement patterns in Leeds in Northern England reveals similar shifts as the interactions of social, economic, generation and cultural security factors create a dynamic of residential change and movement. They explore the history of the complex transitions associated with Jewish identity and the ways in which Jewish communities live in Leeds, their relationship to the city and perspectives on adaption and cohesion. What their work highlights is, first, the heterogeneity of the Jewish population in Leeds (consistent with points made above about other minority ethnic group populations) and, second, the tendency for there to be a direct correlation between the articulation of segregation discourses about a minority group and the extent of deprivation and poverty within that group. In other words as Jewish communities have become more middle class and dispersed within Leeds, the local cultural and religious anxieties about the Jewish communities in the city have diminished.

Although scale of dispersal and residential mobility is a more recent feature of the ethnicity–residence relationship it is not a completely new phenomenon. A study of minority ethnic housing in Bedford in South-East England by Sarre, Phillips and Skellington (1989) and Sarre (1986) revealed similar dispersal and suburban preferences to those more recently identified by McGarrigle and Kearns (2009). For example, Sarre observed that their research participants showed that

> The locational preferences for more recent moves and especially those stated for future moves show an increasing similarity between ethnic groups. In particular, the immigrant groups increasingly reject the areas of ethnic concentration and state aspirations for residence in areas previously reserved for whites. As yet only small numbers have had the resources to realise these aspirations but in the light of past success in reaching objectives, particularly owner occupation, some decentralisation seems inevitable. (Sarre 1986: 83)

What Sarre argues, and is explored later in this chapter, is that the ethnicity–residence relationship is multifaceted. It is shaped by economic prosperity, lifestyle and aspirational intentions, readiness to live in more ethnically mixed areas, generational cultural shifts within minority ethnic households, as well as factors such as employment, education, perceptions of cleaner, safer, quieter environments and proximity to amenities such as schools, parks, health centres and so forth. The dispersal and suburban shifts in the patterns of multicultural residency can generally be read as indicators of relocation into better quality housing. The areas of traditional ethnic residential settlement – inner urban areas – are usually associated with greater indices of deprivation including older, smaller and often poorer quality housing stock especially in the owner-occupied sector. The next section explores the impact of these outwards mobilities on the areas being left behind.

New migrant residential settlement patterns

Understanding where more recent migrant populations have tended to settle and in what type of housing is highly complex. This is because new migrant populations are highly diverse – not only in terms of their national and ethnic origins but also in terms of their gender, familial status, migratory status and migratory intentions. Clearly there are distinctions between migrant populations who are living in the UK through asylum and refugee process (Robinson, Andersson and Musterd 2003, see also Chapter 3) and those who are living in the UK for other reasons. Variations in residency status are reflected both in geographies of settlement and types of housing tenure. The patterns and trends that are indicated by the available data are emergent and partial. The data are still limited and notoriously difficult to accurately collect around migration and asylum. As Perry notes, the lack of information has been widely acknowledged not only by social researchers but also in official reports such as *Our Shared Future*. Knowledge gaps notwithstanding, some tentative conclusions about new migrant housing patterns and trends are being mapped by researchers (Hickman, Cowley and Mai 2008; Perry 2005; 2008; Robinson, Reeve and Casey 2007; Rutter and Latorre 2009).

For many new migrants there has been a clustering around those areas in major UK cities with which established culturally diverse communities have long been associated. These new patterns of settlement help to generate super-diverse multicultural formations, giving rise to new dynamics (Hudson et al. 2007). Deborah Phillips' (2010a) study of the localised social relations between established Muslim communities and newer Eastern European migrants in Leeds found processes of both hospitality and tension between the populations, with Muslim participants' senses of belonging to the city and the creation of safe space having been hard won over time leading to a cautiousness – even an unwillingness – to facilitate an easy settlement for new arrivals. Tensions were particularly apparent in Phillips' study in relation to gender with some of the male Pakistani partici- pants being anxious about young male Eastern European migrants interact- ing with young Pakistani women. Hickman et al.'s (2008) research in the city of Peterborough in East England, which has seen a high settlement of Eastern European migrants, similarly testifies to the clustering of the new migrants in those areas of the city where Pakistani migrants had earlier set- tled, becoming owner-occupiers and subsequently landlords to new Eastern European migrants. The study (see also Erel 2011) also showed that ethnic/ ethnicised tensions in Peterborough were often expressed around housing and in everyday social practices – new migrants were perceived by both local white English and local English–Pakistani residents as not behaving in 'neighbourly' ways, for example, not putting rubbish out properly, making noise and so on.

What these studies show are new and emergent mixes of populations cre- ating the new geographies of multiculture and disrupting the old geograph- ies of multiculture that we discussed earlier. These studies also show that these shifts are not without their tensions and strains.

There are other factors in the population-migration-housing relation- ship which affect residency patterns and localities. Some EU-based migra- tion is for agricultural and food processing industries which have rural and semi-rural locations. As we saw in the case of Thetford discussed before, this is changing what are often remote and previously predominantly monocul- tural localities. Some of this agri-business migration is organised and 'man- aged' however, and temporary migrant workers may live in purpose-built camps or in poor quality multioccupancy housing provided by employers. In 2007 a survey of local authorities reported that more than half of the reported problems are with private landlords exploiting migrant workers, particularly in rural areas (Local Authorities Coordinators of Regulatory Services 2007). Research found evidence in Cornwall and Scotland of up to eight migrant workers sharing a room in converted farm buildings that had no multioccupancy permission and overcrowding and poor living condi- tions were reported across Derbyshire, Leicestershire and Nottinghamshire (Shelter 2008: 5).

Conversely, a rather different type of population movement has also impacted on housing and urban localities of established BME and migrant populations. These urban areas are mainly, but not only, in London and have seen a significant arrival of white middle class populations as processes of urban gentrification have become consolidated and significantly affected the social, economic and cultural nature of those areas (Butler and Hamnett 2011; Butler and Lees 2006; Butler and Robson 2003a).

With these spatial complexities in mind the available evidence on the hous- ing tenure of new migrants shows that they are overwhelmingly represented within the private rented sector (Table 4.1). The figures for new migrants in social housing are particularly low. In their research examining housing tenure and new migrants Rutter and Latorre (2009: 19) found that, despite public perceptions about social housing allocations and new migrants, since the mid-2000s only 2 per cent of those living in social housing are new migrants and that over 90 per cent of social housing tenants are UK born. They go on to note that 'some migrants do benefit from social housing but only when they have been settled for several years and acquire settled status, refugee status or become British citizens' (2009: 19).

The reliance of new migrants on private rented housing means that they are disproportionately living in poorer housing. The private rented sector is often multioccupancy and more likely to be of a very poor quality and condition than social housing but still demands high rents. Robinson et al.'s (2007) study of migrant housing experiences revealed that overcrowding and substandard basic amenities are a common part of their housing experience. Their study also highlighted the instability of residence patterns with migrants having frequent moves and 'complex housing pathways' as they moved between properties, sometimes renting and sometimes staying with friends or relations and sometimes being in employment 'tied' accommodation.

The type and quality of housing available to new migrants is, then, shaped by a number of factors – most obviously the availability of housing and financial resources. But also influential are factors such as migrants' knowledge and perceptions of areas; migrants' demographic status (single or with dependents), migration status and the accompanying uncertainties, whether in relation to asylum procedures or because of the temporary or long-term nature of migrants' aims and plans or because the jobs in which migrants work – particularly in agriculture and hospitality – provide accommodation. Lack of advice and knowledge about housing and other social services and entitlements also shapes migrant housing experiences. However, research by Viv Cuthill (2010) has shown degrees of migrant social capital. Some of the migrant workers in the Cuthill study had detailed knowledge of welfare rights and entitlements and used their networks to share this and mediate their marginality as migrant workers. Robinson et al. (2007) also found that the unstable and unregulated nature of the housing experiences of new migrants became more manageable as migrants' status, knowledge and networks increased over time.

In many ways there are echos of the older housing experiences of established BME populations within the housing narratives of new migrants. The chapter now briefly examines some of the historical context of this housing experience and the associated residential patterns. Not only do these housing histories influence the current ethnicity-housing relationship but they also allow us to ask how is it that, despite all these changes that we have documented above, some of the housing divisions/patterns remain stubbornly the same.

Earlier geographies of race, housing and localities

Cultural difference, residential mix and multicultural populations living in the UK are not just a feature of contemporary England or even of the England during the second-half of the 20th century (see Dabydeen 1985; Fryer 1984 for example). The housing difficulties and challenges that earlier migrants – from Eastern and Southern Europe, Ireland and migrants from the Caribbean, India and Pakistan – faced as they settled in England in the 1950s have now been well-documented and recorded. A combination of migrants' own limited financial resources, shortages in housing stock, housing policy (e.g. 'slum clearance', an expansion of social housing stock and new town development), labour markets, migrant perceptions of and preferences for certain areas and migrant's social capacity, migrants' demographics and racism combined in ways that profoundly shaped multicultural residency patterns in urban England from the mid-20th century onwards. These same broad factors continue to resonate with and impact on the current residency and ethnic settlement patterns that were discussed above.

Certainly the early post–Second World War housing experiences of BME migrants were characterised by a lack of choice and a disproportionate tendency to be occupying poor quality and run-down terraced housing in the most deprived areas of major cities either through private renting arrangements or because of their low-market value through purchase. Not only limited financial resources but also the experience of explicit racism led to the beginnings or the further development of ethnic settlement in areas of cheap housing. Defendable and identifiable community spaces segued into the emergence of ethnic clusters, secured by social and cultural amenities and developed into spatial associations with particular ethnic populations (Henderson and Karn 1987; Ratcliffe et al. 2001; Sarre, Phillips and Skellington 1989). This was not a new phenomenon in the UK – the East End of London has long been a mix of white working class Londoners, refugees, migrants and Jewish populations. The Tiger Bay area in Cardiff, St. Paul's in Bristol and the Toxteth area of Liverpool also have long histories of mixed populations. What became more significant was the scale and extent of multicultural settlement as migration became a very significant process of movement from the 1950s onwards. The 'room for rent' signs in the widows of private properties declaring 'no blacks, no Irish, no dogs' have now become a well-known and notorious part of the history of everyday racism in post-war UK. But other factors – including migrants' own residential preferences, the instability of housing and employment – intersected with experiences of explicit racism and shaped and established the early geographies of ethnicity. Diverse, poor, often overcrowded and deprived, these geographies exemplify the changing nature of urban England and also gave rise to populist connections between migrants and social problems.

John Rex and Robert Moore (1967) explored some of these intersecting processes in their now classic study of Sparkbrook, a poor residential area of Birmingham, in the 1960s. They showed how New Commonwealth migrants experiencing difficulties in securing housing in the private rented sector, with little prospect of public sector housing allocation given residency requirements and limited financial resources, targeted the cheapest housing in the city, which were the once affluent, large Victorian and Edwardian houses. Those migrants who could, drew on family-based resources or on loans from other sources including marginal economy banks charging high interest rates to purchase housing property. Property-owning migrants then became landlords themselves by letting out the rooms to other tenants – invariably new migrants. Thus Rex and Moore argued that migrants owning property and renting them created complex patterns of and social difference between diverse communities. For Rex and Moore these differential relations meant that housing as much as employment had to be understood as a site of race tension and conflict.

The migrant repositioning of the private rented sector – by becoming landlords themselves – in places like Sparkbrook reflected migrants' creativity and social capacity. But the various constraints and racism encountered were not confined only to the private rented sector. Both owner occupied and social housing were also characterised by limited choice, racism and discrimination.

In the owner-occupied sector, vendors would tell BME buyers that the property was already sold; estate agents would, in a process so common and endemic it became known as racial steering, only show and encourage prospective BME buyers to look at properties in particular (already ethnically diverse) areas; banks and mortgage lenders would refuse to offer loans on properties which fell outside of certain areas – the areas they excluded were often those in which BME buyers were interested in purchasing properties. Alongside these practices was the practice of 'red lining' as banks and building societies literally marked out local geographies in which mortgages would not be offered. Not surprisingly red lining corresponded closely to patterns of ethnic settlement that is, not lending on properties that were identified as being in 'minority ethnic areas' (Rex and Moore 1967; Rex and Tomlinson 1979). Over time these heavily racialised processes were tempered (and outlawed) by the development of race relations legislation, community lobbying and activist challenges and also by the alternative financial resilience and resources of BME communities themselves. But explicit and direct racism in owner-occupied housing played an important part in influencing the patterns of BME residential settlement between the 1950s and the 1980s (Sarre, Phillips and Skellington 1989).

The extent of racialised decision-making and processes of direct and indirect racism in the social housing sector have been extensively documented in academic studies (Henderson and Karn 1987) and in investigations by the then Commission of Racial Equality (1984; 1985; Solomos 1989). The allocation of local authority social housing to BME tenants was shaped either by discriminatory processes whereby only housing of the poorest quality, least desired and lowest demand housing stock was offered or by more implicit forms of racism and differention. For example, assumptions that particular BME populations would only want to live in estates and blocks in which particular BME populations were already established – or where BME tenants would be most safe given the fears about racism and the development of 'no-go' housing estates where racial harassment was known to be a problem (Hesse et al. 1992).

Until the late 1970s and the early 1980s housing in the public sector was not much more regulated than the private sector. Although the Cullingworth Report *Council Housing Purposes, Procedures and Priorities* stressed the importance of ethnic record keeping, performance data and the monitoring of ethnicity and housing allocation, processes and practices as far back as 1969, such information was either non-existent or very basic until the late 1980s (Jones 2009). Anti-racist policies (see Chapter 2) in relation to allocations and racial violence and harassment in tenancy agreements were developed and implemented during the 1980s as local councils began to respond seriously to addressing such issues. The spread of good practice in relation to race hate crime was unevenly taken up as some local authorities actively recognised the need for policy intervention and others were slow or resisted generating direct policy initiatives to protect BME tenants (Hesse et al. 1992; Lansley, Goss and Wolmar 1989). The 1980s can be seen as a time when changes meant that BME groups began to have a different experience of social housing. These changes included the local authority engagements with best practice in terms of equal opportunity and anti-racist practice in allocation and service delivery. Also, the increase in BME employees within the public sector meant that cultural changes took place within the housing departments of a number of metropolitan local councils and within housing associations.

During the 1980s housing associations emerged as an important Third Sector provider of social housing (Harrison 1995; Ratcliffe et al. 2001). Community and resident-led housing organisations, lobbying and campaigning impacted the shifts towards anti-discriminatory and reflexive practices and trickled into BME public-housing experiences. Some of the BME community activism in relation to housing and government housing policy in the 1980s converged into the widening of what was to become the other significant aspect of social housing particularly for Caribbean and Bangladeshi communities. Housing in association schemes was of better quality and some associations were progressive and innovative in their social housing service provision aims and intentions and were often tenant and community/BME led or highly inclusive (Law 1996).

The relationship between BME populations and social housing was shaped by a combination of factors including broader housing policy developments and the emergence of more neoliberal approaches to welfare during the 1980s. In these wider policy and political contexts social housing was profoundly affected by reduced government funding on the one hand and the introduction of the *Right to Buy* policy on the other. In this way social housing capacity was reduced – not just overall in terms of the new building of social housing stock but also in terms of its quality as the *Right to Buy* process ensured that the best quality social housing, disproportionately (but not only) lived in by white tenants, was the housing that was purchased and left the public sector altogether.

What this overview of the earlier histories of the race-residency relationship has shown is the collision of different but related processes that continue to resonate in housing outcomes today. Many of those early migrant settlement patterns survive today in changing but recognisable forms. For example, there are echoes of the earlier migrant housing experiences, particularly in the private rented sector, in the housing experiences of current migrants. However, it is the residential geographies established by the migrants of the 1960s and 1970s that are the most obvious legacy of the previous settlement patterns. It is these that continue to cause controversy and debate as the current anxieties around minority ethnic segregation show.

Explaining ethnicity and residency patterns

The myth of increasing segregation

As discussed in Chapter 1 the events of 2001 have led to an ongoing concern that there is entrenched and increasing ethnic polarisation based around where populations live. The Cantle Report suggested there was extensive residential segregation between ethnic groups in Northern England towns and this was directly implicated in the explanations of the unrest. As we saw in Chapter 2 this report and its findings of 'parallel lives' marked the beginning of the community cohesion agenda and a dominant policy focus on cultural difference, localities and neighbourhoods. So, for example in support of the parallel lives finding of the Cantle Report the inquiry quotes two residents

> A Muslim of Pakistani origin summed this up: 'when I leave in this meeting with you I will go home and not see another white face until I come back here next week'. Similarly, a young man from a white council estate said: 'I never met anyone on this estate who wasn't like us from around here'. We believe that there is an urgent need to promote community cohesion, based upon a greater knowledge of, contact between, and respect for, the various cultures that now make Britain such a rich and diverse nation (Cantle 2001: xx).

Despite the political impact of the notion of increasing ethnically based segregation the available data that evidences this is highly contested (see Chapter 1). In the last 20 years or so the segregation arguments in the UK have predominantly involved quantitative researchers, due to the availability of comparative ethnicity data collected in the census. This has meant that the arguments have centred on methodological tussles almost as much as on the interpretations of the data. There has been a body of quantitative research that robustly rejects any suggestions of increasing ethnic residential segregation. The *State of English Cities* report argued that ethnic segregation had declined overall in the UK between 1991 and 2001, finding that it had fallen in 48 of 56 cities while it had risen slightly in eight and only significantly in two locations (Office of Deputy Prime Minister 2006). Similarly Deborah Phillips (2006a; b), Nisa Finney and Ludi Simpson (2009), Ceri Peach (2009) and researchers based at the Cathie Marsh Centre for Census and Survey Research at Manchester University (see Sabater 2008 for example) have all consistently argued that the available data show that there are no 'ghetto style' ethnic concentrations within the UK. Rather, the minority ethnic residential patterns can be understood as patterns of overall growth – minority ethnic populations have a much younger age profile – with more dispersed and mixed but less clustered settlement.

In relation to segregation, Finney and Simpson also make the obvious but understated point, that there are 'no very high concentrations of particular minority ethnic groups other than white because the areas with fewest white residents are diverse and becoming more so'. They go on to note that only six out of 408 districts in the UK have wards with more than three quarters being minority ethnic residents, and even in the least white wards such as Southall in the London Borough of Ealing 12 per cent of the population is white (Finney and Simpson 2009: 187). The work of these researchers argues that it is possible to track the movement of *all* ethnic groups away from areas of high deprivation to more affluent, white and/ or mixed areas and away from established areas of migrant settlement. As Sabater reminds us 'the combination of increased population and increased residential evenness confirms that non-white groups are also taking part in outward migration to suburban areas' (Sabater 2008: 39).

However, these evidence-based repudiations of increasing segregation have not managed to contain arguments as to how to measure segregation *or* arguments that segregation is increasing. The former are exemplified in the measurement debates between Ceri Peach (2009) and Mike Poulsen, Ron Johnston and James Forrest (2010). Poulsen and Johnston (2008) and Johnston, Poulsen and Forrest (2010) avoid more traditional single number segregation indices such as the Index of Separation or the Index of Polarisation which were used in the *State of English Cities* report and instead develop a gradation of segregated-to-mixed *area* typology methodology (Type I = exclusively white and Type VI = areas with over 70 per cent of the population defining themselves identifying as belonging to BME categories) in order to respond to complex and shifting population structures and their geographies.

Analysing the data from this approach Poulsen and Johnston (2008) argue that on the one hand there has been an increase in the number of people living in segregated areas in the UK between 1991 and 2001 but on the other, that there was a significantly greater increase in the numbers of people living in ethnically mixed areas. Because of the overall increase in ethnic minority population in most places in the UK large cities have become more ethnically mixed (evidence from the 2011 Census suggests that this process has accelerated). Poulsen and Johnston found a decline of Type I (almost exclusively white) areas as these had increasingly become Type II (have an ethnic mix between 20–50%) areas in the 1991 to 2001 period. However, within these changing population configurations Poulsen and Johnston also argue that there are specific geographies in which greater levels of ethnic polarisation are evident. Some places in the West Midlands and Northern Pennine towns (e.g. Bradford, Keighley, Birmingham, Smethwick) show rise in the numbers of population living in Type IV, V, VI (have an ethnic minority population is 70 per cent or more) areas which are larger than the rises in populations living in ethnically mixed areas. This kind of data leads Poulsen and Johnston to argue that 'residential segregation remains an important urban issue within a limited set of British cities and towns' (Poulsen and Johnston 2008: 176).

It is clear from looking at the Poulsen and Johnston findings that the data show complex and contradictory patterns of residential settlement and illuminate the extent to which these shift and change. Acknowledging the complexity of their evidence Poulsen and Johnston point to the importance of qualitative studies in order to gain small scale and more nuanced insights into these geographies and state that 'our concern is not whether residential segregation is permanent or problematic but rather that an appropriate methodology be used to measure levels of residential segregation' (Poulsen and Johnston 2008: 159).

However, this attempt to disconnect race politics from research method is immediately problematic because of the highly politicised context into which segregation data are received and interpreted by a range of audiences. For example, Trevor Phillips's ' sleepwalking to segregation' speech (see Chapter 1) was based on his (mis)understood reading of the arguments being made by Poulsen and Johnston (Johnston, Poulsen and Forrest 2010). The volatile and politicised nature of the segregation debates was perceptively identified by Ceri Peach who noted that 'there is a gulf between the understanding of segregation as an academic, technical term (meaning a scale of high to low segregation) and its everyday meaning (high segregation)' (Peach 2008: 2). More broadly, as Chapter One notes, the escalation of anxieties about ethnic segregation is a concern in itself, given that the overwhelming residency trends are not towards segregation but dispersal and that some low levels of ethnic segregation are not automatically problematic and may not signify cultural withdrawal (Husband and Alam 2011). Meanwhile other researchers and theorists have argued that residentially mixed localities do not necessarily mean that other aspects of social life are mixed and integrated (Butler and Hamnett 2011; Butler and Robson 2003a; Ettlinger 2009; Valentine 2008).

However, what the segregation arguments also highlight is the interaction between individual agency (choice) and structural forces (constraint). It is to this relationship that the chapter now turns.

Choice and constraint dynamics: towards an iterative understanding

Understanding and explaining the ethnicity-housing relationship has traditionally emphasised either individualised preferences as to where people live or the ways in which structural factors dictate where people live. For example, a constraints or structuralist explanation can be clearly seen in Rex and Moore's Sparkbrook study in which low-income migrants' housing 'choices' were profoundly reduced and shaped by external process such as racism, limited capital and low-economic status. An individualist explanation can be seen in the work of researchers such as Ballard and Ballard (1977) who argue that migrants' housing choices reflect individual plans and intentions – the cheapest housing was sought not because there was no alternative but rather as a strategy to accumulate the maximum capital. An extension of the active choice model can be found in self-segregation arguments (see Carling 2008 for example).

More recent work on race and residency patterns has looked to work through a combination of these two positions and focuses on the idea of a combination of choice and constraint factors shaping where minority ethnic groups live and in what forms of housing tenure. We have been using such an approach in this chapter. One of the early advocates of the argument that race and residency patterns reflected a choice and constraint hybridity is offered by Sarre (1986) and Sarre et al. (1989). The latter noted, from the data collected in their Bedford study, that migrant housing narratives were ones in which migrants' agency was clearly present but alongside and interacting with institutional processes including intentional and unintentional racism. However, Sarre stretched the combination model further by arguing that emphasising both choice and constraint were relational only took the analysis of housing and ethnicity so far as there was a need 'to clarify *how* they combine and *how* such apparent opposites as cultural choice and economic determinism are in practice mutually reinforcing' (Original emphasis, Sarre 1986: 73).

For Sarre these questions are best addressed through a focus on what happens between the abstract concept of structure and the agency of individual practices and actions because, 'with our everyday experiences as citizens of advanced societies we are both limited by a complex set of forces (including economic pressures, the law, various arms of the state and the more mundane influence of friends and neighbours) and faced by many opportunities (for example in obtaining information, using services or tools, travelling or participating in voluntary organisations)' (Sarre 1986: 75). Emphasising that the ongoing, iterative and varying interplay between individual practices/opportunities and structural processes/closures as a particular characteristic of the ethnicity-housing relationship is an argument taken up by Ratcliffe (2009). Noting that housing markets and household formations are in processes of flux and change – increasing property prices and growth of single person households for example – Ratcliffe argues for a more finely grained and co-constitutional understanding of social structure and social agency, in which each might inflect the other and in which neither is static and monolithic but potentially transformative of the other. Importantly, Ratcliffe also cautions us to take into account the uneven nature of the structural-agency interactions and different minority groups. Certainly the structural factors may be more dominant in the housing experiences of new migrants or for different minority populations in different geographical areas. As Ratcliffe notes, 'those negotiating the housing market do not do so purely in terms of ethnicity, nor is their 'ethnicity' defined by a single marker or for that matter a cluster of fixed markers' (Ratcliffe 2009: 446).

This is consistent with much of the discussion, examples of places and evidence examined in this chapter. The residential aspirations and tensions within South Asian households in Glasgow shown in the McGarrigle and Kearns study reveal some of the interactions and different experiences among established BME populations and among new migratory groups. The findings in Sparkbrook, while fitting into the constraint model, can be reread through a much more iterative dynamic. For example, the experience of structural closures created an environment in which some migrants drew on fringe, family and community resources to purchase properties and then became landlords to other migrants. The social housing experience also provides a setting in which choice–constraint interactions can be identified. Despite the reduction in social housing through the *Right to Buy* policy and reduced government funding, well-organised and knowledgeable community and tenant activist and lobby groups were able to take advantage of the policy emphasis on housing association provision and tenants' choice (Watt 2009: 218). The mention of policy here is important as it raises the role and influence of policy in the shifting interplays between choices and constraints. It is government interventions in the ethnicity-housing relationship which are considered in the final part of this chapter.

Housing policy interventions and responses to race and residence

It is obviously not possible to do full justice to the debates and details of housing policy in the UK in the space here. What we want to suggest, however, is that housing policy is often a marginalised part of the race and housing debate despite being very much a part of the housing opportunities and closures afforded to BME communities. It is important to recognise the ways in which housing policy per se and housing policy in relation to race equality interact and affect BME and migrant populations. Also, wider housing policy developments and interventions will also differentially impact on minority housing experiences and trajectories. For example, the post-war policy of creating new towns, like Milton Keynes and Runcorn effectively relocated a white working class away from London and Liverpool and contributed to a wider depopulation of poorer inner areas of cities making housing cheaper and more available to new migrant populations. Similarly, the neoliberal shift in welfare approaches in the late 1970s and early 1980s repositioned government housing policy from state provision to owner occupation, dramatically reducing social housing stocks on which some BME groups rely. This policy legacy remains largely intact as a key driver of the current housing landscape in England and Wales (Rutter and Latorre 2009).

However, in this same housing policy context the expansion of, and an emphasis on, housing association provision and tenant responsibility created some openings and opportunities for BME organisations to establish small but nevertheless significant provision for some minority populations (Law 1996). Similarly the dynamics of the localised and national housing markets affect BME populations differentially. Some of the inner city areas where migrants had settled in the 1960s have now, through various regeneration strategies and gentrification processes, become sought after and redesired as spaces of residency. This in turn creates social and economic polarisations as well as super-diverse population mixes (London Borough of Hackney 2010).

It is also possible to identify direct links between developments in race policy and BME housing experiences. As we noted earlier the emergence of the race relations legislation in the 1960s and 1970s curbed some of the most explicit racist and discriminatory processes affecting housing provision for BME populations. Similarly some local authorities and Third Sector organisations committed to anti-racist and equal opportunities initiatives (monitoring, racial harassment and employment) brought about changes in the housing-ethnicity relationship (Lansley, Goss and Wolmar 1989). This chapter has shown how legislation regarding migration status and entitlements also impacts BME and migrant housing experiences, particularly in terms of regulated access to welfare entitlements and social housing.

Housing policy changes were also brought about by 'race crisis' events (the urban unrest in inner cities in the early 1980s; the police investigation of the murder of Stephen Lawrence in 1993; the unrest in Northern England in 2001; the London bombings in 2005) and the policy responses to these (the Scarman Report, the Macpherson Report, the Cantle Report and the *Our Shared Future* Report of the Commission on Integration and Cohesion) all recognised, in different ways and to greater and lesser extents, housing and race connections. Scarman highlighted the problem of the quality and quantity of housing in Brixton and recommended that housing, along with education and employment, needed to be addressed. Nearly 20 years later, the Macpherson Report led to the Race Relations (Amendment) Act (2000) and the statutory requirement that organisations be able to demonstrate how race equality was being achieved in process and in practice. While social housing has, as we saw above, been one of the sectors to develop a track record – albeit uneven – on implementing progressive and inclusive approaches to race equality (Hesse et al. 1992), the Macpherson Report was influential. As Harris Beider notes

> the Housing Corporation clearly regarded race equality as an important policy priority in the aftermath of the Macpherson Report [...]. Discussion, consultation, project development and evaluation are required. The Housing Corporation and other organisations commissioned research and projects aimed at raising awareness of the scale of problems and engagement of black and minority ethnic groups in housing associations. (Beider 2009: 412)

However, it has been the cohesion agenda marked by the Cantle Report with its worries about segregation and 'parallel lives' and the Commission on Integration and Cohesion's focus on neighbourhoods, localities and civic interactions that have most recently impacted on housing policy. Both reports make links between investment in housing and regeneration and community cohesion. To counter division and polarisation Cantle stressed the need for housing agencies to deliver more mixed housing, and in one of its explicit housing related recommendations *Our Shared Future* states: 'all affordable housing providers receiving investment funding should demonstrate how this funding will assist in promoting cohesion and delivering mixed communities' (Commission on Integration and Cohesion 2007: xx). The cohesion agenda was central to the strategies of the Homes and Communities Agency (HCA), set up in 2008 under the Labour government but substantially scaled back by the Coalition government elected in 2010, which had a remit to oversee regeneration in 'underperforming' areas and the delivery of 3 million new homes by 2020.

While the current policy emphasis on cohesion, integration and mixed neighbourhoods is envisaged as being delivered through the establishment of ethnically and socially mixed housing this is not a particularly new vision. As Chapter 2 detailed the assimilationist policy approaches of the 1960s worked within a similar policy frame. More recently in England and Wales, the community cohesion-social mix policy approach can be seen in the Labour government's New Deal for Communities Programme and the Housing Market Renewal Pathfinder Programme. This latter programme saw large swathes of low demand, low-value housing and properties in the Midlands and North England either demolished or redesigned and rebuilt with an intention of attracting new, and more socially-economic diverse residents to these 'transformed' areas (Allen 2008). Started in 2003 and initially intended to run until 2018 the Pathfinder Programme was abandoned by the Coalition government.

The programme was not without its controversies – the clearance and regeneration work meant major emotional and housing disruptions for those involved and the areas and communities affected were often among the poorer, more vulnerable and were often places with established BME populations (Cole and Flint 2006). The extent to which issues of racial equality and the ethnicity were integrated into the Pathfinder implementation was questionable (Hilditch 2006). A government Audit Commission report on the Programme (Audit Commission 2006: 42) accused one Pathfinder area of failing BME communities and others of making only limited progress. It argued that BME communities may be disproportionately affected by the regeneration work, yet there was still a need to develop clear polices on racial equality. Some agencies and areas in the Pathfinder Programme were implementing best practice on race and ethnicity issues (see Robinson et al. 2004) but in their Joseph Rowntree Trust funded research into the various consultation, relocation, support, and financial aspects of the Pathfinder Programme Cole and Flint found that

> A number of issues that require to be addressed as support packages are developed. First, both Pathfinder officers and interviewed residents suggested

that there was still a lack of awareness about housing options, housing finance packages and available support amongst some groups of residents, especially BME households. This lack of awareness needs to be addressed, both to maximise the support available to households and to ensure equity in the treatment that each household receives. (Cole and Flint 2006: 32)

The impact and outcomes of the cohesion agenda on the ethnicity and housing relationship is still not clear. The cohesion emphasis on mixed housing provision in England and Wales can be seen in social housing initiatives in other national contexts (Beider 2009; Popkin, Levy and Buron 2009). For example, in the US the Hope VI (Housing Opportunities for People Everywhere) Programme which was set up in the early 1990s aimed to tackle the extremely poor conditions of public housing and rebuild and revitalise high-poverty communities. African–American and Latino populations are disproportionately represented as public-housing tenants in the US, so the Hope VI Programme is a race and class based policy intervention. In order to redevelop the neighbourhoods and properties the programme relocated residents on either temporary or permanent basis to improved housing and more mixed income areas with an intention of avoiding spatially and socially concentrated poverty. Voucher schemes allowed former public-housing tenants to enter the private housing markets and 'better' neighbourhoods. The evidence as to the success of Hope VI policy has been mixed. Popkin et al. (2009: 485) argue that

> for the most part the long term results show tremendous improvements in quality of life for former residents: most are living in neighbourhoods that are dramatically safer and offer far healthier environments for themselves and their children. However, some are struggling with the challenges of living in the private market and a substantial minority continues to live in traditional public housing developments that are only marginally better than the distressed developments they left behind.

In the US context the urban geographer Nancy Ettlinger (2009: 218) has highlighted the limitations of top down, 'desegregating' urban policy interventions which crudely attempt to create more mixed communities because different social and ethnic proximity does not necessarily or automatically transfer into 'meaningful interactions and shared experience' across diversity and division.

Conclusion

This chapter has argued that the relationship between housing, race and ethnicity can be most effectively understood by incorporating a range of other variables and interactions – for example, social and economic status, generation and age, individual and household aspirations and intentions, national and local policy, housing and labour markets, localities and geographies, migration status. The various reasons as to why any straightforward correlation between place, housing form and ethnicity is difficult and problematic is at the heart of this chapter and is discussed through a number of its debates from segregation and multicultural dispersal, to migration patterns and residential mobility. This not to argue that there are no direct connections between race, multiculture and patterns of residency. Clearly there are and much of this chapter has examined the nature of these connections, but these connections are complicated. We have seen something of the constant and shifting interplay between ethnicity, diversity, social and economic status, racism, locality and age in earlier parts of the chapter. The ways in which the race-ethnicity-housing relationship is shaped by wider housing policy interventions – those that relate directly to race and multiculture and those that have indirect and differential impacts on BME and migrant communities – was the focus of the previous discussion. We argued that the choice–constraints model for understanding the housing experiences of BME and migrant populations can shed explanatory light on the residential geographies of multiculture. But its value is only realised if it moves away from an understanding of choice and constraint as discrete binaries and acknowledges the co-constitutional nature of choice and constraint factors and contexts in shaping housing experiences, patterns and outcomes.

It is the nuanced, diverse, differential and dynamic nature of the BME housing experience that this chapter has emphasised.. It is only through a concept of relationality that racism and discrimination *and* aspiration and agency *and* the differences between older and emergent housing experiences and trajectories of diverse BME populations can all be accounted for.

Chapter 5

Policing

Questions about the policing of urban multicultural communities have been an integral part of policy and civil society discourses about immigration and race in British society since the 1960s and 1970s. Given the wider context of the politicisation of immigration and race issues, it is perhaps not surprising that the policing of those localities in which migrants were beginning to settle and develop a sense of community should become an arena of intense debate. Early studies of this phenomenon by John Lambert, Gus John and Michael Banton focussed on the context of specific communities and the growth of tensions between the police and minority ethnic communities (Banton 1973; John 1970; Lambert 1970a; b). Other studies focused on the role of the media in the amplification of moral panics about black youth and crime in specific localities and on the intersections between urban deprivation, youth unemployment and criminalised youth subcultures (Critcher, Parker and Sondhi 1975; Hall et al. 1978; Solomos 1988). At a broader level the emergence of policing as a key contested issue in this field also highlighted the concerns about the emergence of alienated youth subcultures among young West Indians (Cashmore and Troyna 1982; Hall 1967).

In developing the analysis of this issue, this chapter focuses first on this early period of debate about race and policing in urban multiculture. This will allow us to situate the racialisation of debates about policing in the wider context of the changing agendas of immigration and race that emerged during the 1970s and 1980s. This will then lead on to the second theme, the question of the policing of urban unrest, which has been a recurrent matter within policy debates since 1980–1981, with significant outbreaks of urban unrest occurring in 1981, 1985, 2001 and 2011. The third question we shall address is the impact of the controversies that followed the death of Stephen Lawrence in April 1993 on debates about race and policing. As Chapter 2 noted, this event and the subsequent Macpherson Inquiry, shaped wider policy agendas around race as well as the policies of successive governments on racism and policing.

The chapter then explores the intersections that have emerged in the early part of the 21st century between policing and questions about terrorism and security. The terrorist attacks on New York in 2001 and the suicide attacks in London in 2005, along with recurring concerns about other terror attacks more generally, have played an important role in the development of policing strategies and the increasing trend towards the securitisation of cultural difference. The chapter concludes by analysing the debates on the riots of August 2011 and the way questions about policing were framed in response to the disturbances.

Policing multicultural communities

The issue of policing multicultural communities and ideologies linking immigrants with crime have a long history in British society, certainly dating back to the debates on Irish and Jewish migrants at the end of the 19th century. This is not to say that these ideologies have been constant throughout history, or that they were fixed and unchanging. They have undergone numerous transformations over the years, and ideologies which link immigrants to crime have not been universally accepted even by those who are opposed to immigration. But it is certainly true that whether one looks at the Irish immigrants of the 19th century, Jewish immigrants in the period of the late-19th and early 20th centuries, or other significant groups of immigrants the issue of policing and crime has been a common theme in the construction of ideologies and policies towards them (Gartner 1973; Holmes 1988; 1991; Panayi 2010). Indeed, a recurrent theme in the histories of immigration more generally, not just in British society, has involved the intersection between concerns about immigration with fears about criminality and disorder in migrant communities (Smith 1986; Spickard 2007).

For much of the 1960s and 1970s fears about the increasing alienation of young BME and migrant people – and in particular young black men, of African Caribbean origin – from the mainstream British society were regularly expressed in the media and policy documents, and became a constant refrain in both academic and policy writings on the subject (Hall 1967; Hall et al. 1978; Solomos 1988). Such concerns were evident locally in areas such as Brixton and Handsworth, and also in the coverage of these issues in both policy and media discourses. What also became evident by the 1970s is that this was not merely a passing phenomenon which would disappear with the integration of young black men into the mainstream institutions of British society but was likely to remain an ongoing issue in multicultural communities. This was so for at least two major reasons. First, it became clear that the calls for action to help 'coloured school leavers' gain equality of opportunity in education, employment and other arenas did not necessarily result in the development of effective policy measures to put such calls into practice. Evidence of high levels of unemployment and low levels of achievement in schools among BME and migrant communities continued to accumulate (see Chapters 7 and 8). A number of reports from the late 1960s and 1970s highlighted the continuing impact of discrimination and inequality on the life opportunities of young BME people at a time of economic and social dislocation (Clarke et al. 1974; Select Committee on Race Relations and Immigration 1969; 1972; 1977).

At the same time it had also become clear that the exclusionary and discriminatory experiences of young African-Caribbean men were rapidly becoming a key concern within black minority ethnic communities. In various forums, both local and national, black political activists were discussing issues such as education, employment and policing. They were also questioning the failure of the government to take positive measures to tackle the root causes of the growing tensions between the police and young black people in areas such as Handsworth and Brixton (John 1970). Such political debates from within the black communities helped to emphasise the centrality of policing as a concern within minority communities and to raise the issue of what measures could be taken to improve relations between black minority ethnic communities and the police.

Public debate about this issue came to the fore in the 1970s through a number of studies that focused on the changing dynamics of policing multicultural communities. Two of the earliest studies focused on the situation in Birmingham. First, Gus John published his influential study of Handsworth called *Race and the Inner City*, which was based on an account of the attitudes of young African-Caribbean men towards the police and society more generally (John 1970). Second, a more detailed study of race and policing in Birmingham by John Lambert was published in the same year, entitled *Crime, Police and Race Relations* (Lambert 1970a). Both studies attracted attention because they came out at a time when the question of relations between black minority ethnic communities and the police and the involvement of young black men in crime were topical and widely discussed in the press. This was a time when the issue of the growing tension between the police and the black communities, both at a national level and in relation to specific communities, was the subject of much media coverage as well as the subject of community mobilisation in localities such as Handsworth, Tottenham, Brixton among others (Humphry and John 1972; John and Humphry 1972). The complaints against the police from within BME and migrant communities themselves, which had been articulated as early as the 1960s, reached new levels through the 1970s and 1980s when the issue of policing came to the fore in debates about race and community relations.

John's study of Handsworth was a particularly important document in this growing debate. It was written by a black researcher who had spent some time living within the black community in Handsworth. It highlighted the question of policing and the position of young black men as the core concerns of local residents. It was written at a time when the police were discussing their role in the policing of multicultural inner-city areas and formulating their ideologies and practices on this issue. Additionally, media coverage at the time talked of the growing tensions between the police and BME and migrant communities, and saw a number of minor street confrontations with the police in areas such as Notting Hill in 1969–1970. John began his account of Handsworth with an analysis of the area and the contrasting perceptions offered by local residents of the post-war period. But the core of his report, and the issue which gave rise to a full debate in the press, is the description it offers of relations between the local black community, particularly younger African-Caribbean men, and the police. John reported that one police official had pointed out to him that the 'growth of black crime' in the area was the work of a 'hard core' group of 40 or 50 youngsters. But his own perceptions of the situation were more complex, and he summarised them as amounting to three main issues: the prevalence of rumours, fears and explanations of black involvement in criminal activities; a tendency by police to blame the 'hard core' group of young black men for 'giving the area a bad name'; and a deep resentment by older and younger black people of their social position and the discrimination they had to endure. Additionally he warned that there were signs of 'a massive breakdown in relations between the police and the black community', and that if nothing was done the situation was likely to lead to confrontations between black residents and the police and outbursts of urban unrest.

> In my view trends in Handsworth are a portent for the future. A decaying area, full of stress and tension, which also happens to be racially mixed, is going to find it increasingly difficult to cope with the root problems because racial animosities and resentments have taken on an independent life of their own. The problem is not, and can never be, simply one of law and order. (John 1970)

It was this context, argued John, which explained why both young black people and the police saw the situation in the area as one of open 'warfare'. Some aspects of John's account of relations between the police and the black community were criticised as overstated and impressionistic. Yet there is a certain symmetry between his account of the situation and that described later on in the 1970s by John Rex and Sally Tomlinson in their detailed empirical analysis of the political economy of race and class in Handsworth (Rex and Tomlinson 1979). Additionally, other studies of the interplay between race and policing during the 1970s and 1980s indicated that the relationship between BME and migrant communities and the police was becoming an issue of public concern in other areas similar to Handsworth.

Evidence from black communities across the country highlighted three particularly contentious issues. First, complaints by BME and migrant communities that they were being categorised as 'problem populations' by the police and that they were therefore more likely to be questioned or arrested. Second, there were allegations that the police used excessive physical violence in their dealings with black suspects. Finally, it was argued that such attitudes and forms of behaviour by the police were helping to fuel popular rumours about the involvement of young black men in crime, and to drive a wedge between the police and the BME communities.

These were issues that were to remain at the heart of debates about the policing of multicultural localities during the 1980s and 1990s. At the same time the police themselves were required to respond to the fears that were circulating in particular localities about the involvement of some young black men in forms of street crime such as mugging and in the emergent drug subcultures. During the 1980s, for example, the Metropolitan Police became increasingly concerned about the racial breakdown of those arrested for street robberies, the statistics having been collected for some time. These figures showed a marked rise in street robberies, but the crucial statistic picked up by the press and other media was the disproportionate involvement of young black men in crimes such as mugging, purse snatching and robbery from shops (Bowling and Phillips 2002; Rowe 2004). The linkages between race and crime thus became the subject of public debate as well as sensationalised media coverage (Hall et al. 1978).

This issue was intimately linked to wider discourses about the impact of immigration on the social fabric of British society. Fears about urban criminality and violence were seen as a by-product of immigration. Media stories in the 1980s were often framed in terms of a direct linkage between immigration, crime and violence. The *Daily Telegraph*, commenting on the role of young African-Caribbean ('West Indian') men in street crime, articulated this viewpoint succinctly,

> Over the 200 years up to 1945, Britain became so settled in internal peace that many came to believe that respect for the person and property of fellow citizens was something which existed naturally in all but a few. A glance at less fortunate countries might have reminded us that such respect scarcely exists unless the law is above the power of tribe, or money, or the gun. But we did not look; we let in people from the countries we did not look at, and only now do we begin to see the result. Many young West Indians in Britain, and, by a connected process, growing numbers of young whites, have no sense that the nation in which they live is part of them. So its citizens become to them mere objects of violent exploitation. (*Daily Telegraph*, 11 March 1982)

Such a direct linkage between race and crime was not necessarily articulated by the Metropolitan Police or other police forces themselves. Nevertheless, an ethnographic study of policing conducted by Michael Keith in the early 1980s highlighted the ways in which commonsense ideas about young African-Caribbean men's involvement in criminalised subcultures had become an established theme in shaping the relationship between the police and minority ethnic communities in areas such as Tottenham, Hackney and

Brixton (Keith 1993). In this context the involvement of young black men in criminal or quasi-criminal activities became a key area of concern for the police and other institutions, both locally and nationally.

The widespread portrayal of young African-Caribbean men as being heavily involved in mugging and other forms of street crime prompted the development of strategies to keep them off the streets and maintain police control over localities that were identified in popular and official discourses as crime-prone or potential trouble spots. However it also drew attention to the social and economic alienation of young people in BME communities, as reflected in debates on the impact that unemployment was having on them (Cashmore and Troyna 1982). Whether in terms of specific concerns about street crime or more general concerns about the development of subcultures among young black men, the interplay between race and crime continued to be of symbolic importance in political language (Small 1983).

Policing race, policing urban unrest

The second major transformation in policy debate about policing and race occurred in the period of the early 1980s through to the 1990s and was closely linked to the outbreaks of urban unrest that occurred in 1980–1981 and 1985. The 1980s were an important period in the racialisation of debates on law and order, crime and policing in at least two ways. First, the politicisation of the issue of social exclusion of young black people helped to focus attention on the interrelationship between unemployment and crime. Second, the riots of 1980–1981 and 1985 forced the issue of crime and violence on the streets onto the mainstream political agenda. The extensive coverage given to the issue of race in connection with the riots opened up a wider debate on issues such as mugging and black crime under the broad rubric of the future of British society (Joshua and Wallace 1983; Kettle and Hodges 1982).

During 1980 and 1981 there were three major outbreaks of unrest. First, in April 1980 violent confrontations took place in the multicultural St Paul's district of Bristol between groups of predominantly, but not only, young black men and the police. Second, during April 1981 violent confrontations between the police and crowds of mostly black youths occurred in Brixton in London. Finally, in July 1981 there were widespread outbreaks of unrest in the Toxteth area of Liverpool, the Southall area of London and various other localities in London, including Brixton. Other, smaller scale, disturbances took place and attracted some attention in the media and within government (Benyon 1984). The violence in Brixton from 10 to 13 April 1981 caused the Thatcher government to set up the Scarman Inquiry which sought to determine what had happened and to suggest what should be done by governmental and other agencies in the future (Benyon 1984; Scarman 1981a; 1985). The more widespread events during July 1981 led to a flurry of activity at both the central and local government levels, and the employment of real and symbolic interventions to prevent the disorder and violence from spreading further. For example, after years of inaction many local authorities actively sought to develop equal opportunity policies (Chapter 2), and promises were made to reform police training to take account of multiracialism and to tackle the roots of racial disadvantage and discrimination (Joshua and Wallace 1983).

All of these responses were examples of the symbolic reassurance noted by American analysts of the race riots that took place during the 1960s, which also involved the role of policing as a core issue (Bergesen 1982; Fogelson 1971; Knopf 1975). At least four explanatory frameworks were used to frame the riots of 1980 and 1981, namely emphasising race, violence and disorder; the breakdown of law and order; social deprivation and youth unemployment; and political marginalisation. At the core of these frameworks, however, there remained the issue of the contentious relationship between young black men and the police. The Scarman Report itself highlighted the issue of policing multicultural communities such as Brixton as perhaps the key conditioning issue in shaping the underlying processes that led to the violent confrontations between young African-Caribbean men and the police.

In September and October 1985, there were serious outbreaks of violence in Handsworth in Birmingham, Tottenham and Brixton in London, and in Liverpool. Smaller disturbances took place in 1986 and 1987 (Benyon and Solomos 1987). The scale and locations of the 1985 riots seem to have surprised even some of the most astute observers. Handsworth, for example, was widely perceived as a success story in terms of the efforts made by the police in the late 1970s and early 1980s to improve police-community relations, and therefore the outbreak of violence in this area was seen as an aberration. Similarly the spread of violence in London to areas such as the Broadwater Farm Estate in Tottenham constituted a break from previous events, which had centred on areas such as Brixton (Gifford 1986).

In the aftermath of the 1981 and 1985 riots it was generally thought that a key objective of the state, the police and local authorities would be to ensure that similar events would not happen in the future. This was certainly the assumption behind the recommendations made in the Scarman Report and a whole range of other official reports on the riots (Gaffney 1987; Gordon 1987). Perhaps because the unrest was perceived as an atypical deviation from British culture it was expected that, as long as appropriate remedial action was undertaken, violent protest and social disorder would not become a regular feature of urban life (see Chapter 2). For most of the late 1980s and 1990s this seemed to be the case as there were no large-scale outbreaks of urban unrest. However smaller outbreaks did occur. For example in July 1992 there were violent confrontations between groups of young people and the police in Burnley, Coventry and Blackburn. In June 1995 similar confrontations took place in Bradford, with reports that stated that 'alienated Asian youth' had engaged in battles with the police. The Bradford events were the first time when public attention was focused on a young South Asian rather than African-Caribbean men, and were the forerunner of a series of events in the late 1990s that led to increasing public concern about the drift of some young South-Asian men into criminality and confrontations with the police. The images projected did not necessarily present a rounded picture of the changing position of young South Asians in British society, but they helped to politicise and amplify existing concerns about minority ethnic communities in general. While these events were not on the same scale as the unrest in 1981 and 1985 and did not attract the same amount of media or government attention, links were made between them and the circumstances that had led to the violent protests of the 1980s, particularly the treatment of BME and migrant communities by the police.

A new contributory factor in the 1990s was death in police custody. For example the death of Wayne Douglas while being held in police custody in Brixton in December 1995 sparked violent confrontations with the police on a scale that the area had not witnessed since 1985. There was particular concern about this because after the Scarman Report the police and central and local government had worked closely together to prevent any future recurrence of the tensions that had developed in the area during the 1970s and 1980s. The unrest that took place in the 1990s kept the subject of urban unrest on the public agenda, although it was generally thought that such localised outbreaks were containable and it was generally agreed that they were not on the scale of the riots of 1981 and 1985. Certainly in both academic and policy discourses we find little expectation that there would be urban unrest similar to the scale of that of the 1980s.

The outbreak of urban unrest in Bradford, Oldham and Burnley during April and July 2001 thus took many commentators by surprise. Although in scale the 2001 events were similar to those of the 1980s there were two important differences to note. First, in terms of location and context the events in 2001 were markedly different from the unrest of 1981 and 1985. In 2001 the core events took place in a number of relatively deprived towns in the north of England, and the minority participants were largely from South-Asian Muslim backgrounds (Alexander 2004; Hussain and Bagguley 2005; Rhodes 2009b). Second, although confrontations with the police remained at the heart of the unrest there was the added dimension of conflict between local South Asian and white communities. It is interesting to note in this context that the British National Party (BNP) and other extreme right-wing groups were implicated in the events. Certainly in Oldham and

Burnley there was evidence that the BNP was gaining support in local white communities, and it garnered a respectable vote in the June 2001 General Election (Rhodes 2009a).

Given all this it is not surprising that the events in 2001 were seen through a somewhat different lens than the unrest of the 1980s. In Oldham and Burnley, and to some extent Bradford, the unrest was seen in a number of ways; as 'race riots' involving conflict between different racial and ethnic groups; as partly the result of mobilisation by the BNP and extremist ethnic groups; as the product of decades of segregation and lack of contact between white majority and minority, particularly Asian, communities (see Chapter 2).

While media coverage and official reports produced after the events looked at the state of police-community relations in these localities, this was seen as a less central factor than it had been during the 1980s and 1990s. Therefore rather than seeing the events of 2001 as a continuation of the unrest of the 1980s and 1990s, it is better to put them in the context of the political, cultural and social changes that had taken place since then in the towns in question. If we look at the BNP, for example, it seems clear that in Burnley and Oldham it played at least some part in shaping of the tensions that were ignited in 2001. It is also evident that it has remained active in these localities and has attempted to gain the support of the white electorate by nationalistically claiming to represent their 'rights', as opposed to those of the minority communities. Such mobilisations need to be analysed in terms of the specific contexts in which they emerged, and they represent a significant break in the pattern of urban unrest of the 1980s (John et al. 2006; Rhodes 2011).

It is interesting to note in this regard that a core concern in the series of official reports that were produced after the 2001 unrest was the theme of cultural polarisation and a lack of community interaction (Burnley Task Force 2001; Cantle 2001; Oldham Independent Review 2001; Ouseley 2001). In this context community cohesion became the policy framework that has helped to shape much of the wider political debate in the period since 2001, as we have argued in detail in Chapters 2 and 9. The main reports on the 2001 disturbances focused on what they perceived to be a 'white English–Muslim divide', meaning that there was relatively little contact between these populations and no shared sense of belonging to and pride in the local community. These concerns were most clearly articulated in the report by the Ministerial Group on Public Order and Community Cohesion, chaired by John Denham.

> Our central recommendation is the need to make community cohesion a central aim of government, and to ensure that the design and delivery of all government policy reflects this. We recognise that in many areas affected by

disorder or community tensions, there is little interchange between members of different racial, cultural and religious communities and that proactive measures will have to be taken to promote dialogue and understanding. (Home Office 2001: para 7)

This argument did not represent a radical departure from previous government policies on race relations. What was new was the concern about the consequences of social segregation, the entrenchment of cultural and religious differences and the erosion of 'common values'. These concerns had been shaped by the social and political changes that had come to the fore in the 1990s, most notably the emergence of new patterns of racialised inequality, ethnic differences in terms of opportunities and employment, and tensions over new patterns of migration and transnational identity politics. The riots of 2001 were thus read through a political language that was deeply imbued with concern about the emergence of new forms of conflict and tension in British society.

The terrorist attacks in New York and Washington in September 2001, which took place in the aftermath of the 2001 riots, also helped to focus attention on the issue of emergent radical religious movements among South-Asian Muslim communities. In this context the question of policing South-Asian communities came to the fore during the early 2000s, alongside the existing discourses about the policing of multicultural communities more generally. This is an issue we shall return to later on in this chapter.

Stephen Lawrence and institutionalised racism

In response to the emergence of race and policing as a core issue in social policy debates, two main sets of policy responses emerged in the 1980s and 1990s. First, there were initiatives developed within local police forces to improve relations between the police and black minority ethnic communities. These initiatives were framed around the notion that efforts to improve relations between minority communities and the police needed to be based on a grounded knowledge of local conditions. Second, we have seen a wide range of initiatives over the past two decades to attract more police officers from black and minority ethnic backgrounds. Over the years a number of initiatives have been launched to overcome the reluctance of ethnic minorities to join the police, but with only limited success. More fundamentally perhaps, the police have also attempted to develop long-term strategies to improve relations with various minority communities and to manage unrest and violence in inner-city areas (Keith 1993; Rowe 2004). In this context the period since the 1980s has been characterised by a search for policy interventions that would allow the police to better manage contentious issues in the policing of multicultural communities and allow for the development of a more diverse police force, in terms of race and ethnicity.

These initiatives have been characterised as having some impact, both nationally and in specific localities. Certainly the 1980s and 1990s can be seen as a period when policy initiatives on race and policing became a key facet of multicultural social policies. Yet the question of racism within the police remained a live issue. This was highlighted over the next two decades by perhaps the key symbolic event in this field, namely the death of Stephen Lawrence in a racist attack on the streets of Eltham in South East London on 22 April 1993 (Cathcart 1999; Cottle 2004; Hewitt 2005; Solomos 1999). What seemed at first a seemingly random example of racist violence became a cause celebre that focused both on the anger at the impact of racist violence and the failures of the police in handling the aftermath of the attack. While much of the discussion on this particular event focused on the horrific nature of the crime, of equal importance in many people's eyes were the inadequacies of the police response. In the period after the murder of Stephen Lawrence his case became the object of mobilisation about both the phenomenon of racist violence and the management of the case by the police. Lawrence's parents and other activists within black minority ethnic communities took up the case and agitated for a public inquiry into both his death and the wider issue of how the police managed the investigation into possible suspects involved in his murder (see Chapter 2). This eventually led to the establishment of an inquiry into the case by the Blair Government in 2007, which resulted in the publication of the Macpherson Report (Macpherson 1999b).

During the period of the late 1990s and the early part of the 21st century the Stephen Lawrence case and the mobilisations that surrounded it helped to politicise the issue of racist violence and more generally about how the police perceived minority communities. It also helped to highlight the limits and contradictions inherent in the reforms instituted in response to the 1981 and 1985 riots and the Scarman Report (Cottle 2004; McLaughlin and Murji 1999; Rollock 2009). The main weakness of these reforms was that, despite the rhetoric and the promise of a radical new direction, many of the promised initiatives were only partially implemented, if at all. As Chapter 2 suggests, in the aftermath of the Macpherson Report, however, there was a more concerted effort to address the issue of institutionalised racism within the police as well as in society more generally (Neal 2003). The Stephen Lawrence case thus helped to move the issue of racist violence, which had been a recurrent theme through the 1980s and 1990s (Bjorgo and Witte 1993; Bowling 1998), higher up the policy agenda. A case in point is the Metropolitan Police Racial and Violent Crime Task Force in London, which was set up after the killing of Stephen Lawrence and helped to change everyday police practices in relation to racial violence and racist attacks (Bennetto 2009; Rollock 2009).

Although much of the political debate on policing was dominated in one way or another by the Stephen Lawrence case in the 1990s and 2000s, a number of other issues rose to prominence during this same period. For example concern about drugs and gun-related crimes was sparked by the emergence of a new folk devil, namely the 'yardies': criminal gangs from Jamaica who were linked to drug dealing and murder. One of the main themes in public discourses on the yardies was 'black on black' crime, particularly shootings. This was a recurrent cause of police operations during the 1990s and led to the setting up of a special operation, Operation Trident, to deal with gun crimes and murder in black communities (McLaughlin 2007; Rowe 2004; 2007).

Interestingly enough some of the most vocal support for measures to tackle black on black crime have come from traditionally radical voices. For example Lee Jasper, the Race Adviser of Ken Livingstone, who was then the Mayor of London, called for tough action against crime in black neighbourhoods. Commenting on the emergence of a 'gangsta' culture among young African-Caribbean men, he warned that 'black neighbourhoods have become free trade zones for every kind of drug and illegal contraband, including guns' (*The Observer*, 17 February 2002). Popular images of black gun crime may at one level be seen as feeding a stereotype that has been around for some time, but they also reflect real problems that have emerged in many socially deprived urban areas over the past two decades or so. Crime and the fear of crime and violence have become a core concern in many multicultural communities, and the everyday occurrence of street crime and drug-related crime has put crime and violence in multicultural communities firmly on policing agendas. What is less clear is whether adequate and non-discriminatory measures have been taken to intervene in these patterns and address wider community-level worries about crime and violence in culturally mixed urban environments. We return to these issues later in the chapter in our discussion of the disorders of 2011.

Policing, race and terrorism in the 21st century

Following the debates on urban unrest during the period from 1981 to 2001, the beginning of the 21st century saw another important issue come to the fore in relation to policing and minority ethnic communities, namely the question of terrorism and security. The emergence of this issue can be traced back to the terrorist attacks on New York and Washington organised by Al Qaeda in September 2001. It was also linked to the fear that was raised in the aftermath of the 2001 riots about the seeming lack of 'community cohesion' in towns such as Burnley, Oldham and Bradford. In the aftermath of the events in 2001, and the subsequent 'war on terror', there was an increasing preoccupation among both the police and the security services about the possible threat from within Britain posed by radicalised Muslim activists influenced by the ideas of Al Qaeda and other movements. In this context there has been a vilification and criminalisation of Muslim communities. In a post-Macpherson criminal justice system it is interesting to note that in the period since the early 2000s there have been a greater number of complaints about the use of stop-and-search powers by the police in relation to Muslim communities from South Asian and other origins. Certainly Ministry of Justice, Race and Criminal Justice (2010) statistics show dramatic increase in the stop-and-search practice and arrest levels for all ethnic groups and except for the BME groups the increases are significant (see Webster 2012). In relation to arrests, the trend in the Ministry of Justice data shows that there was a 4 per cent increase in arrests of white people between 2004–2005 and 2008–2009; a 16 per cent increase for black people and a striking 26 per cent increase for Asian people. The suicide attacks on London transport in July 2005 amplified the concerns about the threat 'from within' posed by home-grown terrorist cells working in collaboration with globalised terror networks. The attacks of July 2005 have been followed by a number of other potential terror attacks which has helped create an atmosphere of fear about the threat of both domestic and external terror threats (Allen 2011). The beginning of the 21st century saw the emergence of the figure of the 'Islamic suspect/terrorist' in policing and 'ethnic imaginaries' (Husband and Alam 2011; Noble 2010; Poynting, Noble and Collins 2004). As Jock Collins (2010) argues, this coupling of the dangerous 'other' with Muslim communities connects wider and multiscale themes: the global (the bombings in New York, Bali, Madrid and London); the national (immigration debates and segregation controversies) and the local (problem youth, polarised ethnic communities and multicultural conflict in the post-industrial towns and cities of Yorkshire and Lancashire). In this new landscape the preoccupation of both the police and the security services with the threat posed by radicalised activists within Muslim communities has led to a securitisation of policing strategies towards sections of black minority ethnic communities that are seen popularly as providing a base for radical groups to gain support for their activities (House of Commons Communities and Local Government Committee 2010; House of Commons Home Affairs Committee 2011). As we discussed in Chapter 2 this was manifested in the counter-terrorism strategies, most notably in the Prevention of Violent Extremism programme under the New Labour government and revised under the current coalition government. There have been inevitable policy tensions produced by implementing a crime-control policy that associates Muslim communities with violent extremism while also seeking to implement a social policy that aims to mobilise those same communities around cohesion initiatives. While PVE has been highly controversial and difficult to implement (see Husband and Alam 2011) it is indicative of and reflects wider policing agendas and the development of strategies of securitisation. Linking security, social cohesion, cultural difference and threat has particularly marked a new development in the relationship between policing, crime-control policy approaches and multiculture. It is in this context that 'issues of threat and security have become widely extended to issues that are well beyond the immediate remit of terrorism' (Husband and Alam 2011: 85). It is in this way that securitisation permeates and impacts on everyday multicultural environments and community relations as well as within local, national and transnational policy worlds and political sensibilities (Huysmans 2009).

In the period since 2001 we have seen not only a profound shift in the focus of policing towards the issue of terrorism and national security, but a marked politicisation of the policing of Muslim communities both within and outside of national borders. Eugene McLaughlin has emphasised the construction of the threat posed by 'home-grown Islamist terrorism' as an important theme in both governmental and police discourses in this period, particularly in the aftermath of the 7/7 terrorist attacks in London arguing that, 'because terrorism is no longer defined by the territorial boundaries of the nation state, domestic intelligence hubs are now networked with border security and immigration controls and emergent transnational policing and security arrangements' (McLaughlin 2010: 106).

This reframing of police discourses to prioritise terrorism and counter-terrorism measures has by no means replaced other strategies and practices in the policing of multicultural communities as the upward trajectories of stop-and-search and arrests within all BME categories evidence. However it does help to emphasise the ways in which the period since the 1950s has seen important changes in both the language and the practice of policing in this field, often merging concerns about race, migration and cultural difference with wider preoccupations in the society more generally.

Urban unrest, policing and social cohesion

Although many of the public policy debates about policing, race and multiculture during the early part of the 21st century have been over-determined by the issue of terrorism and security, the riots in England in August 2011 have helped to bring the issue of urban violence back onto the agenda. The riots have led to another flurry of public debate and media speculation about the reasons for the violence and their impact in terms of criminal justice policy and wider policy agendas. While the last major round of unrest in the 1980s and 2001 resulted in reports and investigations that focused on questions about race and ethnicity (Cantle 2001; Hussain and Bagguley 2005; Ouseley 2001; Rhodes 2009b; Scarman 1981b), the August 2011 events have usually been seen through a lens that has emphasised cultures of criminality and looting. Although the events in Tottenham, in North London, after the shooting of Mark Duggan by the police bear a remarkable similarity to the Broadwater Farm (a social housing estate in Tottenham) riots of 1985, which took place in protest at the death of Cynthia Jarrett, the question of race and ethnicity has tended to be discussed in an ambivalent and more limited way (Murji and Neal 2011; see also Chapter 1). Given the range of the events that followed the initial outbreak of violence on the streets of Tottenham this is perhaps not surprising. The initial violence in Tottenham started in the evening of 6 August 2011 after a march to the Tottenham Police Station to protest the death of Mark Duggan, which had occurred on 4th August. As the riots spread geographically in the period from the 6 to the 10 of August, however, the media coverage and public debate about the events shifted away from issues about race and policing to a wider set of social and cultural symbols.

It is clear from research on riots and violent disturbances in a variety of contexts that although they may share some characteristics they are not a singular phenomenon (Collins 2008; Wilkinson 2009). In the period since the 1980s the various outbreaks of collective violence we have seen on the streets of British cities have taken a variety of forms, including violent confrontations with the police, street violence, confrontations between groups in a specific community and looting of shops and property. Indeed, it is clear that there is often disagreement about what kinds of events are covered by the term 'riot', and some scholars seek to use other terms such as 'rebellions' and 'urban unrest' to describe events such as those in 2011. It is perhaps this complexity that explains the range of attempts to describe, analyse and explain what actually happened during those few days in early August 2011. The riots and disturbances that took place in Tottenham and across a number of cities and towns in England have been seen through a variety of lenses. More specifically they have been seen as: (i) a product of a 'Broken Britain'; (ii) 'consumer society riots'; (iii) a product of criminality and gang culture; (iv) shaped by the social media technologies, such as *Twitter* and *BlackBerry Messenger*.

The idea of the riots as a product of a 'Broken Britain' became a strong undercurrent in the commentaries on the riots almost as soon as they had started. David Cameron was one among a number of politicians who focused on this dimension when he talked of the need to develop a response to the riots that linked tough policing to measures to 'mend our broken society' (Stratton 2011). This was a theme Cameron had used before the riots in formulating the agenda of the coalition government, but after the violence of August 2011 he was also keen to use this notion to distance the violence from any policies initiated by his administration. He constructed them as the outcome of a breakdown of morality and a sense of order in some families and communities in sections of a criminal urban underclass. In the immediate aftermath of the events *The Sunday Telegraph* framed the riots as an expression of the 'erosion of morality' (McCulloch 2011).

Another strong theme in the media coverage of the riots was the focus on issues such as looting and the idea that they were in some sense 'consumer society riots'. Although images of looting and arson had been a theme in previous outbreaks of collective violence in the 1980s and in 2001, it became perhaps the dominant image of the August 2011 riots, as both TV and newspaper coverage focused on images of shops being attacked, looted or burned down. Sections of the media also picked up on the theme of the riots as an expression of 'rampant consumerism' and the notion that the rioters were engaged in forms of shopping by looting. Indeed the work of the sociologist Zygmunt Bauman was cited by some as evidence that the riots of 2011 were essentially a product of the growth of social inequality in a context where groups of young people feel left out of 'consumer culture' (Bauman 2011).

Much of the official and media response to the riots has been to see them as merely acts of looting and criminality, as the actions of feral children, as the work of criminal gangs within the urban underclass. This theme was not in itself new. Indeed, in both 1981 and 1985 the immediate response of the Thatcher government was to see them as 'criminal acts' and to refute any attempt to see them as linked to issues such as urban deprivation, racial inequality and youth unemployment (Benyon and Solomos 1987). Some facets of the official response in 1981 and 1985, however, accepted the need to bring issues such as racial inequality and the position of black youth into account as the causes of the riots (Scarman 1981b; 1985). In the context of August 2011, however, the emphasis on criminality and gang culture had been much more central in public discourses. Thus a strong theme in the official response to the riots has been to see them, in Gary Marx's term, as essentially 'issueless riots' (Marx 1970). In other words the riots were seen as having little to do with wider social or economic issues, and the rioters were essentially engaged in 'criminality'. From a similar angle *The Sun* commented that 'The mob that turned the centre of Tottenham in London into a smoking ruin were not seeking justice. They are criminal thugs who were hell bent on theft, arson and violence' (Editorial 2011).

An important new theme relative to previous accounts of riots in Britain focused on the role of social media technologies such as *Twitter* and *BlackBerry Messenger* as a means by which the riots spread from Tottenham in London to other parts of London and also to other cities and towns. The use of the internet and social media technologies as tools for political and social movement mobilisation has been widely discussed in recent years. Indeed, it had been a recurrent theme in coverage of anti-globalisation protests and in the student protests in 2010. The 2011 riots highlighted the role of new technologies in both disseminating information about acts of collective violence and in encouraging participation in looting. Given this context it is not surprising that media coverage both during the events and in the weeks that followed constructed the rapid spread of the riots as being intimately linked to the widespread use of *Twitter* to spread news of specific events and to encourage looting. *The Express*, for example, expressed the spread of violence with the headline 'Now the Riots Spread as Twitter Thugs Fan Flames' (Twomey and Reynolds 2011).

Taken together these four frames have been important in much of the discussion that has followed on from the events in August 2011. They have a clear presence in the political language used by politicians to talk about the events and also run through the mass-media coverage of the events.

What then of the role of race issues in the construction of responses to the riots? As argued above, in the context of the August 2011 events race played a there/not there role in most of the media discussion and even in the policy responses to the riots. This is to say that it was a presence and that the discussion of issues such as criminality and a breakdown of morality were inflected with some elements of a racialised discourse (see also Chapter 1). If one follows the media coverage of the events it is certainly possible to trace some elements of racialised discourse about particular events, such as the initial riots in Tottenham and Wood Green. The controversy over David Starkey's construction of the riots as a sign that a 'nihilistic gangster culture' had become a dominant norm in Britain was perhaps the most infamous example of such taken-for-granted racialised discourses being integrated into broader social and political explanations of the riots (Merrick 2011). But much of the discussion of events outside of Tottenham and the surrounding areas was not focused on issues of race and ethnicity and as such it is worth reflecting on how we can explore the role that questions about race, policing and related issues played a role in shaping atleast some aspects of the unrest during August 2011. Perhaps some important ways in which questions about race seem to link up with what happened in August 2011 can be found in relation to the following issues: (i) race and policing; (ii) poverty, unemployment and education; (iii) political inclusion and exclusion.

In his account of the 1981 riots in Brixton Lord Scarman was able to conclude that the riots were essentially an outburst of anger against the police in a context where there were widespread grievances about the role of the police in the local multicultural community (Benyon 1984; Scarman 1981b). While this diagnosis of the riots was not universally accepted it helped to focus attention on the role of local policing cultures in shaping outbursts of collective violence. In the three decades that followed there have been numerous attempts by the police, by governments and by other bodies to address the sources of these grievances and to develop strategies for managing urban unrest (Keith 1993; Rowe 2007; Waddington, Jobard and King 2009). These efforts were reinforced after further unrest in 1985 and 2001, and by the public debates on the death of Stephen Lawrence. The Macpherson Report on the death of Stephen Lawrence provided a policy focus for some of these debates on race and policing (Macpherson 1999a).

Such efforts led to both local and national initiatives to reform the police, to implement race and cultural awareness training, to recruit and retain more minority officers and to develop links and liaison techniques between the police and local communities. Post Macpherson, there has been recognition of the need to develop critical incident management and liaison work with the families involved in such incidents (Murji and Neal 2011). Yet the initial unrest in Tottenham on 6 August highlighted the apparent failure of these initiatives and the important role that the actions of the police, and even rumours about their actions, can play in providing a spark for collective violence to break out. Following the shooting of Mark Duggan by the police, rumours circulated in the wider community linking his death both to other examples of deaths in police custody and related grievances about the police. It is clear from the historical experiences of urban riots in the US during the 1960s and from the earlier events in England during the 1980s and in 2001 that such rumours and stories about the police become an important factor in providing a spark for the violence that follows (Fogelson 1971; Olzak and Shanahan 1996). It was partly as a result of such rumours and a local protest march on Tottenham Police Station that the initial unrest in North London broke out. The sequence of events leading up to the initial violence and looting in Tottenham were thus deeply inflected by highly charged rumours about the police and their role in the death of Mark Duggan, but more generally about the role of the police in relation to local BME and migrant communities and young black men in particular.

Given the importance of discourses about 'Broken Britain' and criminality in accounts of the riots, it is perhaps not surprising that poverty, racialised inequalities, deprivation and youth unemployment were marginalised in the initial political responses to the riots. In their official responses to the events the coalition government used political language that sought to portray the rioters as criminalised looters. This was a theme that was taken up in wider media coverage of the riots that constructed them as a kind of orgy of 'looting' and 'thieving'. In this atmosphere few politicians, either nationally or locally, articulated a link between the riots and wider social inequalities, though there was some discussion in media discourses of the disorders, social exclusion and urban deprivation. It is interesting to note, in this context, that soon after the riots died down the Labour Opposition leader, Ed Miliband, argued that: 'Both culture and deprivation matter. To explain is not to excuse. But to refuse to explain is to condemn to repeat' (Stratton 2011). In an echo of this Ian Duncan Smith (currently the coalition government's Work and Pensions Secretary) also accepted that

> We cannot simply arrest our way out of these riots. We also need a robust social response that members of all political parties can sign up to. (*The Times*, 15 September 2011)

Yet public responses have continued to be dominated by cultural deficit models and 'Broken Britain' narratives as is evidenced in the coalition government's development of its 'troubled families' initiative which involves the development of a national network of local-authority organised teams to work with families who have 'multiple problems'. For researchers, policymakers and the communities affected it seems important to explore the possible links between the wider social and economic conditions in the localities in which the riots took place, policing and local community and police relations and outbreaks of forms of collective violence. The situation in places such as Tottenham, before and after the riots, bears some similarity to what Harris and Wilkins have defined as the 'quiet riots' of unemployment, poverty, social disorganisation and housing and school deterioration (Harris and Wilkins 1988). For example, Stafford Scott, a community activist who has worked since the 1980s within the Broadwater Farm Estate in Tottenham argues that, in the period since August 2011 the emphasis on seeing the riots as linked to criminality and gang culture has made it difficult to give voice to calls to provide more social and economic resources for the communities that live in the most deprived areas of Tottenham. He argues that

> Equality, fairness and justice must be on the table, for without this the regeneration of Tottenham High Road will be meaningless to many of its inhabitants, and the likelihood of another riot erupting will remain a distinct possibility. (Scott 2011)

In the current climate voices such as Scott's remain relatively isolated since the dominant discourses about the riots have given little credence to any links between the riots and issues of equality, fairness and justice. For example, the Department of Communities and Local government's integration strategy describes the riots and subsequent policy challenge as being 'how to respond to the criminality and lack of social responsibility that lay behind the actions of a small number of people' (Department for Communities and Local Government 2012: 4). As with the responses to the 2001 riots in Northern England, in 2011 it has been the nature of the communities involved that has been the focus of political and policy attention. While it was the unrest of the 1980s that was used as common reference point in the initial August 2011 riots – in which policing was a focus of inquiry (Scarman 1981a) – policing has not been addressed as a official concern in the most recent disorders. The absence of a post-riot focus on policing is significant given the role of policing in the initial disturbances in Tottenham and also given that recent research with those involved in riots have cited their relationship with the police – often in the form of frequent stop-and-search experiences – as a site of tension and frustration and a key factor in the disorders (Newburn 2011).

Conclusion

At the beginning of the 21st century the issue of policing multicultural communities remains at the heart of both policy debates and media discourses about race relations. Indeed, it can be said that it remains a deeply contested issue and a source of tension between the police and sections of minority ethnic communities. Ongoing debates about street crime, urban unrest, racism in police subcultures, stop-and-search, deaths in police custody and the policing of terrorism have helped keep the issue of policing very much alive at both national and local levels. A good example of the intense emotions that arise in relation to this issue can be seen in the controversy that still surrounds the Stephen Lawrence case. The trial and eventual conviction in 2012, of two of the five suspects who have been popularly portrayed as involved in Stephen Lawrence's death has led to intense debate once again about institutionalised racism in the police force and the extent of the changes that have taken place in the aftermath of the 1999 Macpherson Report. In this context there are renewed, ongoing and emergent concerns as to the continuing over-representations of BME groups within the criminal justice system in the UK (Sveinsson 2012). These inequalities reflect wider events and social shifts but also the limited impact and/or failure of the various initiatives taken over the past two decades not only to address racism and differential police treatment of BME populations, but to also improve complaint and disciplinary procedures, implement effective cultural competency training for officers, to increase the recruitment of police from within minority ethnic communities, retain BME staff and use a multicultural police force to bring about broader changes in policing multicultural populations (Barot and Jussab 2012).

It is likely that the trends and issues outlined in this chapter will continue to have an impact on policy debates about policing, race and multiculture for some time to come. Although crime and the fear of crime, violence and urban unrest, and racism within the police forces remain key areas of public concern, questions about policing, and specifically the relationship between the police and black and minority ethnic communities, will remain as a substantial issue in both official discourses and within the popular media. There will be continuing policy worries about institutionalised racism within policing institutions and the ethnically differential impact of police practices such as stop-and-search and anti-terrorism measures and ongoing debates on how to most effectively address and intervene in these.

Chapter 6

Health

As with the other fields of social resource and policy considered in this book understanding the relationship between health and ethnicity involves recognising its multidimensionality and complexity. This chapter considers a number of connected although distinct concerns ranging from variations in ethnically differentiated patterns of physical well-being, access to quality health provision services, the employment and status of black, minority and migrant ethnic healthcare professionals within the NHS and healthcare services to mental health provision and the psychiatric systems in the UK. These concerns are embedded in broader contexts of structural and socio-economic relations and compounded by a tendency within some medical models to either marginalise and neglect those illnesses that disproportionately affect BME populations or, conversely, ethnicise illness and culturally pathologise black, minority ethnic and migrant communities health needs.

These complex processes and issues have their antecedents in a long history in which ideas of 'race', science, genetics and medicine (Gilman 1985; Malik 2008) were problematically connected and a more recent history of minority and migrant communities being linked with disease, threat and high health needs. As Glass and Pollins commented in 1960, 'coloured people are feared as competitive intruders; they are thought of as promoters of crime and carriers of disease' (cited in Fryer 1984: 375). These racialised linkages between the categories of 'ethnicity' and 'disease' raise questions about how to debate, research and make policy interventions in the area of ethnicity and health. The field of health policy and health services has been particularly drawn to and embedded in fixed and biologised notions of ethnicity and on that basis made simplistic and/or unproblematic connections between ethnic identity and illness. As Karlsen (2004) and Ahmad and Bradby (2007) note much of the research work in health and epidemiological studies is based on medical science rather than social science and thus tends to operate from untheorised assumptions of ethnic difference. These assumptions view culture as being innate, primordial and genetic and lead to a position in which ethnic categories – defined by country of origin and/or skin colour – are understood as undifferentiated 'blocks' of comparative populations – white, South Asian, Black – and culture itself becomes the 'total' cause and explanation of health differentials. It is then, in relation to debates about health, illness and healthcare provision, that the importance of viewing ethnicity as socially located and heterogeneous becomes especially pronounced (see Chapter 1).

Despite this array of challenges the sociology of health has, historically, been slow to engage with ethnicity. Recently there has been a development of social science based inquiry into the multifaceted relationship between health and ethnicity but there are still areas of contestation and under-developed research. As the composition and constitution of multiculture becomes increasingly diverse and fragmented with the arrival of new migrant populations and with social and spatial changes taking place in older migrant BME communities, health and ethnicity research is struggling to keep pace with these complications.

Reflecting this multidimensional nature of the health-ethnicity relationship this chapter is organised into five broad parts. The first part examines the ways in which social and economic factors interact with ethnicity and shape and impact health and well-being of BME populations. Ethnically based health differentials are the focus of the second part of the chapter. Reviewing the existing data on the established and emergent key medical conditions that appear to evidence particular ethnic over-representations the chapter highlights the differences within and across ethnic categories. Parts three and four of the chapter examine the racialised contexts of ill health. This racialisation has a duality to it: the marginalisation of BME and migrant health needs on the one hand and 'ethnicisation' of illness on the other. The chapter then explores the organisation of NHS-based healthcare in the UK and in particular reviews the extent to which BME and migrant populations provide healthcare services and medical skills in the UK. The final part of the chapter focuses on the long-running concerns about ethnic disproportionality, race and mental healthcare.

Social conditions and well-being: the class-ethnicity-health relationship

To be in a state of good health involves much more than the obvious requirement of the absence of illness and/or disease. It requires an environment in which core human needs are adequately met (World Health Organisation 2010: 7). As Waqar Ahmad argues,

> health is fundamentally located in the socio-economic and environmental contexts of people's lives. Poverty is the most important single determinant of ill health. Struggles for better health are therefore essentially struggles for better jobs, adequate housing, access to education, a safe environment, good public health facilities and civil and legal rights. (Ahmad 1993: 7)

Historically, the broader social context of well-being has often been obscured and dominated by the first, the medicalisation of health – a process which reduces health to a series of individualised, disease-orientated, and scientifically and technologically dominated models (Illich 1975) – and second, a preventive-based health policy approach centred on lifestyles and behaviours. However, the evidence of the correlation between social determinants and health is extensive. In the UK context such data was famously provided in the *Black Report* (Townsend and Davidson 1982) and in subsequent studies (Benezeval, Judge and Whitehead 1995; Davey Smith, Barlety and Blane 1990) and most recently in the *Fair Society, Healthy Lives* Report (Marmot et al. 2010). This report argued in its Foreword that 'the link between social conditions and health is not a footnote to the "real" concerns with health – health care and unhealthy behaviours – it should become the main focus'. The Report, the outcome of a Commission Review Team set up by the Labour Government and chaired by the epidemiologist Michael Marmot, produced findings which show that, despite increased general prosperity, the NHS and the New Labour government's programme of increased health spending, the social determinants of health inequalities were pronounced and entrenched. For example, they note that 'in England, people living in the poorest neighbourhoods, will, on average, die seven years earlier than people living in the richest neighbourhoods' (Marmot et al. 2010: 10).

While Salway et al. (2010) criticised the Marmot Review as it did not explicitly address ethnicity and health, the review process did include a Task Group focus on social inclusion and mobility that had a focus on ethnicity and asylum seekers and refugees. The Task Group confirmed that socio-economic inequalities experienced by BME and migrant populations were reflected in ethnic patterns of ill health and added that the experiences of racism and discrimination are likely to be highly detrimental to their health and well-being. A related set of concerns were expressed in terms of asylum seekers and refugees whose health may be more vulnerable given conditions of flight and migration and who are likely to face particular challenges in accessing health services (Marmot et al. 2010). These findings reflect those of earlier research.

For example in the late 1990s, Nazroo argued that the evidence from the Policy Study Institute's (PSI) Fourth National Survey demonstrates that 'ethnic variations in health are overall most likely to relate to differences in socio-economic position'. The PSI data showed a direct correlation for all (majority and minority) ethnic groups between the reporting of fair to poor health and living in a household with a manual or unemployed worker. Households with a non-manual worker reported the best health. A similar correlation for all ethnic groups was found in terms of reporting only fair to poor health and being a tenant, and higher rates of good health corresponding with being an owner-occupier (Modood et al. 1997: 89). As the social and economic status of BME and migrant populations continues to diversify the social heterogeneity of minority ethnic groups is likely to affect ethnically differentiated health patterns. In the US, for example, where there is a well established African-American middle class, there are correlations between higher income African-Americans and better health (Nazroo 2010)

However, the relationship between health and ethnicity cannot be explained only through socio-economic factors. For example, Smaje argues that race and ethnicity cannot be 'simply emptied into class disadvantage' (Smaje 1996: 153). In this context key studies such as Nazroo's (1997; 2001) have sought to engage with the complex interfaces between ethnicity, social and economic determinants and health.

The socio-economic effect on ethnic health patterns presents two key challenges to understanding the ethnicity-health relationship – avoiding 'over-classing' the patterns that is, explaining ethnic health variation entirely through a social and economic frame and conversely, avoiding an epidemiological 'over-ethnicising' or 'over-culturising' ethnic health variations. With this double bind in mind Nazroo (1997; 2001) has cautioned against an over-reliance on social and economic disadvantage as a single logic defining the relationship between ethnicity and health. Raising questions as to how a socio-economic framework is able to account for the different forms of poor health among different minority ethnic groups that carry the heaviest burden of ill health – for example, the disproportionately high rates of hypertension for African-Caribbean women and the disproportionately high rates of heart disease for Pakistani and Bangladeshi men (see below) – Nazroo (2001) emphasises a number of crucial caveats. These include geographical location and access to, and quality of, health services, heterogeneity within ethnic groups and the social nature of ethnicity and the negative impact of experiences and/or perceptions of racism and discrimination on health. The consequences of experiences and/or perceptions of racism on health has received some research attention which has shown that these can be considerable (Benezeval, Judge and Whitehead 1995; Karlsen and Nazroo 2002). This leads Karlsen and Nazroo to argue that

> not only do we need measures that adequately account for the different forms of social disadvantage experienced by ethnic minority groups, we also need to explore the various ways in which racism itself can impact on physical and mental health. (Karlsen and Nazroo 2002: 18)

The complexities of the relationship between ethnicity, social and economic status and health is further highlighted by the area of infant mortality. Infant mortality is often taken as a key indicator for assessing health and well-being, and high levels of infant death have traditionally been shown to have a connection with social and economic disadvantage. There are significant inequalities in the rates of infant mortality across, and between, ethnic groups. Pakistani and Caribbean groups had the highest rates of infant mortality. Babies in these groups were twice as likely to die before the age of one than white British babies. Babies born to Bangladeshi groups had the lowest rates of infant mortality of all non-white groups (Gray et al. 2009). Bangladeshi and white British groups were comparable in their levels of infant mortality. Not only are infant mortality rates within the Bangladeshi population declining but they are also falling at a faster rate than other minority groups despite the Bangladeshi population comprising one of the most socially and economically deprived communities in the UK. In their research on infant mortality rates Gray et al. argue that socio-economic position must be viewed as a multidimensional concept that incorporates a cluster of components for example, educational attainment, housing tenure, single parenthood as well as the more common indicators of income, employment and occupation, and even then its explanatory power remains limited (Gray et al. 2009: 6). For Gray et al. the ethnic variations in infant mortality can only be explained through the complex 'interplay of deprivation, physiological, behavioural and cultural factors' (2009: 1)

It is clear that, in order to better understand the ways in which social determinants impact on ethnic variations of health more sophisticated analytic tools are required that allow better methodologies and greater understanding of measurement, causality and impact within and across heterogeneous categories of ethnicity.

Mapping ethnically differential patterns of well-being and health

Established data trends in BME health

Data sources since the mid-1990s consistently reveal a pattern in which minority ethnic groups experience a higher degree of ill health compared to majority white groups. The census data replicates patterns found in earlier studies (Benezeval, Judge and Whitehead 1995; Nazroo 1997) showing that after age standardising, Pakistani and Bangladeshi men and women were twice as likely as white British men and women to report not being in good health, and Bangladeshi men were three times more likely to visit their GP than any other ethnic groups. However, while this may be the meta-trend within the health data when minority ethnic groups are considered as an overall homogenised category the pattern is far more complex when it is reconfigured to focus on the significant variations between different minority ethnic groups and levels of ill health. When these variations are taken into account then it no longer is possible to discuss the relationship between health and ethnicity in a generalised or reductionist way. The findings of the Fourth National Survey and the 1991 census offered an early demonstration of the extent and ongoing health differences among different minority ethnic populations and among minority and majority populations. For example, from the age standardised data from these sources 40 per cent of Pakistani, Bangladeshi and Caribbean groups reported that they had fair to poor health, they either had a long-standing illness or were registered disabled. However, the numbers of African-Asians, Chinese and Indians who reported fair to poor health, a long standing illness or being registered disabled were much lower. Similarly, the variations between different minority ethnic populations and majority populations were significant with 50 per cent of Pakistani and Bangladeshis and 30 per cent of Caribbeans more likely than white respondents to report only fair or poor health. In contrast, the rates of reporting fair to poor health for Indians, African-Asians and Chinese reflected the same rates as whites (Nazroo 1997: 130–131). Gender adds a further layer of complexity to the heterogeneity in the patterns of ethnicity-based health (see below). Additionally the recent settlement of white migrants from East Europe in the UK may impact the ethnic health differentials. Certainly the data on Irish populations does reveal health differences. Nazroo (2010: 113–114) confirms that the available data sources have shown that Irish migrants have higher mortality rates across coronary heart disease, stroke, respiratory disease and lung cancer. Along with Pakistani women, Irish women had the highest rates of GP consultation of any ethnic group.

What emerges from the data are established patterns of poor health that disproportionately affect *some* minority ethnic and migrant populations. In particular, Bangladeshi and Pakistani groups had the worst health followed by Caribbean groups. The Indian, African-Asian and Chinese groups reported being in better health. Looking at BME and migrant health and particular health conditions emphasises the differential trends in health conditions and it is these that the chapter now considers.

Established and emergent areas of concern in ethnicity and health patterns

Table 6.1 shows the complex patterns and variations of ethnicity in relation to disease though these health dispositions and differences remain only partially understood. One reason for this is the lack of data for ethnicity and mortality because, in the UK, mortality data records an individual's country of origin and not their ethnicity. Other contributory factors resulting in partial knowledge is the slow response of health intelligence in gathering information and data on ethnicity, the social not biological basis of ethnicity and the rapid changes in the geographies and composition of

Table 6.1 Health conditions more prevalent among minority ethnic groups in UK

Condition	Summary of patterns
Diabetes	Lower rates of Insulin Dependent Diabetes (Type I) in South-Asian and Caribbean populations but poor life expectancy where found. Significant rates of Non-Insulin Dependent Diabetes (Type II; later onset) in Black and South-Asian groups. Higher rates of diabetes also linked with other conditions such as renal failure and coronary heart disease, and consequent service needs.
Tuberculosis	High mortality amongst people born in Ireland. Higher incidence amongst non-UK born Black African and South-Asian populations.
Coronary Heart Disease	Mortality rates are high in South Asian and white populations
Stroke	Higher mortality rates amongst African and Caribbean populations.
Thalassaemia	More common amongst people from Southern Europe, Middle East and South Asia.
Sickle Cell	More prevalent in populations of African and Caribbean ancestry.
Cancers	Mortality rates are high amongst people born in Ireland. Generally lower rates for major cancers for those born in Indian subcontinent and Caribbean and African Commonwealth although some recent evidence of rise in some cancers in some minority ethnic groups.
HIV	HIV diagnosis has increased significantly in heterosexual groups – over 52 per cent of all people with HIV in the UK are heterosexual. Black African communities are the heterosexual group most disproportionately affected by HIV in the UK.

Source: Adapted from Johnson et al. (2004).

BME and migrant populations in the UK. The available data is always likely to lag behind the current health conditions and patterns among different populations.

Coronary heart disease and diabetes

These have consistently stood out as key areas in which some minority ethnic groups experienced especially high rates of poor health, and the connective chain between different diseases is important and is reflected in patterns of ethnic disproportion. For example rates of end stage kidney renal failure – which is related to diabetes and hypertension – are three times higher in South-Asian and African-Caribbean groups than in general white population of the UK (Johnson et al. 2004; Johnson 2006). The patterns of ethnic disproportion are significant in cardiovascular disease or coronary heart disease (CHD) rates which are approximately 50 per cent higher in South-Asian ethnic categories than the general population. Levels of stroke (cerebrovascular disease) among African-Caribbean groups are much higher than in other ethnic groups. In terms of diabetes and in particular Type 2 diabetes the available data (Diabetes in the UK 2010) shows that the disease is up to six times more common in people of South-Asian descent and up to three times more common among people of African and African-Caribbean origin. Disaggregating the 'South-Asian' category, the NHS Health Survey for England reported that doctor-diagnosed diabetes is almost four times as prevalent in Bangladeshi men, and almost three times as prevalent in Pakistani and Indian men compared to men in the general population (National Health Service 2005). Adding in gender complicates but maintains the pattern of BME groups being more vulnerable to the disease. Among women, diabetes is more than five times as likely among Pakistani women, at least three times as likely in Bangladeshi and Caribbean women, and two-and-a-half times as likely in Indian women, compared with women in the general population (Diabetes in the UK 2010). Again a caution with this data has to be linked to the nature of diabetes and Type 2 diabetes in particular in which genetics and lifestyle do matter but social and economic deprivation is a key factor related to the disease – as the Diabetes in the UK (2010) report notes 'the most deprived people in the UK are two-and-a-half times more likely than the average to have diabetes at any given age'. While it is crucial to avoid an ethnic reduction there is a need to recognise that ethnicity is a pattern in those living with diabetes.

National organisations such as Diabetes UK and the British Heart Foundation have both developed resources for raising awareness of CHD and Type 2 diabetes in South-Asian populations living in the UK. These resources include various fact sheets, including one on fasting during Ramadan and interactive training initiatives to help health advocates, as well as statutory and voluntary organisations, convey health messages to minority ethnic populations (Astin and Atkin 2010). While not diminishing the importance of these awareness-raising tools and preventative steps the emphasis of these initiatives is overwhelmingly cultural and somewhat obscures the complex interplay of multiple risk factors including social exclusion. Social and economic deprivation, access to services, age, migrant history and gender are all involved in CHD and Type 2 diabetes. The need for a multifaceted approach to understanding CHD is reflected in the ongoing confusion as to both the relationship and the need to avoid approaching the category of South Asians as fixed and homogenous.

Cancers

Overall the dominant pattern in terms of ethnicity and cancers has been that non-white populations tend to show lower representations in cancer mortality rates. However, cancer research and data in relation to ethnicity are still limited. While recent data, for example the National Cancer Intelligence Network and Cancer Research UK Report (2009), confirm this trend, the report also reveals a more complex picture and 'highlights the increased risk of certain cancers in the Asian and Black ethnic groups'. A key finding from this research shows an upwards trend in breast cancer diagnosis in Asian and Black women in the younger (50 years and below) age group and 'shows that the Asian and Black women have lower survival than the white ethnic group for females diagnosed with breast cancer aged under 65 years'. The Report, the first major study of ethnicity and cancer diagnosis between 2002–2006, also found differential patterns for black men and stomach and prostrate cancers and a high incidence of mouth cancer among Asian women. On the basis of this pattern the report argues for the need to target 'public health messages to the ethnic communities around the signs and symptoms of cancer. It is also crucial for healthcare commissioners deciding how best to spend their budget in areas with large ethnic groups' (www.cancerresearchuk.org/cancer-info/news/archive/pressrelease/2009–06–25).

The concerns that are only just beginning to emerge about the relationship between cancers and ethnicity reflect either – or both – the changing nature of health conditions and of populations and the increase in research intelligence on certain illnesses and their diagnosis (and treatment) within different ethnic groupings. The ethnic-health variations in the contemporary Britain raise a key challenge – when does ethnicity makes a difference and mediate a person's health experience, and when it does not. Ensuring that policy and practice reflects this complexity and recognises a range of other possible causal factors while maintaining an appropriate evidence base, represents an ongoing challenge for policy interventions and healthcare practices (Astin and Atkin 2010; Phillimore 2011).

HIV and AIDS related illness

This challenge is perhaps especially pronounced in relation to HIV infection. Black Africans have the highest rates of HIV diagnosis compared to anyother BME group including gay, lesbian and transgendered BME groups. Despite being one of the smaller minority ethnic groups in the UK, Black Africans are about 1.7 per cent of the UK population, the Health Protection Agency figures show that 38 per cent of new HIV diagnoses are Black Africans. A complex range of factors and issues lie behind this statistic, namely most HIV positive Black Africans tend to be young (20–49); more women are tested for HIV probably due to their contact with health services via antenatal care and late diagnosis – with implications for treatment – is more common among this group (Health Protection Agency 2008). As Owuor explains this late diagnosis is multifactored with cultural, social and structural barriers all affecting access to testing and care (Owuor 2009). The fear of testing positive, of HIV related stigma and discrimination and worries about migration status and rules may all also impact on pathways to diagnosis and treatment. Research has consistently shown that a majority of Black Africans who tested positive had been resident in England on an average of five years (Dodds et al. 2008; National Aids Trust 2008) which challenges – and undermines – the 'health tourism' media discourses that led in part to the 2004 legislation to tackle the so-called problem of migrants seeking free health treatment and introduced NHS charges for HIV care for migrants. As the National AIDS Trust (2008: 3) states 'HIV is the only serious communicable condition or sexually transmitted infection where certain migrants are subject to NHS charges – for all these other infections NHS care is always free on public health grounds irrespective of residency status'. The vilification of migrants with HIV – and disproportionately – migrants from sub-Saharan Africa has meant that healthcare in relation to HIV can be identified as deeply racialised. This follows a much longer history of healthcare in the UK either stigmatising or marginalising health conditions and it is this that the chapter now considers.

Racialised contexts of health

Ethnicising and marginalising illness: some case study examples

The previous section has indicated variations in incidences of diseases by ethnicity. However, a major concern is the way in which the medical and healthcare profession has tended to veer between either pathologised models of ill health and health inequalities which use ethnicity as their central explanatory axis or a complete negation of genetic or inherited conditions which are known to disproportionately affect particular ethnic groups. A well-cited example of the *ethnicisation* of the health of minority ethnic populations is rickets. In the 1970s, high incidents of rickets were reported in South-Asian communities settled in inner-city areas. In particular, the disease affected the younger population and pregnant women (Ahmad 1993). Whilst poverty had previously been identified as a key causal factor in relation to incidents of rickets, health professionals in the 1970s attributed it to cultural rather than structural factors. Stereotyped notions of a deficient 'Asian diet' and modes of dressing causing Vitamin D deficiency were mobilised to explain the prevalence of the disease. The process of ethnicisation was so complete that rickets was renamed 'Asian rickets' and was targeted by two high-profile campaigns, the Stop Rickets Campaign and the Asian Mother and Baby Campaign, which placed the responsibility for illness on South-Asian communities themselves and urged the adoption of Western diets and lifestyles (Rocheron 1988).

Another example of the ethnicisation of health has been the use of consanguinity (marriage between first and second cousins) to the explain the high levels of infant mortality due to congenital abnormality in babies born to mothers of Pakistani origin (see our earlier discussion on infant mortality). Despite other possible explanations – socio-economic disadvantage, relatively low take-up of antenatal services, age, lower rates of childhood immunisation against rubella, migration status – consanguinity received particular medical attention (Bundey, Alam and Kaur 1991). The existing data is unable to confirm a causal link between rates of congenital abnormality in infants and consanguinity. For example, Proctor and Smith note that 'there seems to be disagreement about the long term effects of consanguinity on a population' (Proctor and Smith 1997: 63), and Hobbiss argues that 'the majority of infants born to consanguineous marriages are perfectly healthy and the extent of consanguinity and genetic predisposition to congenital anomalies [needs to] be considered in this context' (Hobbiss 2006: 11). The dominant place of consanguinity in explanations of the relationship between infant health and ethnicity demonstrates the tendency to emphasise cultural practices and neglect other structural and material circumstances as causal factors (Ahmad 1993).

In relation to the *marginalisation* of minority ethnic health experience a key example of this has been the health care response to haemoglobinopathies – inherited sickle cell and thalassaemia disorders. These are the commonest genetic conditions in the UK where it is estimated that about 12,500 people die due to sickle cell disorder and researchers argue that these numbers are likely to increase (Keenan 2008: 4). Sickle cell disorder primarily affects African/Caribbean populations and to a lesser extent Mediterranean and Middle Eastern populations. Thalassaemia primarily affects South Asian, Mediterranean and Middle Eastern populations. While it was formerly the Cypriot population that was primarily affected by thalassaemia in Britain, the population now most affected by the disorder are infants of couples of Pakistani origin.

There is a discrepancy between the high numbers of carriers of the sickle cell and thalassaemia traits and the much lower number of those who develop the blood disorder which makes awareness and screening important. Without treatment both the sickle cell and thalassaemia conditions can be fatal – death in infants with thalassaemia occurs before they are two years old and 30 per cent of deaths related to sickle cell disorder occur prior to a diagnosis (Keenan 2008: 2). In this context of high healthcare need it has been the ways in which haemoglobinopathies of sickle cell and thalassaemia have been managed and treated in the UK which provides a particular insight into the exclusion of the specific health needs of minority ethnic populations from medical agendas and from service provision. The response of the health service and the professionals to sickle cell and thalassaemia conditions which require, at a minimum, the provision of effective screening, support, education, information and non-directive counselling has historically been characterised by reticence (Anionwu 1993; Anionwu and Atkin 2001). Despite the high percentage of carriers of the trait, within Britain but also globally, sickle cell has been under-researched and research programmes poorly funded. Until relatively recently it was rare for UK based GPs to have any knowledge of sickle cell and the misdiagnosis of the symptoms of a sickle cell crisis was common throughout the 1970s and early 1980s. Since the 1990s there has been a general shift in the quality and extent of healthcare responses to the sickle cell disorder though this has mostly been in London and Greater London areas, where the majority of people with sickle cell and thalassaemia diagnosis were located, where healthcare providers began to be responsive to need and offer haemoglobinopathy services and integrated approaches to care. This shift was due in no small part to BME sustained campaigning over the quality of the health provision and specialised information around the sickle cell disorder (Anionwu and Atkin 2001; Dyson 2005).

Campaigns and policy responses to ethnicity and healthcare needs

The demands for improved health services for sickle cell incorporated thalassaemia into the campaigning agenda as evidence showed that information and screening campaigns about thalassaemia targeted at London based Cypriot communities during the 1970s had a significant impact on the number of Cypriot infants affected by the disorder and raised awareness and knowledge about the condition. The impact of access to information and care on the decline of thalassaemia in Cypriot communities contrasted with the rising thalassaemia figures among Pakistani communities, predominantly located in Northern England. Studies in the early 1990s (Ahmed et al. 2002) showed that contrary to the medical professions' stereotyping of Muslim communities as being unwilling to be screened or to have prenatal diagnosis, Muslim families, often socio-economically deprived, had had little information about these services, and little-to-no opportunity to discuss the disease with specialist health professionals.

The relative success of these long campaigns for appropriate care and treatment is reflected in the current developments in NHS policy regarding sickle cell and thalassaemia, which has taken the form of a nationwide screening programme offered in early antenatal care stages to all pregnant women and to new-born babies as part of their routine blood checks. As well as the universalism of the screening it is the availability of information, support and specialist/doctor–patient partnership models that reflect the extent of the shift in healthcare approaches to sickle cell and thalassaemia in the UK in the 21st century (Keenan 2008). Sickle cell and thalassaemia provide a 'classic' example of the historical marginalisation of the specific health needs of particular minority groups. Although there is clear evidence of health policy shifts in response to haemoglobinopathies since the 1990s there is still some spatial and conceptual unevenness in the levels, forms and strategies of care management. As the geographies of multiculture in the UK expand and as the composition of multicultural populations becomes more complex through current migrant patterns and the rise of mixed ethnicity groups the genetic based health conditions and related care needs will remain a key policy and service concern.

Health policy responses have been highly varied. In some instances responses have been absent or marginal, often policies were hard-won by community-based lobbying, at times policy responses have been shaped by culturalist explanations and at times by epidemiological approaches. What has become increasingly apparent in the 21st century are the ways in which health policy remains 'in development' in its thinking and approaches to ethnicity but does display a recognition that it is a policy domain operating in a context of a multiethnic population with diverse health requirements that are complex and mutating and specific and universal. Examples of this would include HIV organisations who have been increasingly active in campaigning for provision, care and awareness around HIV diagnosis and African migrant groups; research into cancers beginning to engage with ethnicity; the NHS's universal screening for haemoglobinopathies; the targeted Bangladeshi and Pakistani awareness campaigns; and work of CHD and diabetes organisations and the NHS. The recognition that healthcare policy and service delivery is for a multiethnic population is also reflected in the dominance of the concept and language of 'cultural competency'. This has become the key benchmark and standard for health policy intervention and service provision in the UK.

Cultural competency is broadly taken as an approach in which health policymaking and health providers integrate an awareness of, and sensitivity to, cultural diversity into all levels of health policy formation, health research and healthcare practice (Papadopoulos 2006: 5). While cultural competence has its antecedents in multiculturalism (see Chapter 2) it is an extension of this approach. An import from the US where it has had a much wider application across private and public sectors, the focus in cultural competence is not on knowledge of other cultures but is much more broadly on a capacity to operate in a context of multiculture. Unlike multiculturalism cultural competence works with multiculture as the norm and does integrate a wider sociological recognition of structural factors and their impact on healthcare experiences and practices (Holland and Hogg 2001). It combines this with a broader level of culture and places an emphasis on self-reflection, communication and research. Cultural competence has been overwhelmingly located in healthcare in the UK context and has become part of the everyday policy and practice discourse in the NHS and the Department of Health, although understanding of its efficacy and impact on health provision is as yet limited. Early research showed some unevenness in application and confusion over the ways in which cultural competency strategies were distinct from earlier cultural diversity approaches (London Deanery 2008).

As health research, policymaking, service delivery and practice can be understood as evolving in relation to the increasingly complex compositions of multiculture it is the broader structures and architectures of healthcare in the UK and how these relate to issues of race and ethnicity that the chapter now considers.

The NHS: a multiethnic, super-diverse, ethnically segregated organisation?

Since the late 1940s the structures and systems of health provision in the UK have been overwhelmingly organised through the National Health Service (NHS). While private healthcare is an established and increasing part of the healthcare landscape, the NHS still dominates healthcare. It is the core system of healthcare provision within the UK and the NHS historically, and currently, relies on migrant and overseas labour. A study of NHS hospitals in the early 1980s showed that 30 per cent of doctors and 20 per cent of nurses were born overseas (Doyal, Hunt and Mellor 1981). This pattern has not only persisted but also increased. Connell (2010: 51) notes that there were 20,923 foreign trained doctors in the UK in 1970 and in 2003 this number had almost tripled to 69, 813. Foreign doctors account for approximately 33 per cent of medical workforce and a significant number of these (15%) are from Nigeria and South Africa. The employment of migrant nurses also remains high. Since the early 2000s approximately 37 per cent of nurses registering to work in the UK were educated outside the EU, mostly in India and the Philippines and increasingly from Sub-Saharan Africa countries – mainly Nigeria, Zimbabwe, Ghana and Zambia. The UK is not alone in this globalised 'brain drain' pattern of employment of skilled health workers who migrate to the rich world from the poor world. While the UK and the US dominate, Australia and EU countries such as France and Germany are also receiving countries for skilled health workers from Global South countries (Connell 2010; Raghuram 2009).

The post-colonial, and highly uneven, relationship or the 'inverse care law' (Connell 2010: 18) that characterises the contemporary medical labour market extends beyond the overseas recruitment and employment of skilled health workers. Unevenness also characterises the experiences of migrant workers in the healthcare system in the UK. Kyriakides and Virdee (2003: 283) note that 'migrant doctors from specific geographic locations have historically played a fundamental, but paradoxical role in the maintenance of the NHS: they are integral to its running but not awarded the status that such a position would seemingly confer.'

There is an established body of research that documents the historical and continuing segregation of BME and migrant health workers employed in the NHS. From its early days migrant health workers have been disproportionately employed in the least popular specialities, worked longer hours, evening and weekend shifts, come into the NHS at the lowest entry points despite often having higher qualifications and been paid at lower pay grades (Alexis and Vydelingum 2007; Connell 2010; Doyal, Hunt and Mellor 1981; Gish 1971; Robinson and Carey 2000; Xu 2007). There is evidence of deskilling and skill loss among migrant nurses in the NHS and in social care more widely. For instance, Nigerian nurses find themselves employed in nursing homes doing basic carework despite being over qualified for such work (Dyer, McDowell and Batnitzky 2008).

Leroi Henry's (2007) study of the NHS career trajectories of Ghanaian nurses and midwifes found widespread perceptions of discrimination, as the NHS promotion procedures operate through systems of patronage and informal processes and networks of support rather than transparent, formal systems and facilitative career mentoring and feedback. A number of the respondents in Henry's study describe being demoralised as well as withdrawing from careers. He concludes by stating that day-to-day work-based experiences become 'processes and practices [that] institutionalise disadvantages and have discriminatory outcomes which could well account for the under-representation of overseas trained nurses in senior posts' (Henry 2007: 203).

In many ways the experience of migrant and BME doctors has echoed that of migrant and BME nurses in the UK. While the levels of deskilling are not quite as systematic, research has consistently revealed familiar patterns in which migrant and BME doctors tend to be under-represented at the top of the medical hierarchies (senior registrar and consultant) and over-represented in the lower medical hierarchies (registrar and senior house officer). Kangasniemi et al. (2007) found that almost 50 per cent of their sample of migrant doctors were working at a lower grade after migration and Indian doctors in particular experienced this reduction. These patterns of under and over-representation and deskilling also bore a relation to areas of healthcare with a tendency for migrant doctors to be working in the unpopular, lower status areas such as geriatrics and psychiatry rather than in higher status, more popular areas such as general surgery (Ward 1993).

There has been some recognition of these inequities in the healthcare industries and there have been several attempts since the late-1970s to intervene in the racialised and disadvantaging practices operating within the NHS. Despite the NHS being a highly multi-ethnic organisation with marked internal discrimination, it has been slow to implement equality policies. Historically the Commission of Racial Equality (CRE) and successive governments have urged the NHS to take up equality policy and codes of practice (Ward 1993: 177). In 1991 the CRE issued a guide for NHS employment (*NHS Contracts and Racial Equality*) but a follow-up survey by the Commission discovered that only 29 of the 600 district health authorities were planning to implement the Guide (Law 1996). In the late 1990s, the Labour Government made a series of public announcements outlining governmental concern about racial equality issues within the NHS and a commitment to their improvement with the *Vital Connection* programme. This was a five-year, eight-point Department of Health initiative for tackling racial inequality and racism within the NHS, ranging from improving the coverage of ethnicity monitoring, developing a set of equality standards for the NHS, and tackling racial harassment to launching an equality award schemes to promote and reward best practice, fund positive action projects and develop schemes to maximise opportunities for BME health workers to compete for senior posts.

The NHS also has a legal obligation under the 2000 Race Relations Amendment Act to promote and implement race equality initiatives. The cultural competency approach and its take up in the healthcare industry can be read as an acknowledgment by the industry of the need to respond to its multiethnic constituency. There have also been policy initiatives by the UK and other countries such as Norway and the Netherlands which recruit overseas skilled health workers to manage these migration processes in more ethical ways and at the same time develop national sources of recruitment. But, as Connell (2010: 206) notes, 'despite occasional "good intentions" only minimal evidence exists which shows that the UK has modified health worker migration and realistically increased nationally sourced health workers'.

The limited impact of the equalities agenda seems to reflect a range of factors from the very entrenched and often informal micro nature of exclusionary and/or discriminatory practices, the nature and scope of the equality strategies, variations in the policy reticence or willingness within of health authorities to tackle inequalities to limited resources, globalisation, healthcare reforms and an expanding private health industry to an ever expanding demand for skilled health workers as the age demographics of the UK shift. Such factors have all meant that unequal and racialised employment patterns and experiences of migrant and BME skilled health employees have not radically altered. The persistency of such patterns is also apparent in the final aspect of healthcare that the chapter now considers.

Mental health: systems of social care or systems of racism and social control?

Perhaps more than any other area of health and ethnicity it is mental health diagnosis and mental healthcare that have had a particularly high public profile, have been the focus of intense concern and been the most controversial and contested.

Ethnicity and disproportionality in mental health diagnosis

Much of the controversy over the ethnicity-mental health relationship surrounds the diagnosis of psychotic illness – schizophrenia and bipolar disorders – in particular ethnic groups. While the occurrence of psychotic illness in the general population is relatively rare – about one in 200 – the disproportionately high rates to which young African and African-Caribbean men have been diagnosed as psychotic has caused widespread concern for African/Caribbean communities and organisations since the 1970s (Leese et al. 2006). Recently it has become a concern for more 'mainstream' mental health lobbying groups (see for example, MIND 2009). Government responses have remained slow and uneven and the collection of ethnic monitoring data in mental health systems was not instituted until 1995. The 2000s saw government-level recognition of the problematic relationship between race and mental healthcare. For example, the Department of Health (2005) launched its Delivering Race Equality (DRE) strategy which sought to address a range of concerns including the reduction of the levels of psychotic diagnosis and hospitalisation of BME groups.

While different studies reveal different figures, what is consistent across all of the data is the finding that African/Caribbean men are diagnosed with mental illness at about five times the rate of the general population (Karlsen et al. 2005). Recent figures available through the Care Quality Commission's Count Me In Census (2009; 2010) show that 23 per cent of mental healthcare inpatients were from BME groups. The Count Me In Census was a key monitoring part of the Labour government's five-year Delivering Race Equality in Mental Healthcare plan to tackle worries about inequalities in mental healthcare, particularly the over-admission, detention and treatment of BME groups into mental healthcare services.

However, The Count Me In (2005–2010) figures show admission rates for Other Black BME groups (White and Caribbean; White and Black African, Black Caribbean and Black African) are at about six times higher than average and that detention rates are increasing. The failure of the five-year DRE policy intervention to make any impact on the patterns of ethnic disproportion in diagnosis and detention are indicative of the extent and systemic nature of the problematic relationship between ethnicity and mental healthcare (MIND 2011).

As Nazroo (2010) notes, apart from Type II diabetes, mental health is the largest area of health disproportion between ethnic populations. Mental healthcare is surrounded by controversy as the debate about the relationship between mental illness and ethnicity and race becomes polarised between those that highlight the role of racism within the system and those that focus on ethnicity itself and argue that particular minority groups have a particular vulnerability in relation to certain forms of mental disorders. Historically, the absence of sustained and consistent evidence made it difficult to confirm the exact rates of diagnosis and to substantiate either explanatory model. For example, Smaje (1995), while broadly sympathetic to the racism model, notes that direct and systematic racism would need to be operating on a massive scale in order to account for the differential rates of over-diagnosis of psychotic illness (see also Singh and Burns 2006). However the consistency of the most recent data, and the formal recognition of institutional racism (Macpherson 1999), has meant that racism and discrimination have become much more widely accepted in recent policy environments as explanations of disproportion. Although, as with physical health, the process of racism may be multifactored and not only constituted by direct discrimination on the part of mental healthcare professionals at the point of diagnosis (McKenzie and Bhui 2007). In addition connections between social and economic disadvantage and experiences and perceptions of racism and discrimination and negative impacts on well-being and mental health have been evidenced (Karlsen et al. 2005).

Explaining disproportionality: continuing controversies and arguments

The reductionist or 'ethnic vulnerability' notion is highly problematic, relying as it does on a biological interpretation of ethnicity and this being casual. Not only is there a lack of available data to qualify this notion of a 'schizophrenia epidemic' but the data that are available actually militates against such a position. For example, studies of psychosis in the Caribbean do not reveal any higher-than-average rates of occurrence (Hickling 1991) and in the UK context the incidence of anxiety and depressive illness is lower in the African/Caribbean population as are rates of attempted and 'completed' suicide (Balajaran and Soni Raleigh 1995). In examining the validity of the ethnic vulnerability model Sashidharan (1993) and Sashidharan and Francis (1993) argue that much of the existing research data from epidemiological studies of psychiatric disorders among black people, based on hospital admissions, is flawed for a number of reasons. First, using hospital admissions as the evidence base is unreliable as a measure of disposition – studies based on community samples rather than hospital admissions and treatment shows a much reduced prevalence of psychotic illness (Nazroo 2010). Second, the unreliability of clinical diagnosis: professional identification and treatment of patients for psychosis does not necessarily mean patients have psychosis. Third, the geographical area where the study is conducted needs to be accounted for as mostly these studies take place in urban areas which have significant black populations. And fourth, the failure of the research to take into account particular features of populations for example, social and economic status; gender, migrant/non-migrant status and age. The BME population has a significantly younger age profile than the majority white British population and schizophrenia rates are generally higher in younger (15–44 year old) age groups (McCrone et al. 2008).

The process of hospitalisation – admission and detention – is central to concerns about ethnic disproportionality and mental healthcare. Research has shown that BME groups, particularly the African/Caribbean group, were far more likely to enter the mental health system through contact with the police or other forensic services and through compulsory admission, via the 1983 Mental Health Act (amended in 2007), than the general population (Sashidharan 1993). It has been Section 136 of the 1983 Act and Sections 2 and 3 of the amended Act that have become particularly notorious as these are the non-voluntary detention routes into mental healthcare systems. In particular Section 136 has been a focus of concern as it allows the police powers to arrest and place within the mental health system anyone who is deemed to be a danger to themselves and/or the public for up to 72 hours. Section 2 and 3 can then be used to detain people for longer. The combination of the racialised notion of 'danger', police power and compulsory mental health detention has led a number of commentators in the area to argue that the combination amounts to a specific form of the social control and incarceration of pathologised minority groups (Department of Health 2005; Cope 1989; Sashidharan and Francis 1993). Once hospitalised, studies have shown that minority ethnic groups tend to come under harsher or more containing forms of coercive psychiatric treatment (Department of Health 2003; Leese et al. 2006). In their study of high security psychiatric hospitals in England Leese et al. (2006) found that black patients were eight times more likely to be confined to these types of hospitals, were more likely to be male and more likely to be diagnosed with a mental illness rather than a personality disorder or learning disability. The Leese et al. study also found that patients' 'unmet needs' were significantly higher for black than white patients. This echoed earlier studies which showed differential treatment and care in that white mental healthcare staff tended to view white patients diagnosed as schizophrenic as suicidal and black patients diagnosed as schizophrenic as volatile, aggressive, chronically psychotic and potentially dangerous to others, thereby requiring larger dosages of medication and to be in locked in wards (Department of Health 2003; Littlewood and Lipsedge 1997).

Some of the efforts that mental health professionals have attempted to develop as strategies to challenge racism within the system and intervene in discriminatory care practices have been problematic. The most obvious example of such a response has been the development of transcultural psychiatry that sought to incorporate notions of multiculturalism and cultural competence into psychiatric practice. Theorists such as Sashidharan (1993) and Mercer (1986) have noted that transcultural psychiatry has been unable to tackle the notions of power and the processes by which various forms of bias and racism are manifested and instead has been drawn into a reductive position in which culture becomes identified as predominantly causal. However, those policy approaches in mental healthcare that do attempt to directly address bias and racism in mental healthcare systems reflect the same mixed outcomes as other social institutions (Care Quality Commission 2009; 2010; Department of Health 2005; Neal 1998a). For example, the Christopher Clunis case demonstrates the complexities and contradictions which exist in relation to race in mental healthcare systems as well as the confusion around anti-discriminatory practice within mental health systems. Christopher Clunis, a young African/Caribbean man, diagnosed with schizophrenia but being cared for within the community, randomly and fatally stabbed Jonathan Zito, a passenger on the London Underground, in December 1992. Public anxieties about what had happened to Jonathan Zito resonated with wider public anxieties over the changes in mental healthcare that were shifting from institutions to the community as part of the then Conservative government's NHS and Community Care Act.

In this policy context, media coverage of the tragedy and those involved in it and a well-orchestrated campaign by the *Independent* newspaper for an inquiry culminated in an NHS six-month investigation, led by Jean Ritchie QC, into Christopher Clunis's care and treatment within the mental health system (Neal 1998a). The findings of this Inquiry indicated that throughout Clunis' seven-year history of contact with healthcare system in South-East London there were numerous examples of healthcare professionals being reluctant to diagnose him as schizophrenic despite the actual severity of

Clunis' mental illness. Commenting on Clunis' discharge from a hospital before he had had any psychiatric assessment in 1988 Ritchie et al. (1994: 19 emphasis added) note that, 'it seems to be an example of the desire *not* to *stigmatise* a patient or *label* him in any way as a violent or difficult person which it was felt might work to his disadvantage'. While anti-racist perspectives of psychiatric services have emphasised the domination of racialised notions of black dangerousness as the basis of psychiatric practice, the actual care and treatment of Christopher Clunis demonstrates some of the complexities and the contradictions of treatment within mental healthcare (Neal 1998a).

Recent policy interventions in ethnicity and mental healthcare

It is these complexities that resonate in the failure of the recent Delivering Race Equality (DRE) in Mental Healthcare plan (2005–2010) that was discussed earlier. The DRE intervention was an action plan conceived in the wider context of the inquiry into the death in 1998 of David Bennett a 38-year-old African-Caribbean who died in a medium secure psychiatric unit in Norfolk after being restrained by staff. The Bennett family successfully campaigned for the inquiry and this inquiry identified institutional racism as characterising David Bennett's inpatient care and treatment. It made a series of recommendations relating to the need to reform treatment regimes for BME inpatients and train staff around issues of racism and diversity and to place strict limits on restraint techniques of inpatients. The findings and recommendations of the Bennett Inquiry (Department of Health 2005) echoed many of those made in the Ritchie Inquiry in 1994 as well as those made in an even earlier government inquiry by the Special Hospitals Service Authority (SHSA) (1993) into the care of young African-Caribbean men in mental health system in the UK. This SHSA inquiry examined the deaths of three African-Caribbean prisoners Michael Martin, Joseph Watts and Orville Blackwood, who died at Broadmoor psychiatric hospital. While SHSA report from the inquiry subtitled *Big, Black and Dangerous* was focused on Broadmoor, it identified a range of issues affecting BME groups in contact with mental health services including training around restraint, diagnosis and treatment of psychotic disorders and training around cultural competence and racism. These were to re-emerge eleven years later as findings in the Bennett Inquiry. The long running, systematic nature of the findings of these formal inquiries into individuals within mental health services and the legislative requirements of the 2000 Race Relations Amendment Act provided the broader policy context for the 2005 Delivering Race Equality in Mental Healthcare strategy (McKenzie and Bhui 2007).

Conceived as an action plan the DRE focused on 12 areas of concern ranging from a reduction in BME admission rates to psychiatric units to more balanced treatment regimes and a more trained, ethnically mixed and culturally competent body of mental healthcare staff and targeted these as areas for improvement by 2010. However, there is an uneven picture of impact. As we noted above the continuing disproportionately high rates of particular BME – Other/Black – groups in mental healthcare systems and the continuation of compulsory routes into those systems for this group testify to the limits of the DRE initiative (Department of Health 2009: 22–23).

The failure of the DRE strategy to impact on rates of admission, detention and forms of treatment highlights the extent and nature of racism within mental healthcare services but it also highlights the need to recognise how wider contexts, availability of and access to resources and environments affect mental health. The review of the DRE argues that poverty and social exclusion mean that BME populations will be more likely to encounter mental health issues (Department of Health 2009: 9). This focus on the wider environment and combinations of factors affecting mental health and mental healthcare echoes the arguments of Karlsen et al. (2005) when they suggest that experiences of racism impact on mental well-being. Also, there are concerns that ethnic inequities in broader health services may mean that certain minority groups do not – or cannot – access preventative services and thus only come into contact with health systems at a point of crisis.

What is clear is that there continues to be an urgent need to open up mental healthcare systems to policy scrutiny, reflection and intervention in order to the impact on differential rates at which particular BME groups enter these systems, the coercive nature of that entry and the forms of clinical diagnosis, treatment and care that are then made available.

Conclusion

This chapter has focused on the multidimensional relationship between ethnicity, race and health. It has moved from identifying and understanding the shifting ethnic differentials in health and illness, the role of structural factors and contexts on health outcomes to racialised inequities in the organisational, employment and delivery patterns of health services to the over-representation of BME groups within mental healthcare. But each area has evidenced patterns of ethnic variation and inequality as well as a shared story of the generally limited efficacy of equality and diversity policy interventions.

While BME and migrant populations disproportionately carry the burden of ill health compared to white British populations, that burden is carried differentially *between* different minority groups and carried differently *within* the 'same' ethnic group. In other words there is an increasing heterogeneity that characterises defined ethnic categories. In emphasising the degree of health variation between and within BME and migrant populations we have emphasised the importance of multiple factors – most obviously socio-economic divisions but also gender, age, migration status, locality and environment – in determining health outcomes.

This raises the key question of whether there is a relationship between ethnicity and health or whether the relationship is really between social and economic position and health. Nazroo concludes in answer to this that, 'despite the importance of socio-economic status in explaining ethnic variations in health, a consideration of the position of ethnic minority groups will still benefit from an understanding of their relative health. Indeed if we are to improve on the delivery of healthcare to any group in our society it seems crucial to consider its health needs' (Nazroo 1997: 144). Clearly there is every need to be cautious in how the concept of ethnicity is mobilised in explaining variations in health and every need to be critical of how the concept of ethnicity informs health policy and practice. We have argued in this chapter that sometimes ethnicity is central to understanding health needs and outcomes – and, crucially, sometimes it is not. Working in this way requires a relatively sophisticated interpretation of, and approach to, ethnicity. But, such competency will become increasingly urgent as multicultural populations continue to geographically disperse and the composition of multicultural populations becomes more diverse.

Chapter 7

Education

The relationship between race, ethnicity and education is particularly contested. The relationship has changed and reconfigured over time but it remains high-profile, troubled and emotive in the UK. For example, in 1990 Paul Gilroy argued that it was not in crime and policing but in the class and staff rooms of inner-city schools that race politics and conflicts were most visible. The uneasy nature of the education and ethnicity relationship has continued as the compositions, geographies and social and economic status of multicultural populations have changed and as educational attainment and ethnic correlations have increasingly diversified. In the current educational landscape long-standing concerns about the educational experience of BME children and adolescents remain but are accompanied by newer, albeit fragmented, narratives of educational success. This landscape is also one in which there is a high degree of policy activity. Since the 1960s and into the 2000s, changing educational policymaking and interventions in England and Wales have differentially affected the ethnicity-race-education relationship.

This chapter is divided into four parts. First, it explores why and how education became such a contested site of race politics, polarised debate and achievement concern for BME communities between the 1960s and early 1990s. Second, the contemporary configurations of ethnicity and education are examined particularly in relation to the changes and continuities presented by current BME pre-16 educational experiences. The third part explores educational policymaking over the last decade and the effects and impacts of such policy interventions as school choice, faith schools, league tables and social cohesion initiatives on schools, on their localities, on BME populations and on current race-ethnicity debates. The final substantive part of the chapter turns to the post-16 education world and assesses the ethnicity-education relationship in a non-compulsory context detailing the apparent contradiction of over-representation of BME populations in UK universities. The chapter concludes by suggesting that education is a relational sphere of social policy delivery – schools, educational policies, class room relations, attainment outcomes, communities and localities all interact with each other in complex and contested ways and are embedded in the wider social world.

Historical race-education controversies

1960s–1970s: establishing an 'ethnic paradigm' in education

We have already suggested that education has been a particularly potent policy landscape to which race politics have been integral and around which they have been articulated. The popular 1967 film *To Sir With Love* starring Sydney Poitier as a black teacher in a mainly white inner London secondary school was an early cinematic engagement with the relationship between race, education and schooling. While this film only lightly touches on race issues it was an early presentation of ethnically mixed classrooms and the perils and possibilities that this delivers. During the 1960s and 1970s the educational experiences of ethnically mixed classrooms were mostly defined by perils rather than possibilities. Three of the most immediate recognisable examples of these perils were first, the disproportionately low educational qualification outcomes for children from some BME populations; second, the high levels of children from particular BME communities being formally labelled as Educationally Sub-Normal (ESN) and consigned to specialist teaching and remedial classes and the third, the 'bussing' or dispersal of migrant children to non-local schools as part of early assimilationist race policy (see Chapter 2). While the latter was largely abandoned by the end of the 1960s, concerns about educational achievement and unequal educational experiences became increasingly controversial as policymakers, politicians, academics, teachers, parents, families, local communities and activists variously lobbied, campaigned, organised and argued about the dynamics and nature of the ethnicity-education relationship.

There was little focus on what the effect of factors such as social class, locality and gender might be on the ethnicity-education experiences of BME children. Race and ethnicity became *the* dominating filters through which educational debates and explanations of schooling experiences took place. An exemplar of this process was the issue of educational outcome. The under-achievement of African-Caribbean pupils became a wide-ranging concern, from parents worried about their children to politicians and policymakers worried about social order and cohesion. Since the late 1960s and early 1970s African-Caribbean parents, families and communities articulated concerns about the failure of the schooling systems to provide an environment in which their children could succeed. The publication of Bernard Coard's campaigning pamphlet (*How the West Indian Child is made Educationally Sub-Normal*) in 1971 summarised concerns about the ways in which low teacher expectations and culturally biased and inaccurate 'testing' systematically harmed the education of black children (Coard 1971). Coard's work sold thousands of copies and became an early public marker of the extent of African-Caribbean anxieties about the nature of the race-education relationship and it was effective in getting the issues of African-Caribbean educational achievement and racism onto educational agendas. The connection between an education system in which certain populations appeared to fail and social exclusion was later to be commented on in the findings of the Scarman Report (1981) which stated that above all it was schooling and education that disadvantaged African-Caribbean communities and it was education where urgent change had to take place (see Chapters 2 and 5).

In this context research and statistics repeatedly confirmed the relationship between African-Caribbean pupils and low achievement. Department of Education (1985) figures for (the then) 'O' level and CSE attainment in England showed that in 1981–1982 only 6 per cent of 'West Indian' pupils attained 5 or more qualifications at A-C compared to 23 per cent of all maintained school leavers and 17 per cent of 'Asian' pupils (Troyna and Williams 1986: 126). This seemingly entrenched pattern of differential attainment became part of an accepted and reified 'norm' and it was overwhelmingly understood that ethnicity was *the* causal factor of the poorer performance of African-Caribbean pupils. This narrative was officially reinforced by the Swann Report (1985) – the outcome of the Conservative government's inquiry into educational attainment of BME children which relied on the notion of culture as the determinant of educational performance. As Troyna and Carrington (1990) argue, in this reductionist logic, or 'ethnic paradigm', the complex and compounded interaction of racism, racialisation *and* factors such as social class and also geography, type of school, and gender on educational performance were ignored in the analysis of underachievement.

This is not to argue against the centrality of ethnicity to understanding educational experiences and outcomes but to suggest that ethnicity should not be treated as the only explanatory category that drives and defines educational trajectories. The struggle between those debates that attempted to position race and ethnicity as either causal or as an issue which colour-blind approaches would eventually resolve; those that emphasised racism or those that suggested multidimensional and intersecting social divisions have – as this chapter demonstrates – largely remain part of the contested educational landscape (see Gillborn and Rollock 2009 for example).

1980s–1990s: the escalating politicisation of race and education

During the 1980s and early 1990s these contestations became condensed and narrowed into arguments as to how to make effective interventions in the race-education relationship. The more complex patterns of differential migrant and BME school experiences and achievements and the intersections of social divisions were obscured as the arguments became increasingly controversial and polarised between those who advocated multicultural approaches in education and those who supported anti-racist approaches. This polarisation meant that a range of complicated processes and dynamics were swept up into simplifying debates that advocated either the need for multiculturalism in classrooms or the need to address racism and the structural impacts of social division. In practice there were some convergences between the two approaches (see below and Chapter 2) but the public and educational arguments between multicultural and anti-racist education were a key feature of education policy and politics in the 1980s.

With its emphasis on cultural awareness and practices multicultural education was often criticised for creating a curriculum and school practices that were overly focused on an essentialised notion of cultural difference (Carby 1982; Troyna and Williams 1986). Cultural difference became the premise for both explaining and making interventions regarding the ethnic educational inequalities. A culturalist focus also meant that minority-culture deficit models crept into multicultural educational approaches. This allowed room for the continuation of formulaic racial thinking in which culturalist assumptions – that African-Caribbean cultures were anti-educational, that South-Asian pupils spoke English as a 'second language' or were caught between 'two (pre-modern and modern/Western) cultures' – could continue to flourish and feed into classroom relations and teaching practices (Brah 1996). Cultural pluralism was, at its best, about recognition of cultural diversity but more insidiously was part of establishing 'us' and 'them' or 'other' categories of cultural difference.

The challenge to cultural pluralism came from more overtly politicised anti-racist educational approaches that focused on the processes and impacts of racism and racial inequality in wider society as well as in school worlds – teaching systems, curriculum and classroom relations. At a time when local politics were particularly turbulent different local authority educational departments took up and pursued multicultural or anti-racist agendas and initiatives in their schools (see Chapter 2). The intensity of the debates, and their very public profile, generated something approaching a moral panic. A series of highly mediated public controversies fuelled this – some were newspaper headline-driven rumours of 'politically motivated teachers', banning the nursery rhyme baa baa black sheep, banning celebrations of Christmas, and complaints about celebrating Nelson Mandela's birthday, Diwali, Eid and so on. Other controversies centred on particular schools and parents' protests and withdrawal of children from ethnically mixed schools. These disputes, detailed below, reflected the intensity of the education debates about race and ethnicity at that time and were to have long-running repercussions.

In Dewsbury in West Yorkshire in 1987, 26 white parents withdrew their children from the local primary schools in which there were significant numbers of South-Asian children. Denying that they were motivated by racism these groups of parents insisted their actions were about culture and their concerns were about multicultural education and not race and cultural difference. In the same year the Dewsbury case was echoed by a similar case in Cleveland in which a white pupil was withdrawn by parents from a mostly South-Asian school (Loveland 1993; Vincent 1992). These cases escalated into legal actions and were forerunners in creating Conservative educational reforms that introduced and prioritised parental choice as a core value in the education system. The chapter will return to this policy development later. In addition to the Dewsbury and Cleveland cases a long-running controversy during the mid-1980s concerning the Bradford school headmaster Ray Honeyford received widespread public attention. Bradford's local education authority sacked Honeyford for criticising the authority's multicultural education strategy. Honeyford then became the centre for of a reinstatement campaign led by local white parents, and supported by Conservative ministers, public commentators and sections of the media.

While each of these controversies and events amplified the intensity, divisions and politicised character of education as a policy site perhaps the most damaging and violent event in the education-race crisis took place at Burnage High School in Manchester in 1986. The murder of Ahmed Iqbal Ullah, a 13-year-old pupil at the school, by another (white) student in the school's playground became the subject of a public inquiry led by Ian Macdonald. It was the school's supposedly crude anti-racism approach that was directly implicated in the escalating racialised tensions between pupils culminating in the death of a pupil. Although the Macdonald et al. report (1989) took a careful line in which anti-racist educational approaches to school life were criticised but not blamed, the events at Burnage and the report itself were widely seen as the outcome of the dangerous politicisation of education and the promotion of race politics within the school gates.

The combination of these catastrophic events, public rows, legal court cases and a central government hostile and explicitly opposed to a number of LEAs culminated in a set of educational interventions and reforms that were to massively reconfigure education policy and set parameters of the educational landscape into the 21st century. The Education Reform Act (ERA) of 1988 marked and embodied these shifts. The Act took power and responsibility away from local education authorities – widely perceived by the Conservative government as too politicised – and replaced their role with a much greater consolidation of educational power within the centre on the one hand and devolved power down to school level on the other. As Troyna and Carrington (1990) suggest, the seeming paradox of combining the central and the local was expressly about undermining LEA control of schools.

The centralising drive of the ERA was also evident in the establishment of a traditionalist 'back to basics' national curriculum and the introduction of key stage targets of attainment in the form of Standardised Assessment Tests (SATs) at 7, 11, 14 and 16. The devolved nature of the ERA was evidenced in the Act's introduction of the Local Management of Schools (LMS) scheme which moved the core and day-to-day responsibilities of schools, including school budgets, admissions, testing and discipline, and staffing procedures, to individual school governing bodies (Troyna and Carrington 1990: 94). The other key feature of the ERA was its introduction of the principle of school choice for parents (see below).

The ERA can be understood as a political response to the educational crisis of the 1980s. It transformed education policy and initiated the marketisation of education. The contemporary education terrain remains largely shaped by the ERA legislation. We have spent some time discussing the historical education and race relationship in the UK because the current education and race relationship is imprinted so heavily with this history. It is this current relationship to which we now turn.

Contemporary race-education experiences

The current issues and concerns that circulate around ethnicity, race and education are both familiar and unfamiliar. One core aspect of the change has been an increase in the BME population in schools in England. In 2004 the Department for Education and Skills classified 17 per cent of the school population in England and Wales as belonging to a minority ethnic group. While the BME school population has increased significantly since the late 1990s the total school population has had a much smaller increase in the same period (Department of Education and Science 2005). In the context of an increasingly diverse educational environment this section of the chapter considers the changing key areas of attainment and education performance: exclusion rates, Special Educational Needs identification rates and assesses how the changing nature of educational provision – a more multicultural teaching body and home–school intiatives – may affect the ethnicity-education relationship.

Ethnicity and differential educational attainment and achievement

We have argued that educational attainment patterns are more likely to be the outcome of a constellation of factors. While class, location, gender and ethnicity are each important factors in educational outcomes none are 'completely dominant' (Gillborn and Rollock 2009: 142). The recognition of the range of variables affecting educational performance is partially reflected in the Department for Education's current collation of data on attainment based on gender, ethnicity, on pupils who have English as a first language, on pupils who are eligible for Free School Meals (FSM) and on pupils who have Special Educational Needs (SEN). The Department for Education's 2010 report on attainment data show that there is an increasing overall attainment of 5 or more GCSEs or equivalent (including English and Maths) at grades A*-C; 54.8 per cent of all pupils achieve this national level (Department for Education 2010a). The data confirm that girls continue to outperform boys – 58.6 per cent of girls attain 5 or more A*-C grades compared to 51.1 per cent of boys (Department for Education 2010a). There is a certain familiarity in the key data patterns. For example, pupils whose first language is English achieved better than those for whom it isn't. Pupils who were not eligible for FSMs performed better than those who were, although the gap narrowed between 2005–2006 and 2009–2010. Pupils who lived in the least deprived areas performed better than pupils in the most deprived areas, although the gap has again narrowed in the stated comparative periods. Pupils with no SENs outperformed pupils with SENs and this gap widened between 2005–2006 and 2009–2010.

In relation to ethnicity the data reveal that pupils of 'any White background' achieved in line with the national level, while pupils of 'any Black background' achieved below it with only 49.8 per cent of black pupils achieving 5 or more A*-C grades. Pupils of 'any Asian background' performed above the national level with 58.0 per cent gaining 5 or more A*-C grades. Within this broad category pupils of Chinese, Indian and Mixed White and Asian origin had the highest proportion in gaining 5 or more A*-C grades. Pupils of Gypsy/Roma and Traveller of Irish Heritage had the lowest levels of attainment.

The DfE data and the patterns revealed in Table 7.1 are significant for a number of reasons. First, earlier studies of ethnic performance relied on more limited ethnic categorisations such as 'White', 'Asian' and 'West Indian'. Studies since 1992 have been more attentive to the diversity of ethnicity; the 18 ethnic categorisations in Table 7.1 and in the report (DfE 2010a) evidence the extent of the official recognition of the complex and proliferating forms of ethnic identification. Second, data that incorporates ethnic diversity has led to the collation of more complex ethnicity-education data sets and more complex patterns of education performance in which significant differences between and within different ethnic groups are very apparent. In particular pupils from Indian, Chinese, Irish and mixed white and black African, white and Asian and any other Asian background are attaining education results above and significantly above the 2009–2010 national average. Third, while the data clearly demonstrate the increase across the

Table 7.1 Key Stage 4 GCSE Attainment by ethnic group

Ethnic grouping	Percentage of pupils gaining 5+ A*-C grade GCSEs in England 2005–2006 to 2009–2010	
	2005–2006	2009–2010
White	44.4	54.8
White British	44.3	55.0
Irish	50.1	63.4
Traveller	11.1	21.8
Gypsy/Roma	3.9	8.3
Any other white background	46.8	50.6
Mixed	42.8	54.6
White and Black Caribbean	32.6	45.3
White and Black African	43.1	55.6
White and Asian	59.4	65.2
Any other mixed background	45.2	57.8
Asian	46.1	58.0
Indian	59.1	71.3
Pakistani	34.6	49.1
Bangladeshi	39.0	57.7
Any other Asian background	51.6	57.6
Black	33.6	48.9
Black Caribbean	29.5	43.5
Black African	37.5	52.8
Any other Black background	31.2	45.8
Chinese	65.8	75.1
Any other ethnic background	41.7	51.2
All pupils	44.0	54.8

Source: adapted from DfE 2010.

board in pupils attainment between 2005–2006 and 2009–2010, there is recurrent pattern in those ethnic categories not attaining the national 54.8 per cent level of pupils gaining 5 or more A*-C GCSEs. To varying degrees it is clear that pupils of Black Caribbean, Pakistani, Bangladeshi and Black African origin continue to fall below the national level. The data show a story not dissimilar to that of the ethnicity-attainment patterns of the 1970s. However, the data show more marked trends of improvement within these groups between 2005–2006 and 2009–2010 of between 14 per cent to 15 per cent compared to an improvement of 11 per cent in white British pupils' attainment rates. To what extent can recent data on the relationship between ethnicity and other key variables explain this continuing outcome?

While the 2010 data provide information on the relationship between pupils' identity characteristics and their education performance, data on the combinations or intersections of these variables is more limited. The report itself does comment on the fact that across all ethnic groups (apart from Travellers of Irish Heritage) girls are more successful, albeit at different rates, than boys and it documents the ways in which deprivation, as measured by Free School Meal entitlement, impacts on education performance. The DfE (Department for Education 2010a) data show that *all* pupils from socially deprived backgrounds (as measured by FSM entitlement) have lower levels of attainment. While the data do not show the interaction between deprivation and ethnicity and gender the DfE note that 22.8 per cent of white British boys eligible for FSM achieved 5 or more A*-C GCSEs compared to the overall national rate of 54.8 per cent. The attainment gap is smaller – but still significant – for black Caribbean boys. For this group 27.6 per cent of those eligible for FSM gain 5 or more A*-C GCSEs compared to the overall national average.

More detailed evidence relating deprivation and different ethnic categories is provided by earlier data from the then Department of Education and Science (2005). These data show the persistency in the patterns noted by the the later report (Department for Education 2010a). For example, white British boys who are eligible for FSM do least well educationally with only 17 per cent achieving 5 or more A*-C GCSEs compared to 50 per cent of white British boys not eligible for FSM. Though only slightly higher, the 19 per cent of black Caribbean boys eligible for FSM achieve 5 or more GSCE measure compared to the 28 per cent of black Caribbean boys not eligible for FSM who do achieve the measure. Although girls in both ethnic categories do perform better, particularly black Caribbean girls, it would seem clear that deprivation does strongly correlate with poorer educational outcomes.

However, class is not a total explanation of differential education attainment. In their study of black middle-class parents and education Vincent et al. (Vincent et al. 2011: 9) found that although 'black middle class parents are able to make use of aspects of their class advantage to mediate the effects of racism [...] social class does not eradicate the consequences of racism altogether'. The difficulties of relying on a single ethnicity or class causal factor to explain educational achievement are apparent in Bangladeshi attainment rates which are higher than would be expected given the Bangladeshi FSM rates. Chinese, Indian and White/Asian pupils also do better than expected when FSM is taken into account. However, the DfES data shows that 'for Black Caribbean and Traveller and Gypsy/Roma groups results are much lower than FSM [levels] indicate. [This] underlines that for Black Caribbean pupils lower attainment is not wholly explained by deprivation factors' (Department of Education and Science 2005).

The complexities of these attainment patterns means that any analysis of education and ethnicity needs to work through a multidimensional lens but in a way that does not discount the impact of ethnicity and race in educational systems, experiences and outcomes. As Gillborn and Rollock argue 'the common assertion that gender and/or class factors explain ethnic difference is demonstrably false' (Gillborn and Rollock 2009: 142). The challenge for education attainment explanations is to avoid a one-dimensional, over-ethnicisation of education performance data *and* avoid adopting an approach which over-allocates explanatory power to other 'colour blind' or non-ethnic variables. Classroom relations and classroom practices – as well as the factors examined above – also contribute to explaining the varying attainment levels of pupils from different ethnic populations. Moreover teacher perceptions of ability and pupil behaviour have been persistent concerns reflected in disproportionate rates of exclusion and Special Educational Needs diagnosis for particular populations. It is these that we now consider.

Ethnicity and school exclusions

The exclusion system for the management of pupil behaviour in schools in England and Wales can and does have a negative impact on educational careers, particularly in its permanent form. Pupils who have been permanently excluded rarely recover educationally and their attainment of 5 or more A*-C GCSE grades is significantly low (Gillborn 2008; Gillborn and Rollock 2009; Parsons 2008). Rates of permanent exclusion in secondary schools, given mainly because of persistent disruptive behaviour (Department for Education 2010b), rose dramatically in the 1990s. Gillborn and Gipps (1996: 53) noted a national picture in which black Caribbean pupils were six times more likely to be permanently excluded than white pupils. The rates of permanent exclusion became a focus of policy concern for the Labour government that made a reduction in permanent exclusions a policy target and overall exclusion rates fell dramatically from 1997 to 2001 (Department of Education and Science 2005). While there was ethnic variation in the declining numbers 'the greatest proportionate reductions was experienced by Black Caribbean students' (Gillborn and Rollock 2009: 153). However, since 2001 exclusions rates for black Caribbean boys have persisted and the reduction trend has begun to creep upwards again (Department for Education 2010b; Department of Education and Science 2005). Black Caribbean boys are currently almost four times more likely to be permanently excluded than the school population as a whole (Department for Education 2010b). As with the attainment and ethnicity patterns there are limits in what the figures reveal but there are patterns that remain tenacious and predominate. Children of Traveller and Irish Heritage and Black Caribbean groups are disproportionately at higher risk of permanent exclusion.

The impact of the Race Relations Amendment Act 2000 (see Chapter 2) – which places a duty on public organisations in which schools are included to examine and review practices such as exclusion policies which appear to have detrimental effects on particular ethnic groups – seems to be uncertain. Parsons et al. (2005) found that some schools were taking successful measures to minimise permanent exclusion rates of black pupils. These measures included ongoing policy reviews, classroom management, training for governors, mentoring schemes and counselling projects and establishing positive school–community relations. While examples of good practice on the use of the exclusion system show that interventions can make a difference, it is clear that these need to be accompanied by a wider political commitment to reducing the negative impact of exclusion practices on particular black and minority ethnic groups. A multidimensional response is necessary in order to understand why a pupil may face exclusion taking into account families, communities, teachers, governors and school policy.

Ethnicity and patterns of Special Educational Needs identification

Concerns have been raised about disproportionate Special Educational Needs (SEN) identification within some ethnic groups. SEN covers a broad range of issues and needs from cognition and learning to emotional and social skills to speech and communication to sensory and physical impairments and disabilities. SEN identification involves pupils being given either a Statement or a School Action Plus, which means they have additional educational support. Filtering these various components of SEN through ethnicity show that at primary school black Caribbean boys are three times more likely than white boys to be on a School Action Plus for Severe Learning Difficulties. Also, black Caribbean and Black Other boys are approximately twice as likely to be on School Action Plus than white boys at primary and secondary levels for Behavioural, Emotional and Social Difficulties. Conversely pupils with English as an Additional Language (EAL) are half as likely to be identified as having a Specific Learning Difficulty and are under-represented in SEN categories. The exception to this are EAL pupils having a SEN diagnosis in speech and communication difficulties. The learning of English as an additional language might affect their communication skills but this does raise issues as to whether EAL pupils are receiving appropriate levels of support and provision in other SEN areas (Department of Education and Science 2005: 25). Certainly social and economic disadvantage has a profound impact on SEN identification. Pupils with FSM entitlement are up to three times more likely to have statements for all categories of learning difficulties, emotional and behaviour difficulties and physical disabilities. However, class does not entirely explain the ethnic SEN disproportionalaties. Black Caribbean and white/black Caribbean non-FSM pupils are still twice as likely as white pupils to have an SEN identification and there is no difference in black African FSM and non-FSM pupils in the rates of SEN categorisation. SEN is a challenging area. Pupils need to be given appropriate provision where it is needed (and there is some evidence with EAL pupils that this is not happening) but inappropriate and over-SEN identification of particular ethnic groups can lead to stigmatisation, low teacher and school expectation and/or the wrong type of support and therapy. The SEN-ethnicity relationship is then fraught. Deprivation, individual LEA and school practices, genetic factors, misidentification of EAL pupils, cultural differences, teacher and school perceptions and the nature of pre-school contact with other services and support are all factors which interactively shape SEN identification processes.

Ethnicity and emergent education initiatives

Making effective interventions to address these various patterns of ethnic disproportionality is a contested and uncertain policy area. Key factors that could be expected to make a difference such as a more culturally diverse and ethnically mixed teacher body and involvement with black and minority parents have begun to be tracked. There is a general consensus that home support and involvement makes a significant difference to pupils' attainment and educational experience. The available evidence indicates that there is significant commitment among black and minority ethnic parents to home-school connections and dialogue. For example, DfES (Department of Education and Science 2005: 38) research shows significantly higher levels of black and minority ethnic parents and carers stating they felt very involved with their child's education. Fifty-three per cent of BME parents compared to 38 per cent of the main sample questioned agreed with this. Reflecting this sense of parental involvement in education, figures were high for those BME participants stating they attended parent evenings (82%) and for senses of home responsibility for education. Similarly, 24 per cent of BME parents compared to 19 per cent of the main sample agreed that education was largely parent and school's joint responsibility. In their study Vincent et al. found that black middle-class parents were highly engaged in their children's schooling and drew on a number of strategies such as initiating meetings with teachers and tutors and accessing professional networks to support their children through the education system (Vincent et al. 2011: 5).

Increases in the diversity of the teacher workforce have also been noted although this is spatially very varied. DfES (2005) data showed that nationally 9 per cent of teachers were from minority ethnic backgrounds. Teachers from Asian and South-Asian groups comprised the largest fraction of this figure at 2 per cent followed by black and black British groups at 1.5 per cent. However in London the levels of diversity rise significantly where 31 per cent of teachers identify as belonging to a BME category. Although the impact of teacher diversity is as yet unknown, it seems likely that a more diverse teaching workforce alone cannot be expected to counter patterns of ethnic disproportion. Nevertheless, any increase in BME teachers is positive and a necessary – and inevitable – part of the current shifts in educational landscapes. Where teacher perception appears to play a particularly influential role in educational outcome a more diverse teacher workforce may contribute to counter racialised and ethicised decision making about pupil behaviour, attitude, aptitude and so forth. This is by no means a given. Social and economic differences, that some BME teachers may hold deficit views of particular groups and socialisation into a predominantly white teaching profession, may limit the changes that a more diverse teaching body can deliver.

In summary, there are many patterns of educational experience and outcome in which some BME groups are disproportionately represented. These patterns are complicated and shaped by a range of factors including race and ethnicity. Deprivation, gender and locality clearly have a profound impact on what happens within schools. What is also clear is that there are some ethnic groups which are consistently featured within unfavourable education categories – lower levels of attainment, higher rates of exclusion and higher levels of SEN identification. Issues of concern in the 1970s continue to be issues of concern in the 21st century. But there are newer contestations and contradictions that need to be recognised – the changing pupil demography and, related to this, the changing educational terrains, increasing diversity of pupils and teachers and the significant attainment differences between different minority ethnic pupils. We have already seen that policy interventions can deliver shifts and change and it is to these we now turn.

Race and educational policymaking

We noted in our introduction that schools had become one of the most contentious sites of race and policy debates. While we looked in detail at some of the obvious reasons for this, the emotive nature of those debates relates to how schools are broadly imagined and conceived that is, as meritocratic institutions in which all children's futures are open and possible. At the same time schools are centrally involved in the 'production' and socialisation of children as future citizens of the nation. As such schools are worlds in which educational competence is part of a broader role in which citizenship, identity and civic learning are core responsibilities – although the policies of the Coalition Government on education since 2010 have stressed that schools should be focused on a core mission of education provision. To some extent, cultural diversity and intercultural mixing have become part of this process and schools can and have been positioned as having wider roles and responsibilities, not only for turning out cosmopolitan citizens but also for contributing to social stability and creating senses of national identity. For example, the Cantle report allocated schools a key role in delivering cohesive, integrated and stable local communities (Cantle 2001).

In this context, the relationship between policymaking, education, race and multiculture concerns can be understood in three keys ways:

- Education policymaking that is directly connected to race and ethnicity issues (e.g. school cohesion and the Education and Inspections Act 2006, faith schooling)
- Education policymaking that has an indirect effect on race and ethnicity issues (e.g. parental school choice and Education Reform Act 1988; Education Act 2002; Education Act 2011)
- Race focused policymaking that has an impact on schools and education policy (e.g. Race Relations Amendment Act 2000).

These policy formations can be viewed in relational terms. For example parental school choice may contribute to more segregated schooling, a situation that may then become affected by cohesion demands. The requirement of the anti-discrimination practice enshrined in the RRA Act impacts on both of the previous processes.

This part of the chapter now looks in more detail at these various policy interventions and the ways in which they have shaped and reshaped the education and race relationship.

Education policy – creating school choice and ethnically segregated schooling?

We argued earlier that the high-profile race-education conflicts of the 1980s were part of the process that led to the 1988 Education Reform Act. At the centre of the Act was the establishment of the principle of parental choice in relation to children's schooling. Making choice the heart of education policy meant a restructuring of the education system as a competitive process between schools. Subsequent educational policy has continued to support – and expand – the principles of school choice. For example, the Education and Inspection Act 2006 emphasised parental demands as the way to generate improvements in educational provision. Similarly, the Education Act 2011 reinforced the parental choice principle through its further diversification of school provision and the creation of more academies and free schools.

An early concern about the 1988 Education Reform Act was that choice would create educational differentiation along social, economic and ethnic lines. This concern has become increasingly articulated over the two decades or so of the choice policy as research appears to consistently evidence class and ethnicity-based segregation in schools in high-density urban areas of the UK (Ball 2003; Reay et al. 2007; Weekes-Bernard 2007). For example Burgess and Wilson (2005: 1052–1053) argue from their quantitative analysis of School and Population Census data that secondary school age children 'are more segregated in school than in their neighbourhood. This seems more clearly true of children with Black Caribbean heritage, children of Indian ethnicity, Pakistani ethnicity and Bangladeshi ethnicity and less true of children with Black African heritage. Our regression analysis shows that the ratio of school to neighbourhood segregation increases with the population density of the area'.

These findings, of greater residential mix (see Chapter 4) but greater educational polarisation, would appear to reflect the impact that parental choice has on schools and their pupil populations. These patterns of class and ethnicity-based educational segregation have emerged and become consolidated through a variety of interacting and complex processes that structure and influence parental choice practices. The competitive, market-based education system driven by school's attainment levels as well as other intelligence made available through league tables, OFSTED reports and 'local knowledge' networks has meant that particular schools become sought after and others avoided by parents. The ways in which school choice is made and eligibility for sought after schools obtained has increasingly preoccupied researchers and concerned policymakers and educational providers, especially in diverse, high-density urban areas where the type and number of schools is greater and where, as Butler and Robson note, there is much social but little spatial distance within local populations (2003a).

In some areas of some cities processes of gentrification and urban regeneration have contributed another dimension to the complex interplay of factors giving rise to segregated education provision. In London in particular, as white lower middle-class and white working class populations have tended to move out of the inner areas of the city to the suburbs, gentrification has led to spatial proximities between affluent white middle-class and ethnically mixed and poorer populations (London Borough of Hackney 2010). The impact and education implications of a high level of social and ethnic diversity in gentrified areas of cities in the UK has attracted attention from both urban geographers and education sociologists (Butler and Hamnett 2011; Vincent and Ball 2006). Based on their work in gentrified areas of London, Butler and Robson argue that 'education markets are now rivalling those in housing and employment as determinants of the nature, extent and stability of middle class gentrification in Inner London' (Butler and Robson 2003a: 24).

A key and shared finding from this body of research is the way in which the white middle class living in culturally diverse urban areas tend to have resources and a repertoire of strategies and practices for ensuring their children have access, predominantly at secondary level, to either fee-paying, selective schools or high-achieving comprehensive schools (see for example Ball 2003). While there are geographical variations, at primary school level, there is a degree of social and ethnic mixing in local schools, but it is secondary schooling that is significantly marked by parental choice processes and polarisation between schools. Some of these parental choice practices and processes amount to a 'white flight' educational outcome in which some urban local comprehensive secondary schools do not reflect the complicated social mix of the local population that surrounds them (Reay et al. 2007).

A significant degree of conscience and ambivalence in the process of white urban middle-class parental school choice has been revealed by a number of studies (Byrne 2006). Research shows that there are some within the urban middle class who are committed to living in a diverse, mixed area of a city and this can extend to parents with this approach making a 'positive choice' of an inner urban local comprehensive school for their children (Reay et al. 2007). However, the findings of the studies examining this 'positive choice' reveal the continuation of privilege and middle-class normativity rather than a socially transformative trend in which social mix delivers social mixing. For example, Hollingworth and Williams (2010) conclude from their qualitative study of white urban middle-class families who choose to send their children to their local comprehensive schools that cultural practices, even in mixed settings, can result in segregation and the persistence of middle-class privilege.

While Hollingworth and Williams (2010) found that many participants identified, through their experience of mixed schooling, an ability to be confident and at ease within very diverse ethnic and class settings they go on to suggest this 'mobility' is always underpinned by choice and by continuing access to white middle-class resources. The emphasis that Hollingworth and Williams put on the cultural and 'out of school' life of pupils is reflected in the findings of other researchers (Butler and Robson 2003a; Vincent and Ball 2007). The importance of 'out-of school' as well as 'in-school' social relations and practices was recognised in the Cantle Report and influenced its recommendations regarding social exchanges between schools – for example school twinning – as well as in extra-curricular activities and inter-actions (Chapter 2).

In contrast to the resources and strategies available to the urban middle classes in their navigations of the education market the concept and agenda of school choice is much more circumscribed and constrained for poorer and for BME parents and families. The process of school choice is far from straightforward for poor parents and for BME parents. For example, in her study of BME parents and school choice Deborah Weekes-Bernard (2007) found that

> Many parents were unable to exercise choice. They were able to express a list of preferences on an application form and many of them, particularly from lower socio-economic groups were successful in getting their first or second choices. For the vast majority, however, the preference expressed did not at all reflect actual choice. And indeed for many of the parents we spoke to, the schools in which their children are now pupils [...] and indeed the schools that the majority of BME pupils are attending are not the schools their parents might have wanted them to attend. (Weekes-Bernard 2007: 5)

Apart from socio-economic constraints that mean going to local schools is simply more manageable in terms of travel and family commitments, Weekes-Bernard highlights the range of interacting factors that can limit the choice as to what schools are available for parents to chose from. These can include a lack of resources for tuition to pass selective school entrance exam; a lack of access to information and knowledge networks about schools and school choice; a lack of resources to fund residential flight into the catch-ment areas of over-subscribed schools; concerns about safety and familiar-ity with localities; considerations around schools having greater or fewer BME pupil populations and schools' educational 'well-being' for example, exclusion and attainment rates among BME pupils; considerations around faith and single-sex school provision. These are all different and connect-ing factors which can affect – and inhibit – the processes and practices of school choice. In this context, school choice and strategies for achieving choice are very differently and mostly negatively experienced by BME and poorer parents.

The combination of the complex social and spatial geographies of urban areas of the UK, an urban middle class and the emerging and aspirational factions of diverse BME populations has neither disrupted or transformed social divisions within education. Rather, it is the interaction of these and broader social and economic factors, with the choice agenda, that contribute to the increasing levels of class and ethnicity-based segregation in current educational provision.

Clearly, the choice agenda is dependent on the seeming availability of a range of schools from which to make choices. The current creation of an 'education market' through the diversification of types of schools continues the 'market' trend in education provision since the late 1980s. The majority of secondary schools in England have now become specialist and academy schools, again reflecting a move away from local authority control. In mid-2012 there were more than 600 academy schools (Department for Education 2012: 12) and the Coalition government policy of continuing to encourage academies and creating Free Schools will again add to the diversity of the forms and types of schools in the sector. Faith schools have also been a central and significant part of this widening education market. Faith schools are not only numerically substantial and increasing but they have been at the heart of a series of contentious debates about the relationship between education provision, ethnicity, multiculture and increasing polarisation. It is to these that we now turn.

An expanding faith school sector

While state-funded religious schools are not a new feature of the educational landscape in the UK, since 1997 the increase in religious schools has been significant. This growth can be understood as the outcome of successive government policy and the organised lobbying of minority groups. For example, in 1997 the Labour government's expansion of the 'school choice' agenda was influenced by the campaigning for parity in relation to religious schooling. The first Muslim school opened in 1997, the first Sikh school in 1998 and the first Hindu school in 2008. The creation of academy schools created further openings for the involvement of religious organisations in education provision and the Free Schools initiative pursued by the Coalition Government from 2010 has also encouraged the involvement of faith groups.

Faith schools make up around a third of all maintained primary and secondary schools; there are more primary than secondary schools that are religious. Around one quarter of UK pupils, mainly in England attend faith schools and they are increasingly popular and often over-subscribed (Bolton and Gillies 2009: 3). Faith schools tend to perform above the national average for GCSE attainment. The majority of faith schools in the UK are Church of England. Catholic schools make up the next largest proportion of faith schools. The figures for non-Christian associated schools are very small. For example, in 2008 there were 38 Jewish schools, 11 Muslim schools, 4 Sikh schools and 1 Hindu school. This pattern is echoed in other education sectors. For example, of those academy schools which are religious most are Christian associated. In the independent sector where there are 2400 schools 957 have a faith designation. Of this number the majority – 786 – are Christian associated. Of the remaining 171 independent schools 118 are Muslim, 49 are Jewish, 2 are Hindu and 1 is Buddhist and 1 is Sikh (Bolton and Gillies 2009: 27; Department for Education 2010c).

While the numbers of non-Christian associated faith schools is very low the increase in faith schools and the demand for them has met with some concern and anxiety. While this anxiety has been expressed as a secular worry about the relationship between state and religion and education policy, there is also a more specific concern about Muslim schools. The passage of the 2006 Education and Inspections Act illustrates the interaction of this broad and specific set of worries. As the Act consolidated the principle of parental choice and foresaw the role faith-based organisations could have in the expansion of school choice, the then Education Secretary, Alan Johnson, attempted to impose conditions of maintained faith schools by requiring them to provide up to 25 per cent of pupil places for pupils of other or no faith. Because this requirement was to be made on all new faith schools but not made on those existing ones it was widely seen as a condition that would disproportionately affect new Muslim and minority non-Christian schools. As Dwyer and Parutis (2012: 7) note the 25 per cent quota played to broad secular concerns and allowed a direct connection to be made to Muslim schools and self-segregation.

The proposed amendment was eventually dropped as it met with sustained opposition from a range of faith schools who argued that imposing such a mandatory condition would be more likely to work against community cohesion and social inclusion rather than encouraging it. The legislative compromise of the 2006 Act was that first, faith schools be voluntarily required to operate a fair and open admissions policy even as they give priority to pupils who are of the faith of the school. Second, the launch of the Faith in the System declaration which presented the joint views of the government and faith school providers and outlined the education contribution faith schools would make alongside their community cohesion commitments and third, that the governing bodies of all schools must be able to demonstrate that they were actively engaged in activities and initiatives which promote community cohesion. Partly reflecting the continued unease, until 2011, OFSTED inspections incorporated this aspect of a school's work in its reviews of schools (Bolton and Gillies 2009: 16).

The faith schools expansion in England and Wales continues to be a feature of the diversifying schools sector. This has been apparent in – and facilitated by – UK Coalition Free Schools education policy. This policy, in which parents, teachers, charities, business community and other interest groups can apply to set up a school which will be outside of local authority control but receive state funding, has seen a number of applications from faith groups. Of the 323 initial applications made in 2010–2011, 115 were faith school applications (Department for Education 2010c). Of the 24 Free Schools which opened for the academic year in September 2011, seven were faith schools. The paradox of the growth and encouragement of religious schools in a secular society reflected the choice agenda and also the increasing role of religion in multiculture and identity politics. Under New Labour, the government managed this paradox through its cohesion agenda.

Schools and cohesion policymaking

The outcome of the debates and controversies between government, education policy and faith organisations and faith-based schools officially (and legislatively) established a direct and active relationship between the education sector and the community cohesion agenda (see Chapter 2). In a reflection of the ambivalence as to what community cohesion meant as a concrete translation into a school's interventions and commitments the then Labour government issued guidance on 'what to do' and underlined the importance of cohesion: 'every school, whatever its intake or wherever it is located, is responsible for educating children and young people who will live and work in a country which is diverse in terms of cultures, religions and beliefs, ethnicities and social backgrounds' (Department for Children Schools and Families 2007: 1).

Between 2008 and 2011 OFSTED inspections of schools' duty to promote cohesion were uneven, as schools' initiatives have reflected the broad scope of the guidelines and expectations. Early analysis of OFSTED data on cohesion performance indicates that faith schools perform strongly – especially at secondary level – on the cohesion targets. Almost a third, 32 per cent, of faith schools received an 'outstanding' grade for community relations while only 16 per cent of non-faith schools achieved the same level. David Jesson (2009) suggests that this finding counters the worries that faith schooling leads to increasing or entrenching social division. The findings of Jesson's study may reflect the ability of faith schools to present themselves as effective education providers (Dwyer and Parutis 2012: 25). It may reflect the sense of extra scrutiny that faith schools may perceive themselves to be under given the earlier debates and arguments with government over admission policies or it may reflect uncertainties within the OFSTED inspection system as to how to actually assess the success and effectiveness of cohesion initiatives and whether the OFSTED criteria were sufficient to objectively measure cohesion initiatives.

The Coalition government's Education Act 2011 ended the duty placed on schools to promote cohesion. It is not yet clear what the consequences of this are likely to be. On the one hand, the ending of what was seen by some to be the technical or tick box nature of the cohesion duty may have positive outcomes if schools pursue initiatives that reflect a broader recognition of being part of diverse communities. On the other hand, in a pro-choice education market in which 'free' schools are being encouraged the division and separation may become even more entrenched (Runnymede Trust 2011).

Even with the withdrawal of schools from community and cohesion responsibilities, the ways in which education policymaking has incorporated schools into approaches for managing cultural diversity and difference is significant. The schools-cohesion relationship – and its abandonment – testifies to the continuation of the political and policy controversies and anxieties as to how to contain and manage the connections between education and ethnicity. While not achieving quite the same high-profile status as the furores over race and education in the 1980s, the education policy approaches to school choice, faith provision and cohesion in the beginning of the 21st century, evidence has reanimated schools 'as spaces for contesting competing narratives of citizenship and integration' (Dwyer and Parutis 2012: 25). It is the ways in which these race-multiculture and education narratives extend to and are a feature of the post-school education landscape that is now considered.

Higher education and ethnicity

Ethnicity and over-representation in post-16 education

Compulsory education occupies, as our earlier discussions have shown, a dominant place at the heart of race and ethnicity debates and controversies in England. However, in something of a contrast the post-compulsory education sector has been a relative newcomer to the ethnicity-education agenda. It has only been in the last two decades that there has been a more sustained focus on the relationship between ethnicity and further and higher education. This relationship has been particularly shaped by one key factor: in the post-compulsory education sector BME groups are increasingly over-represented. The expansion of higher education since the early 1990s has meant a general increase in the numbers of all young people who go to university. But within this pattern, proportionately, a much higher level of BME young people go to university than white young people (Connor et al. 2003; Connor et al. 2004; Gilroy 1990). The Higher Education Statistics Agency (HESA) (Equality Challenge Unit 2010) show that in 2008–2009, 17.8 per cent of UK university students were from a BME background. This is a significant figure given that the overall BME 18–24 age group represents 14.2 per cent of the population. Despite the well-documented problematic relationship between ethnicity and compulsory education, this has not translated into exclusion and under-representation in the post-compulsory education sector in either further education or at universities. In their study of education and BME patterns Bhattacharyya et al. (2003) note the dominant trend for BME young people to stay within education – only 15 per cent of 16-year-old BME pupils intended to leave compared to 57 per cent who intended to go to university. This is compared to 20 per cent of white students who intended to leave education and 46 per cent who intended to go on to university. Bhattacharyya et al. also point to evidence that further education at colleges offer an opportunity for some BME pupils to re-enter the education sector after negative school experiences.

The high levels of BME representation in post-compulsory education can be seen to reflect both the aspirational approaches of BME young people (see Shah, Dwyer and Modood 2010) and the success of the university sector in attracting BME students. However, once the over-representation narrative is unpacked a set of more complex and differential patterns becomes evident (Tolley and Rundle 2006). There are distinct polarisations in the geographies and in the types of higher-education institutions that BME students predominantly attend, in the degree subject areas studied and in degree attainment, moreover, there are marked differences between different minority ethnic groups and between genders.

BME students are most heavily clustered in the modern (post-1992) universities in urban areas in the South-East of England (Connor et al. 2004). Of the ten universities with the highest proportion of BME students only the Universities of Bradford and Aston were outside of London and the Home Counties. The School of Pharmacy, Brunel, Queen Mary and Westfield College, Universities of East London, Middlesex, Westminster and Thames Valley had the highest percentage of students from BME backgrounds (Race for Opportunity 2009). There appears to be a correlation between BME students being attracted to Higher Education Institutions (HEIs) that are in areas in which BME populations are well established. The converse of the high BME student in the mid 1990s populations in some universities is the poor levels of BME representation in others. Recent research found that half of the ten universities with the lowest proportion of BME students in the mid 1990s appeared again in 2007, a finding which is indicative of the extent to which some HEIs continue to either not be attractive to BME students and/or to move very slowly in relation to being able to address and improve their BME student profile (Connor et al. 2004; Reay, David and Ball 2005; Race for Opportunity 2009). Chinese and mixed-ethnicity students are well-represented at Oxford and Cambridge, all other BME students are under-represented at these elite institutions. Apart from Oxford and Cambridge, this elite group of universities – known as the

Russell Group – comprise 20 research-intensive institutions reflected in their attracting around two-thirds of the UK's research grant and contract income. Apart from the London based Russell Group universities (London School of Economics, Kings College, Imperial College and University College London) the under-representation of BME students is repeated at the majority of the other Russell Group institutions. Only Birmingham, Manchester, Nottingham and Warwick managed to attract a representative student proportion of the BME population in 2007–2008. This means that over half (12 of the 22) of the Russell Group Universities (including Oxford and Cambridge) continue to have, overall, disproportionately low levels of BME students: (Race for Opportunity 2009).

It is not easy to straightforwardly explain these trends (Connor et al. 2003; Connor et al. 2004; Reay, David and Ball 2005). The geographies of the HEIs and BME residential patterns do not completely explain this under-representation – for example Warwick and Nottingham with small BME local populations are representative but Leeds, Bristol, Liverpool, Cardiff and Sheffield with established local BME communities are under-representative. That there is evidence that some universities have not made any progress in attracting greater numbers of BME students between 1995–1996 and 2007–2008 implies an institutional failure to engage with and secure representative levels of BME students (Connor et al. 2004).

While it is clear from the existing research (see Ball, Reay and David 2002; Tolley and Rundle 2006) that a significant number of BME students tend to make selection decisions (through choice or constraint) in favour of those universities that are local and/or already have a multicultural student body, the lack of progress among universities with under-representation of BME students is indicative of the approach of some HEIs towards ethnicity and policy initiatives. There is some evidence of policy inertia, overly technical and mechanical approaches to equality policy and uncertainty in terms of what makes effective equality policymaking in the university sector (Neal 1998b). There are also pockets of good policy practice in the form of universities being very engaged with local schools and communities and working to change perceptions of those universities to make them attractive to BME groups (Bird 1996; Law, Phillips and Turney 2004; Neal 1998b).

Ethnicity and differentiations: subject choice clustering and degree attainment

To some extent differential BME student representation connects with institutions and subject specialisms but this does not by any means completely explain these polarisations. However, in terms of subjects that are favoured by BME students there is a clear division between the sciences and humanities – BME students tend to be over-represented in medicine, dentistry, computer science, law and business studies and under-represented in humanities subjects: (Connor et al 2003). There are clear lines of separation in more applied subjects too. While significant numbers of BME students are drawn to business and administrative studies, they are only half as likely to be studying education and even less so agriculture (Bagguley and Hussain 2007; Purcell et al. 2008). This is an area in which there is a direct correlation – agricultural and teacher-training institutions have fewer BME students and it is these institutions that dominate the five HEIs with the lowest proportions of BME students. Concerns about the highly differential patterns of where BME students are studying and in what subjects are mirrored by emergent concerns about differential degree attainment. One study based on data collated in 2003–2004 reveal that BME students graduate with lower degree classifications than white students (Broecke and Nicholls 2007). The attainment gap noted by the Broecke and Nicholls' study was followed by a number of other studies (Fielding et al. 2008; Jacobs et al. 2007) which confirmed attainment differences but argued that the causal factors were not reducible to ethnicity or single variables and were likely to be explained by a range of complex factors including age, gender, socio-economic status, location, entry qualification level, and type of institution. In the quantitative analysis Fielding et al. (2008) found that there was an attainment pattern in which the higher the proportion of BME students in the institution, the higher the differential in degree attainment. Most strikingly, in institutions with low numbers of BME students, BME students outperform White students.

The differentiations in the higher education presence among minority ethnic populations both echoes and disrupts some of the broad patterns identified in the compulsory education discussions in relation to the diversity within ethnic groups in higher education. In terms of echoes there are some familiarities in the trends that the HESA figures cited in Race for Opportunity Report (2009: 6) which show that UK students of Indian descent in the 18–24yrs age category are the most well-represented minority ethnic group. Representing only 2.7 per cent of the total population they make up 3.3 per cent of the student population in 2007–2008. British Black African constituted the second largest minority group (3.2%) in higher education and mixed-ethnicity students (2.1%) the third most represented. Students from Pakistani and Bangladeshi backgrounds are the least well-represented. While Bangladeshi 18–24 year olds constitute 1.1 per cent of the population there are 0.6 per cent of Bangladeshi students in the higher education system. Similarly there are 2.2 per cent Pakistani origin people in this age category but only 1.9 per cent of university students came from this group.

In terms of disruptions there are some patterns that are very different from the compulsory education sector – UK pupils of Chinese origin achieve high levels of educational attainment in compulsory education but are under-represented in the non-compulsory sector. There are 1.1 per cent of Chinese 18–24-year-olds in the total population with 0.9 per cent university students of Chinese origin. Despite the relatively low levels of compulsory education attainment British African-Caribbean students are better represented in universities. While 18–24-year-old African-Caribbeans' constitute 0.9 per cent of the total population there are 1.4 per cent university students who are African-Caribbean (Race for Opportunity 2009: 6).

There are gendered dimensions to some of these representation patterns. A Joseph Rowntree Foundation study by Bagguley and Hussain (2007) examining young Pakistani and Bangladeshi women reported on rising HEI participation, although the study highlights the importance of degree courses that are available locally and the continuing need for schools and career services to challenge assumptions about the education aspirations of young Pakistani and Bangladeshi women. Apart from the African-Caribbean group of 18–24 year olds, young women from BME groups are all slightly under-represented but, in a continuation of compulsory education attainment trends, Black African-Caribbean women are three times more likely to be in university than Black African-Caribbean men.

As with compulsory education the uneven non-compulsory education landscape is shaped by the interaction of diverse structural contexts and variables – location and school choice, social and economic status, gender, perceptions of HEIs – which converge with ethnicity in unpredictable ways as some of the patterns discussed above evidence. For example, even though the number of young Pakistani people in higher education is among the lowest of the minority ethnic populations, recent trends show that young Pakistani women and men are more likely to be at university than their white peers (Shah, Dwyer and Modood 2010: 1110). In their analysis of educational achievement among young working-class British Pakistanis, Shah et al. (2010) suggest that the concept of 'ethnic capital' is useful in understanding social and education aspirations (and outcomes) among socio-economically disadvantaged British Pakistani groups. Drawing on a two-year qualitative study they found that the beliefs and attitudes in middle and working-class Pakistani families and parents held towards education and transmitted to their children overwhelmingly and tended to emphasise the importance and value of education for social mobility. For example, 'Yasmin, a student at Brunel and from a working class family, noted that it did not matter which university she attended as long as she went to university because "I think it's a kind of status that comes with it"' (Shah, Dwyer and Modood 2010: 1114–1115). As we have suggested in relation to compulsory education, Shah et al. argue that education trajectories are complex and relational where class, gender and religion religion all play formative interacting roles in the educational experiences and aspirations of young Pakistani men and women. Importantly their findings highlight the need to take into account the more nuanced contributions that cultural and ethnic capital also make to the non-compulsory education and ethnicity relationship.

Conclusion

This chapter has sought to map some of the key debates, concerns, data and trajectories that define the relationship between education and ethnicity in England and Wales. It has argued that education has had a particular proximity to race and ethnicity debates and controversies. This proximity has meant that anxieties and contestations have occurred on a number of fronts and in a range of ways. Poorer levels of educational attainment, negative school experiences, classroom relations, low expectations, labelling, rates of exclusion and SEN practices have been a long-running cause for concern for parents, families, communities and education providers. The increasing differentiation in education performance between ethnic groups has become increasingly marked in the 21st century. This complexity has been analysed in order to take into account the intersecting ways in which social context and structural constraints combine and interact with ethnicity.

We have argued that ethnicity and race are not always and not *the* explanatory factors for understanding what happens to pupils and students within education systems. Socio-economic constraints do have a profound impact on the educational trajectories and outcomes of pupils and young people. However, like ethnicity, class cannot be reified as *the* explanatory factor. Gender, geography and location, school choice and type of school and religion and migration status must all be considered as potent, relational and intersectional factors in the shaping of educational experiences and outcomes.

As the current education landscape has become characterised by increasing differentiation and diversity in educational outcomes across and within minority ethnic populations, educational provision has itself become increasingly diverse and differentiated. In particular the creation of a quasi market-orientated education sector and school choice have led to a transformed compulsory education sector in which class and ethnicity-based polarisations are particularly pronounced and significant. The chapter has argued that in the urban areas of the UK it has been those parents and populations who are most able to access resources and enact strategies such as private tuition and residential flight who have benefitted from school choice. The school choice agenda has created renewed spaces for religious and faith organisations to influence and be directly involved in educational provision and this has opened up broader debates about social and ethnic divisions in England and anxieties about Muslim schools in particular. If race domi-nated education politics in the 1980s, then religion, parental choice and divided schools have been a key feature of education politics in the 21st century. What is clear in this shift is that the education-race relationship is highly political and policy 'busy' and in a context of diversifying multicul-ture all aspects of compulsory and post-compulsory education will continue to be at the forefront of concerns, aspirations and policy intervention.

Chapter 8

Employment

Having a job is one of the key determinants of a person's welfare. For some even low-paid work can have a positive impact on well-being (Clark and Drinkwater 2007: 19). However, research consistently shows the relative disadvantage of ethnic minorities in the labour market though it also emphasises the diversity between and within groups. While on an average people from minority ethnic groups experience higher levels of unemployment, lower wages and fewer opportunities this is only part of the picture as some groups do better than the white majority. Instead the data shows cleavages between and within different groups (Clark and Drinkwater 2007; Owen et al. 2000). Employment and employment outcomes therefore highlight the complexity of the intersections between multiculture, race and social policy. This is because employment, unemployment, sectors of employment, wages and terms and conditions of employment demonstrate some of the main aspects of structural inequality in the UK based on ethnicity.

It is also the place where immigration legislation operates to segregate, exclude and disadvantage and in doing so creates a division of labour, by immigration status. At the beginning of the 21st century these divisions in the patterns of BME and migrant labour were not always straight forward as the UK and other Northern European countries and the US have also demanded highly skilled migrants from Global South countries (Raghuram 2009). Health is an area in this form of migration and global interdependency that is particularly striking creating what Connell (2010) describes as a 'health worker exodus' from poorer countries in the Global South to the richer countries in the Global North. For example, we saw in Chapter 6 how the NHS recruits and relies on increasing and significant levels of overseas doctors and nurses. Similarly, membership changes within the European Union have also had an impact on the labour market and the nature of migration flows since 2004 (Chapters 1 and 3). There have been significant rises in the number of migrants from those Eastern European countries joining the EU particularly from Poland and also from other A8 countries such as Hungary, Czech Republic, Latvia, Lithuania and Estonia. Employment patterns for EU migrants tend to reflect the high and low-skill polarisations of migrant labour more generally but there is a disproportionate clustering of Eastern European workers within low-paid, low-skilled employment sectors such as agriculture, construction, social care and hospitality.

The divisions of migrant labour, unevenly polarised at the top highly skilled end and the bottom unskilled end of the labour market, as well as the increasing diversity of migrant labour demonstrate the importance of citizenship and the tensions between labour rights, human rights and conflicting social-policy agendas (Wills et al. 2010). For example, McDowell argues that 'Whiteness has once again become an issue in the UK as the number of new migrants from the expanded EU continues to grow, greatly exceeding initial estimates and fuelling a media panic about job competition and community cohesion' (McDowell 2008: 52). The divisions and diversity of migrant workers in the UK context also highlight the importance of employment as a site of mobilisation and contestation about migration in the current environment of shifting mobilities of labour and capital on a global scale.

Centrality of employment

Employment is therefore an important area to explore in relation to global and national social-policy but also within the wider contexts of migration and development. Migratory movements are influenced by employment and wage-earning opportunities in different countries. Early theories of migration focused almost entirely on the economics of migration (Arango 2000) but now theory incorporates the greater complexity of any migratory decision including those associated with persecution, human rights abuses and networks (Castles and Miller 2009). Global inequalities, interdependencies, differential employment and wage-earning opportunities and unemployment are migration drivers while the remittances sent to sending countries have an important role to play in supporting family members and in some cases wider development. The need for low-paid workers in developed countries of the Global North and West provide jobs for migrant workers and has been one of the main contributors to the higher rates of poverty experienced by all ethnic minorities compared to the population average (Platt 2007). Inequality in a globalised and mediated era will ensure that migration and mobility are the key issues of the 21st century. Castles argues that migration is an essential component of globalisation but while capital and commodities are desirable, the flow of people is seen as potentially harmful to identity and sovereignty (Castles 2000). Immigration controls are in place but these policies fail, in part because developed countries have a 'structural dependence on immigrant labour because migrant workers were concentrated in jobs which locals were unable or unwilling to do' (Castles 2004). In the 21st century, migration flows continue to be diverse and are becoming more complex as immigrant legislation changes and develops, as labour-market needs polarise and as population demographics impact social needs and the economy.

While structural inequalities characterise the labour market, these inequalities can benefit both the sending and the receiving countries.

Employment links closely with immigration policy, which during the 20th century has acted as a catalyst for both encouraging and restricting migration. In the post–Second World War period there was a need to attract migrant labour to rebuild the country and this led to immigration of Eastern Europeans from Displaced Persons Camps and then there was the migration of workers from Commonwealth countries in the Caribbean and South Asia (see Chapter 3). The jobs taken up by these new migrants were for the most part low-skilled jobs with poor terms and conditions of employment and low pay but were necessary for the economy. As the numbers of migrants increased, immigration controls were put in place and, as we saw in Chapter 3, these controls included restrictions on work and welfare. Structural inequality, based on migration and ethnicity, have resulted in a tranche of other social policy and legislative interventions in the areas of Race Relations, capacity building, equality legislation and targeted government programmes such as the Ethnic Minority Employment Task Force. Moreover, relative poverty also impacts the experiences in other areas including health, housing, education and criminal justice and these intersections are explored in others chapters.

What this chapter will demonstrate is that labour market experiences and outcomes are very different between and within minority groups and that attempts to understand and explain these differences are complex and require a multifaceted approach that seeks to understand individual rather than more generalisable experiences. The chapter is organised in three parts. Part one will examine the different labour market experiences by ethnic groups and gender. The second part will seek to explain why some of these differences exist by examining the main factors that intersect with labour market outcomes including migration, language, cultural norms, migration aspirations and discrimination. The third part will focus on employment within the social-policy arena as a mechanism that facilitates inclusion and integration as well as its role as a site for exclusion based on ethnicity, immigration and citizenship.

Differential labour market experiences

The shortfall of labour created by the expansion of the economy and rebuilding programmes in the post–Second World War period precipitated the pull factors necessary to attract migrant labour to the UK but the ethnic division of labour was immediately apparent. The dominant trend for the white workforce was upwardly mobile, meeting the labour demands of the more attractive jobs while migrant workers filled the labour market gaps as replacement workers (McDowell 2008). The migrant workers from the New Commonwealth countries in the Caribbean and then South Asia found themselves settling in different areas of urban England, in the low-paid jobs that were considered unpleasant and entailed long and unsocial hours. The geographies of migrant settlement were largely driven by the different employment and industrial needs for migrant labour. For example, in London health and public transport recruited heavily from Caribbean migrant populations and in the Midlands and Northern England manufacturing industries recruited heavily from South Asian countries, particularly Pakistan and India. These social and spatial patterns of post-war migration, where new arrivals took the least desirable jobs, echoed those from the earlier migration periods in which white minority ethnic populations like Irish and Eastern and Southern Europe migrants found themselves similarly structurally located in the labour market. However, the visible differences of the post-war commonwealth migrants moving and living in Britain meant that racism and systematic discrimination also affected their labour market participation and experiences. The result was that whatever the qualifications, experience and social origins of migrants, they were still for the most part confined to low-paid manual work.

Research carried out in 1966–1967 before employment discrimination was banned as part of the 1968 Race Relations legislation showed that ethnic minority workers were steered away from the most desirable jobs with prejudice coming from other workers and employers. Some employers even had a policy of not recruiting ethnic minorities while others said that they would use them only as a 'last resort' when they had been unable to recruit British workers (Daniel 1968). Other employees said that they appointed on merit but it soon became clear that merit was in fact not just qualifications but also how well ethnic minorities would fit in with other workers and, where applicable, how acceptable they would be to customers and representatives of other businesses.

In 1982, a further study was carried out (Brown 1984) which revealed that the relative positions of Britain's white and black populations found some progress but that there was still a disproportionately high level of unemployment among ethnic minorities in spite of increasing levels of self-employment. By the 1990s there was evidence of upward mobility among some ethnic minorities, expanding self-employment and a clear diversity between different ethnic groups (Modood et al. 1997). Three broad groupings were identified: the most advantaged were people of Chinese, African-Asian and White heritage, people of Bangladeshi and Pakistani origin were the most disadvantaged group, and Indian and African-Caribbean people occupied the middle ground. However, the situation is more complex than ethnic group differences; gender and age within ethnic groups was also a source of much diversity (Owen et al. 2000).

More recent research also shows the continuing cleavages between and within ethnic groups. Using data from the Labour Force Surveys (2001–2004), Heath and Cheung distinguished between the economically active, those who are working or seeking work, and the economically inactive that includes people who are not seeking work because, for example, they are looking after the home and family or are students (Heath and Cheung 2006). Exploring the data in these different ways allows for a more insightful analysis by ethnic and gendered divisions. Heath and Cheung found that the average rates of unemployment were 4.8 per cent for those who described their ethnic group as white (Heath and Cheung 2006). Among Chinese (4.3%) and Indians (6.2%) the rates were similar to whites while other ethnic groups experienced higher rates of unemployment. Bangladeshi and Pakistani people fare least well in terms of their labour market experiences especially women (Berthoud and Blekesaune 2007).

Tables 8.1 and 8.2 show the relationships between employment and unemployment by gender and ethnic group. Table 8.1 clearly shows the low rates of full-time employment among Pakistani and Bangladeshi men compared with other groups. British and other whites have the highest rates of full-time employment. There are also variations in levels of self-employment with a quarter of Pakistani men and just under a quarter of Chinese men in full-time self-employment. Research has shown that self-employment can be a route into the labour market, offering an alternative to the lack of employment opportunities available to some groups (Metcalf, Modood and Virdee 1997).

Table 8.1 Patterns of employment and unemployment – men %

	Employed full-time	Employed part-time	Self-employed full-time	Self-employed part-time	Unemployed	Number
Black African	64.2	14.3	6.8	0.7	13.9	961
Black Caribbean	64.6	9.0	9.9	1.5	15.1	1,025
Black Mixed	59.4	9.7	12.9	0.9	17.0	317
Indian	67.0	9.0	16.6	1.1	6.2	2,202
Pakistani	46.3	12.7	25.2	2.9	12.9	1,181
Bangladeshi	47.1	20.1	15.5	0.0	17.3	399
Chinese	59.8	11.0	23.1	1.9	4.3	419
British, other whites	73.2	6.6	13.9	1.5	4.8	124,013

Source: Labour Force Survey 2001–2004, in Heath and Cheung 2006: 81.

Table 8.2 Patterns of employment and unemployment – women %

	Employed full-time	Employed part-time	Self-employed full-time	Self-employed part-time	Unemployed	Number
Black African	59.7	26.0	2.0	0.7	11.6	915
Black Caribbean	62.0	24.9	1.7	0.6	10.8	1,134
Black Mixed	50.6	33.2	1.4	3.5	11.3	347
Indian	55.0	30.5	4.5	3.1	6.9	1,701
Pakistani	42.1	35.5	4.7	2.7	15.1	484
Bangladeshi	48.7	33.3	0.9	4.3	12.8	117
Chinese	49.3	31.4	9.2	4.6	5.5	348
British, other whites	51.2	38.2	3.3	3.2	4.1	98,136

Source: Labour Force Survey 2001–2004, in Heath and Cheung 2006: 82.

Table 8.2 shows that a greater proportion of women, from all groups, work part-time compared to their male counterparts. Black women, from either Caribbean or African heritage, are the most likely to be in full-time employment. In terms of unemployment, the pattern is same among women as it is among men: British and other whites, Chinese and Indian women experience lower levels of unemployment than women from other groups. Bangladeshi women have three times the level of unemployment than their white counterparts and Pakistani women experience nearly four times the level of unemployment.

Turning to labour market participation and levels of economic activity, Figures 8.1 and 8.2 show the lower levels of economic activity among Pakistani and Bangladeshi people compared to others. Included in economic inactivity are retired people, students or others who are economically inactive because they were long-term ill, temporarily sick or disabled (Heath and Cheung 2006). Among men, more than one-fifth of Bangladeshi (22%) and one-fifth of Pakistani men (19.8 %) fit into the other inactive category compared to only 4.9 per cent of Chinese men, 7.5 per cent of black mixed and 8.6 per cent in the British and other white category. Among women the main difference between groups is the high proportion of Pakistani and Bangladeshi women who are economically inactive because they look after the home and family. British and other white women and black Caribbean women have the highest levels of economic activity, 74.8 per cent and 72.8 per cent respectively while Pakistani and Bangladeshi women have the lowest rates, 28.7 per cent and 18.4 per cent respectively.

While gender norms and expectations do affect women's labour market participation among some groups, research with Bangladeshi and Pakistani women show that younger women, born and educated in Britain, were likely to follow a different life course compared to their mothers, seeing paid work as a means to independence and self-esteem (Dale et al. 2002). Moreover, such research provides a warning against reductionist assumptions that low participation can be explained by a homogenous culture and religion. Instead they argue that Pakistani and Bangladeshi groups are heterogeneous and this is influenced by a number of factors including migration and migration processes, individual beliefs and cultural values and norms, economies and areas of settlement and intergenerational factors including education and language. This means that while patterns are evident, generalisations and explanations can be more difficult.

The data does show, however, that a significant gap exists in employment rates between the general population and the ethnic minority population – 14.2 per cent – and the gap is only 1.3 per cent lower than it was in 1987, although there have been fluctuations during the 20-year period (National Audit Office 2008). There are, according to the National Audit Office, three main factors that contribute towards the under-achievement of ethnic minorities in the labour market: human capital, regional differences in local labour markets and discrimination. They also suggest that cultural factors are influential in creating differential experiences.

Among those working, there are clear differences in terms of the kind of jobs and earnings between and within groups. In general, ethnic minorities tend to be over-represented in low-skilled occupations and under-represented in managerial and other high-skill occupations

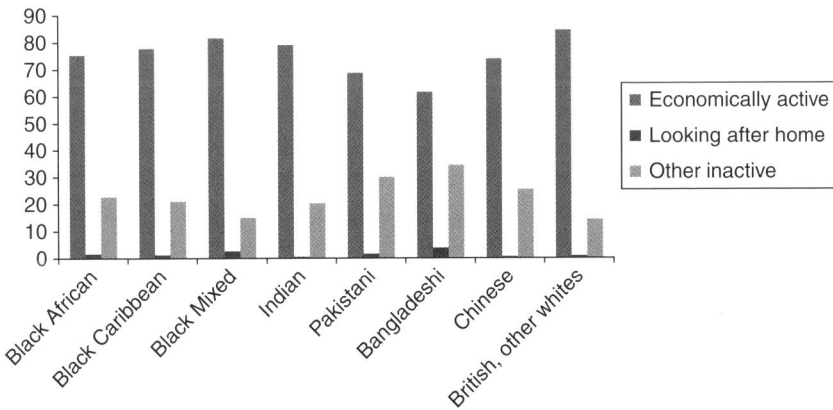

Figure 8.1   Labour force participation – men %
Source: Labour Force Survey 2001–2004 in Heath and Cheung 2006, p. 81.

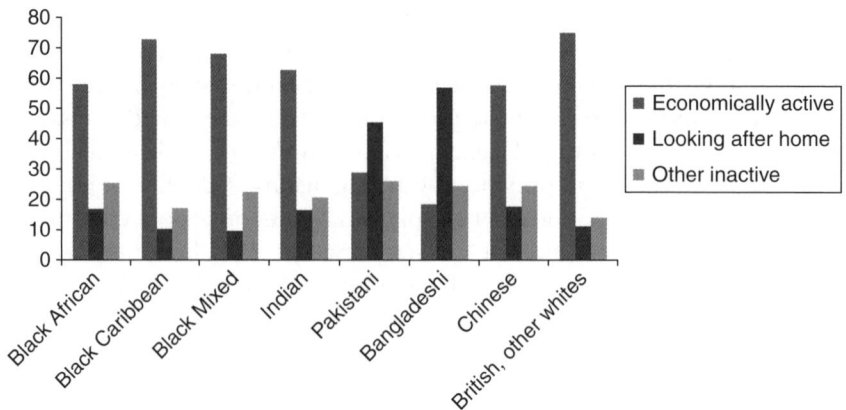

Figure 8.2   Labour force participation – women %
Source: Labour Force Survey 2001–2004 in Heath and Cheung 2006, p. 81.

with strong evidence of sectoral and job clustering within employment. Research carried out by the Commission for Racial Equality found patterns of difference by ethnic group and gender (Commission for Racial Equality 2006). Around a quarter of the people who described their ethnic group as white worked in production compared to less than 14 per cent among ethnic minorities. In contrast 35 per cent of people from ethnic minority groups worked in hotels and catering, distribution and transport and communications compared with 26 per cent of white workers. Eighty per cent of Bangladeshi men worked in the hotels and catering, distribution, and transport and communications industries and more of Chinese men also worked in these industries. Ethnic minority women were disproportionately employed in public sector services (42%) and the highest proportions employed in this sector was found among black Caribbean (54%), black African (52.1%) and Bangladeshi (50.8%) women. However, the research found that women from ethnic minority groups working in public services were over-represented in the lowest grades (Commission for Racial Equality 2006).

There was also clustering in the actual jobs carried out by different groups. Most densely located were the 10 per cent of black African women who worked as care assistants and the 10 per cent who worked as nurses at the time of the 2001 census. Among men, over 23 per cent of Bangladeshi and over 21 per cent of Chinese men worked as cooks. In total, 41 per cent of Bangladeshi men worked in catering, either as cooks, waiters or restaurant owners whilst the proportion among Chinese men was 35 per cent. These kinds of jobs are often insecure, badly paid with poor terms and conditions of employment with little opportunity for training or vertical job mobility.

These jobs also command very low wages and reinforce different experiences of poverty and deprivation by ethnic group.

Using aggregated data, ethnic minority men and women consistently earn less than their white counterparts, on average by occupational groupings, with the income deficit largest within the professional and managerial grouping (Clark and Drinkwater 2007). This suggests that people from ethnic minority groups find it more difficult than white people to penetrate the higher level occupations, regardless of their educational levels (National Audit Office 2008). People from ethnic minority groups are much more likely to live in low income households than others. Around two-thirds of ethnic minority people live in low income households, which is twice the rate experienced by white people. In working households, the variations by ethnicity are also evident, with Bangladeshi and Pakistani households experiencing higher proportions of low income households than other groups. Around 65 per cent of Bangladeshi households live in poverty, which is when income is less than 60 per cent of *median* household income for any year. The larger the numbers in the household the greater the income has to be to ensure that the household is not in poverty, and the larger household size of some groups directly correlates with both low income and household size (Aldridge et al. 2011).

While on average ethnic minority workers are paid less per hour than their white counterparts (£7.50 and £8.00 respectively), there are differences by ethnic group and gender. Black women earn more than black men, while white and Indian men earn more than Indian women. There was little differential, by gender in the other groups though Pakistani and Bangladeshi men and women earned substantially below average (£6.25 and £6.24 respectively) (Commission for Racial Equality 2006). Not surprisingly earnings are affected by levels of qualifications though having a degree had a greater impact on income among ethnic minorities in general than it did among refugees as Table 8.3 shows.

Among refugees, obtaining a degree in the UK had a positive effect on earnings though it did not completely eradicate their low pay in comparison with other ethnic minority groups. Refugees who had obtained their degree

Table 8.3 Mean gross pay per hour (£) by highest qualification

	Minority ethnic groups	Refugees
Degree or higher	13.71	9.04
A' level or equivalent	8.18	8.42
O' level/GCSE A-C or equivalent	7.67	6.09
None	5.67	6.30

Source: Bloch (2002b: 99).

in Britain earned £12.10 on average, compared to the average earnings of £8.23 among those who had obtained their degrees elsewhere. One of the difficulties faced by refugees, and migrants, is that their overseas qualifications are generally not recognised at the equivalent level which means that they are unable to work in the profession for which they are qualified without retraining. Not being able to use skills and qualifications and the associated deskilling is one of the main ways in which refugees and other migrants remain disadvantaged in the labour market. This highlights the inherent contradiction between refugee integration policies and the agendas and concerns of different government departments (Bloch 2008). Refugee integration is linked to achieving full potential which includes 'gaining employment appropriate to their skills and qualifications' (Home Office 2005: 20), and this is not happening.

Zimbabweans in Britain provide an example of a group of highly skilled migrants and refugees who are not employed in jobs commensurate with their skills and qualifications. Prior to migration, Zimbabweans were working in a range of jobs including professional and managerial ones while in the UK the shift was to nursing and care work (Bloch 2008). Data from a Home Office Skills Audit of refugees found that 85 per cent of Zimbabwean men had been employed or self-employed before leaving Zimbabwe and the proportion among women was 69 per cent. Of those working, nearly half had been in management and senior or professional jobs (Kirk 2004). Similar patterns of high levels of education and managerial and professional jobs prior to migration were found in research by the Refugee Council and Zimbabwean Association (Doyle 2009). Becoming deskilled has more than just an impact on an individual, it also has a negative effect on the sending country – should migrants and refugees return – and the amount of money that is remitted – which is an important part of development. Compared to other refugee and migrant groups Zimbabweans are relatively advantaged, because on arrival the majority speak fluent English and do not therefore face language as an obstacle to employment or, in theory, to integration. The next section will explore some of the main factors that affect both labour market outcomes and position among migrants, refugees and established ethnic minorities in Britain.

Explaining differential employment experiences and diversity

In the previous section, the ways in which labour market experiences intersect with ethnicity and gender were examined, but also the impact of immigration status was considered. This section unravels the complexity of different labour market experiences and attempts to explain why these differences exist. Migration and migration patterns, immigration status, language, cultural norms, migration aspirations and discrimination will all be explored in relation to experiences and outcomes.

New migrants fare less well in the labour market than their children and so there are intergenerational factors involved in labour market outcomes. The British born children of migrants do slightly better in the labour market than their parents though British people from ethnic minority backgrounds still do less well than white people with the same level of qualifications (Heath and Cheung 2007). Among the migrant population, recently arrived migrants are less successful in the labour market than those who have been in Britain for longer (National Audit Office 2008). In short, length of time in Britain and being born in Britain does on the whole diminish the inequality, though the inequality of outcomes is still stark. There are exceptions to this pattern, notably the unqualified Pakistani men among whom the British born experience higher levels of unemployment than their overseas born counterparts (Simpson et al. 2006). Moreover, an analysis of the 1991 and 2001 censuses found that the 'ethnic penalty' was more acute among many British-born ethnic minorities than those born outside of Britain (Simpson et al. 2006).

The term 'ethnic penalty' is used by Heath and Cheung to 'refer to all the sources of disadvantage that might lead an ethnic group to fare less well in the labour market than do similarly qualified whites. In other words it is a broader concept than that of discrimination, although discrimination is likely to be a major component of the ethnic penalty' (Heath and Cheung 2007: 19). One of the criticisms of the term is that it distracts from racism and instead focuses on what are seen as human capital deficits such as education and language, among some ethnic minority groups (Virdee 2010). The role of discrimination in differential outcomes cannot be ignored though one of the difficulties is that it is hard to prove, as it happens covertly. Nevertheless, small-scale studies, such as that carried out by Esmail and Etherington to test the hypothesis that British trained doctors with foreign sounding names were less likely to be short-listed for jobs as senior house officers than were others, show the ways in discrimination operates but is largely hidden. A repeat study in the late 1990s told a similar story of discrimination (Esmail and Etherington 1997). The fourth national survey of Britain's ethnic minorities, carried out by the Policy Studies Institute in the 1990s, found that 20 per cent of ethnic minority respondents said that they had been discriminated against by being refused a job on racial grounds (Modood et al. 1997). Because this is subjective, it means that in most cases little or nothing can be done in order to prove discrimination and no amount of Race Relations or Race Equality legislation will, in reality, put a stop to this.

However, there are other reasons why the migrant generation do less well in the labour market than their British born children and these have been attributed to having lower or unrecognised educational qualifications, lacking networks and job references, and difficulties understanding the English language and culture (Berthoud 2000). Methods of job seeking vary within different social and cultural contexts and the social networks that can facilitate employment also differ with newer migrants less likely to have these networks in place. On arrival in a new country migrants often depend on family members or people from the same ethnic group to inform them about jobs and labour market conditions. The consequence of these information sources means that jobs are often within the particular ethnic economy unless the family possesses strong social capital (Nee and Sanders 2001). These initial micro contacts can be either stepping stones for new arrivals while they develop new links or they can limit and restrict access to wider networks as co-ethnic employment does not facilitate language learning or social contacts outside of the immediate ethnic or linguistic group. When migrants expand their networks and develop links with people from other groups the acquisition of this social capital can provide valuable resources for labour market mobility (Lancee 2011).

These patterns while present among many new migrant groups are not generalisable to all groups. Certainly, group history prior to migration as well as traditions and resources can be used to gain mobility. East African-Asians have been used as an example of a group that arrived in Britain with networks, English language and the kind of business experience and acumen that enable them to successfully transfer their skills into the British economy, also using self-employment as a mechanism for upward mobility (Robinson 1993). Other groups, who had come from rural areas or ended up working in mills and factories in the north of England were less successful and found themselves living in deprived regions without labour market opportunities as a result of industrial decline in the 1970s.

Additional factors that result in differential labour market outcomes are aspirations for migration and the desire to return home, making the migration temporary rather than permanent, and immigration status. If individuals see migration as temporary then it will affect decisions about investing in training and qualifications in order to achieve labour market mobility (Bloch 2004). Where a migrant does not have a regularised status, meaning that he or she does not have documents to stay in Britain legally, employment choices are reduced often to the informal economy with its associated low pay, poor terms and conditions of employment and sometimes exploitative working conditions (Wills et al. 2010).

Levels of education and qualifications are important correlates of employment. As the chapter on education clearly showed, there are differential educational outcomes and this will have a long-term and adverse effect on the labour market experience of some groups. Berthoud (1999) for example identified the lower levels of qualifications obtained by some minority ethnic groups in the UK as one factor influencing low rates of employment and earnings. However, it is more complex with education being another site where racialised assumptions based on colonial stereotyping and where relational othering takes place (Phoenix 2009). The effects are discriminatory leading to differential education outcomes, as Warren notes.

> While the experiences of these students can be highly individual, they belong to a larger formation of teacher attitudes and practices towards Black students...which are themselves part of a larger formation of Empire, nation and colonialism. The core problematic I deal with concern the instituting practices of particular oppressive racial settlements in schooling – the 'normal' processes of schooling that produce discriminatory effects. (Warren 2005: 246)

This stereotyping also transfers into the labour market, again affecting assumptions and perceptions about competencies and work attitudes.

Economic restructuring and deindustrialisation and the decline in manufacturing industries, the site for largely unskilled employment for migrants from Pakistan and Bangladesh, also have to be taken into account. Low-paid service sector jobs and an increase in part-time work have replaced manufacturing in areas of economic decline with higher-than-average rates of unemployment and a clustering of people from Bangladeshi and Pakistani heritage such as the old-mill towns in the north of England and Tower Hamlets in east London. Research by Ho and Henderson (1999) found significant variation by region in terms of employment and ethnicity. Their study focused on greater London and Manchester but they also stressed the regional intersections with discrimination, class, origins of the communities in question, local economic structures at the time of migration and settlement, and the uneven nature of educational provision. All of these factors will of course affect the skills and aspirations of localised ethnic groups and hence their competitiveness in the labour market.

While some groups are adversely affected by educational and regional disadvantages other groups are functionally over-qualified for their posts. The reasons are complex and diverse. In some cases language skills are not commensurate with skills and qualifications. In other instances qualifications are not recognised at their equivalent levels and as already noted racism and discrimination is prevalent in the labour market. Policy focuses on the practical interventions of human capital but these interventions do not address the deskilling of highly skilled workers nor do they address or analyse racism and systematic discrimination, especially among refugees where such an approach is largely absent from research and has not been addressed through government integration policy (Archer et al. 2005). This is in contrast to strategies to alleviate the under-achievement of some ethnic minority groups in the labour market where capacity building measures relating to individual human capital are combined with social-policy measures, notably equal opportunities, in recognising discrimination (Cabinet Office 2003; Home Office 2005).

Unemployment, under-employment and low pay is a problem not just for the individual but for society as a whole. Refugees experience these negative aspects of the labour market more acutely than others and have very low levels of employment (29%) and on an average earn only 79 per cent of that earned by ethnic minority groups as a whole (Bloch 2004). Part of the reason for refugee disadvantage is the consequence of being first generation migrants with fewer social networks and less access to or familiarity with statutory provisions. The recent dismantling of integration services for refugees (2011), notably the Refugee Integration and Employment Service (RIES) which was put in place only in 2008 to provide a personalised service to newly recognised refugees and those granted humanitarian protection on integration, employment and training, will further disadvantage this group. The service recognised the need to support refugees in wider areas of their lives, including housing, education and English language, in addition to employment and job-seeking advice and supported and treated individuals holistically rather than in compartments. Refugees are expected to use job centres for employment advice instead though research has shown that these are under-used by refugees and are not an effective mechanism for finding work. Informal networks, especially of friends, are a much more successful route to employment and explain why some refugees are located within the hidden economy in co-ethnic businesses associated with low pay and sometimes exploitative working conditions (Community Links and the Refugee Council 2011). These micro networks therefore perpetuate sectoral clustering in low-paid work with horizontal rather than vertical labour market mobility. All this contributes to under-achievement in the labour market and prevents refugee people from fulfilling their potential.

One of the most cited and researched examples of highly skilled refugees and migrants under-employed in the labour market are Zimbabweans who arrive in Britain, as noted earlier, with English language fluency (Kirk 2004) and higher-than-average UK qualifications. A survey of 292 Zimbabweans in Britain found that 19 per cent had a degree or post-graduate qualification on arrival and that the highest proportion (15%) had been teachers prior to migration (Doyle 2009). Once in Britain, Zimbabweans continued to acquire new qualifications and in a survey of 500, more than half had obtained a formal qualification since living in the UK (54%). Among those with a UK qualification, 69 per cent had obtained a degree or higher of which 22 per cent had a Masters degree and 6 per cent had a Doctorate (Bloch 2010). However, despite premigration skills and qualifications and high-level qualifications obtained in Britain there was clear evidence of under-employment.

While 49 Zimbabweans had been teachers before coming to Britain less than half were teachers in Britain. Under a quarter of the qualified teachers from Zimbabwe were working in the same profession in the UK and half of those had retrained in Britain and taken a degree, Masters or a professional qualification. Instead, former teachers were working well below their skills level in jobs that included carers and care assistants, factory and/or production operatives, domestics and waiters. Half of all respondents said that they had skills and experiences that they had been unable to use (Bloch 2010). When exploring the situation of Zimbabweans in Britain it is hard to ignore the need to address some employer discrimination, race relations and restrictive asylum policy. In the next section, the social-policy arena and it's intersections with employment will be examined.

Employment and social policy: inclusion or exclusion?

Employment has been used and associated with conflicting notions of and interventions around inclusion and exclusion. On the one hand, race relations and equality strategies are concerned with alleviating labour market inequalities while on the other hand, immigration controls are used as a mechanism for excluding and creating a division of labour on the basis of immigration status, where some workers experience exploitative working conditions. This section will first examine the recent inclusive components of employment and integration policies. Second, the ways in which employment is linked to exclusionary agendas will be examined particularly in relation to immigration status, citizenship and rights.

Under the previous New Labour government, refugee policy was both separate and different from the wider social-policy agenda that was concerned with social inclusion and poverty alleviation for disadvantaged groups, which included BME populations. What was formulated was two strands of policy with one concerned with cohesion and disadvantage and the other concerned with using work and employment as a key site for increasing social inclusion. Concerns over the long-term labour market disadvantages of some groups identified in The Cabinet Office's 2003 report *Ethnic Minorities and the Labour Market* resulted in The Ethnic Minority Employment Task Force. The report, like earlier research, had highlighted the differences between and within different groups and found that among those working, the comparatively low levels of income had a negative effect on a social and economic inclusion. They noted disadvantage in four main areas: employment/unemployment rates, earnings levels, occupational attainment and progression in the workplace, and levels of self-employment (Cabinet Office 2003). The report concluded that disadvantage was complex and even groups that were doing well, notably Indian and Chinese, were still not achieving at the levels their education and other characteristics would anticipate. The main facets of intervention to reduce the disadvantages experienced by some groups were focused in three main areas: improving employability, connecting minority groups with work and reducing barriers to the labour market, and the promotion of equal opportunities.

The first area concerned with improving employability was to concentrate on raising education levels and skills. The focus of this strand was very much on human capital, defined 'as the sum of skills, knowledge, experience and educational qualifications a person possesses' (Cabinet Office 2003: 27). The varying levels of achievements and educational outcomes by ethnic group, and also by gender were areas to address. While second generation, British-born ethnic minority groups have closed the gap in terms of qualifications, the Cabinet Office report noted with concern the ethnic and gender differences that characterise outcomes and the relatively large proportion of some second generation groups without any qualifications, more marked among Pakistani women where 25 per cent have no British qualifications. Even among those with qualifications there are disparities in terms of the levels of qualifications and this too adversely affects employability.

The second area of strategic intervention, connecting BME and migrant populations with work, was concerned with alleviating the specific barriers to work in deprived areas such as poor transportation and improving access and effectiveness of employment programmes. Minority ethnic groups are disproportionately located in deprived areas 'which are often characterised by factors that correlate with worklessness' (Cabinet Office 2003: 9). The disorders in the northern towns of Oldham, Bradford and Burney in the early 2000s demonstrated the lack of opportunities, discrimination and the prevalence of gendered inequalities. In fact, in the Cantle Report's analysis of employment, they noted that 'opportunities in some areas are lamentably poor' (Cantle 2001: 43). Part of the community cohesion strategy was in response to Cantle's observations about the 'depth of polarisation' around segregated communities living 'a series of parallel lives' such that improving employment outcomes becomes crucial to addressing marginalisation. The final area of intervention identified in the Cabinet Office report recognised the prevalence of discrimination in the workplace by ethnicity and recognised the need to address this. Promotion of equal opportunities in the workplace was an imperative and one way of trying to achieve this was through better advice and support to employers and by addressing indirect discrimination.

While for BME and migrant groups, as a whole, the strategies for change are diverse, for refugees the language used in the policy discourse is different. Instead of social inclusion, the concern is integration – and the path to integration is closely linked to the labour market with the development of individual human capital portrayed as the solution. Central to refugee integration policy has been the acquisition of skills to enhance employabil-ity. Such an approach ignores the other reasons for employment disadvan-tages as well as the deskilling experienced by refugees with language fluency and professional backgrounds, such as that experience by Zimbabweans, as noted earlier. Refugees occupy a disadvantaged position in the labour mar-ket in terms of employment levels, earning and self-employment.

The Home Office accepts that integration 'begins on day one' and main-tains that integration, 'in its fullest sense can take place only when a person has been granted refugee status so that they can make plans, including those for employment' (Home Office 2005: 14). For refugees to achieve their full potential, the Home Office (2005) focuses on English language skills and the attainment of employment commensurate with skills and ability and in so doing identifies two factors as being crucial, 'the ability to communicate effectively in English and gaining employment appropriate to their skills and ability'. Linked to the integration debates are the opportunities that employment can offer for refugees and other migrants, to make social con-tacts, learn and practice English – for those not fluent in English – and the chance of greater financial independence which links to self-esteem.

From a social-policy perspective, there have been strategies put in place to try and facilitate the integration of refugees and employment is always central to these policies. Included in this was the formation, in 2000, of the National Refugee Integration Forum (NRIF) with five subgroups, including one concerned with employment and training. The NRIF, which was dis-banded at the end of 2006, was tasked with identifying and recommending solutions to the issues faced by refugees. This was replaced by the Refugee Integration and Employment Service (RIES) in 2008 but funding ceased under the coalition government in 2011. Cutting services is likely to have an adverse affect on access to the labour market not least because of the necessity for an integrated approach, not one that deals separately with dif-ferent areas of need and support for refugees. Refugees will rely even more on informal networks especially of friends as a route to employment but these micro networks perpetuate sectoral clustering in low-paid work with horizontal rather than vertical labour market mobility.

Employment while depicted as a crucial component of cohesion and/ or integration and so a priority, ironically, is also the place where exclu-sion and separation are consciously and actively enforced. Access to the labour market is part of immigration policy and legislation but also used as a deterrent to migration and as a mechanism for separating people with different immigration statuses. For example, prior to 2002 asylum seekers could apply for permission to work but changes to the employment rights of asylum seekers in the summer of 2002 affected their labour market par-ticipation because permission to work is granted by the Home Office in exceptional circumstances, notably where asylum seekers have been waiting for a decision on their case for more than 12 months. The delay in accessing training and employment opportunities can result in a loss of skills, especially among professionals such as doctors (Stewart 2003) and has a 'scarring' affect which Clark and Drinkwater (2007) note in terms of reducing the likelihood of entering the labour market.

The situation has worsened as employers are fined for taking on workers without the correct documentation and this added layer of bureaucracy makes employers less likely to employ refugees because it means checking documents or risking penalties (Hurstfield et al. 2004). Moreover, the strategy of raiding businesses thought to be employing people without the correct documents has had a negative effect on employment opportunities but has also decreased wages for some forced migrants resulting in breaches of employment law and standards governing minimum wages (Bloch, Sigona and Zetter 2009). Undocumented migrants are the most vulnerable in the labour market because of their lack of status and as a consequence have to be cautious about where they work, how they find work and who they trust and so rely on micro social networks, often of other undocumented migrants. This group of migrant workers are on the margins of society earning less than other workers and are sometimes exposed to unregulated conditions of work that are in breach of basic health and safety. Accessing union representation or any rights becomes problematic due to their status and their need to remain out of the public gaze.

The migrant division of labour is very real, with undocumented migrants having to take what is metered out to them without complaint because they need to work and lack choices. Research with undocumented migrants shows that some are paid less than other workers for the same job or for jobs that entail more hours and harder work, because of their immigration status (Bloch, Sigona and Zetter 2009). Employers cannot be challenged because it is too risky because of their vulnerable status (McKay 2009). However, joined-up government does not exist when it comes to the employment experiences and labour market vulnerabilities of marginalised groups. Rights, wages, health and safety, so stringently adhered to and applied in theory, are in principle ignored for those without papers.

Returning to the arguments put forward by Castles at the start of this chapter what we have in place are policies designed to fail because labour markets need low-paid workers and so different policy agendas conflict in this arena. On the one hand employment is crucial to social cohesion, economic growth and individual well-being. Societies with labour markets divided along ethnic contours suggest racism, discrimination and institutionalised inequality, all features of fragmentation. On the other hand labour markets are used by governments as a tool to exclude and separate migrant workers and develop highly managed forms of migrant labour. Not only does legislation determine who is welcome as a worker and who is not, but it also facilitates an environment where migrant workers are demonised and seen to be creating social problems, to be adversely affecting labour market opportunities and community cohesion. As we saw in Chapter 3, work visas has been used to determine what kind of workers are welcome to fill the gaps in the economy.

Conclusion

This chapter has analysed the complex and multifaceted ways in which the labour market is a site for intersections between and within BME and migrant groups, one where there are contested and conflicting policy concerns and varied outcomes. It has also shown how complex divisions of labour based on ethnicity and immigration status, racism and discrimination have emerged, shaped and become entrenched in employment patterns. The chapter has emphasised the ways in which policy accentuates these outcomes. A key policy effect has been through immigration legislation and the shifts and changes in this according to both national and global contexts. For example we have seen in this chapter and Chapter 3 how there has been a continual refocusing of immigration legislation in order to manage migration more effectively and meet labour market needs and demands.

While it is difficult to generalise, the patterns of difference and disadvantage in terms of employment, unemployment, jobs, pay and progression are sufficiently evident and well-documented to conclude that the labour market perpetuates inequality between different minority and majority ethnic groups and that social policy contributes to this but is not solely responsible. In the changing labour market environment that is evident in the current period there is a need to understand the impact that transformations in employment patterns will have, particularly in terms of the wider contexts of globalised interdependencies and globalised transformations in migration and mobility of both labour and capital.

Part III
Policy Futures

Chapter 9

Changing Policy Agendas and Future Trends

The core issues covered in this book have addressed the new terms of political and policy debates about race and multiculture in the changing environment of contemporary British society. We have argued through an engagement with key policy arenas that we are now, at the beginning of the 21st century, at a conjuncture from which there is likely to be an intensification of debates about multiculture and social policy. With growing ethnic, cultural and religious diversities at the forefront of debates about a range of social and political agendas we are now at a point where the questions we have addressed in this book are likely to remain deeply contested in the decades to come. The backlash against multiculturalism in contemporary European societies that has been evident over the past decade or so is but one example of the highly contested nature of this arena (Lentin and Titley 2011; McGhee 2008; Meer 2010). In this context it is important that we engage in a meaningful public debate on these phenomena, a debate that both draws on existing research but also open up avenues for future research agendas to pursue.

It is with this wider objective in mind that we want to close this book by taking a look again at some of the central arguments that we have sought to develop and venture to look at some of the future trends that may help shape the dynamics of this ever-changing field. By their very nature these are reflections that are suggestive rather than conclusive, but they are founded on the substantive conceptual and empirical analysis to be found in Parts I and II of this volume. The first part of this chapter revisits a number of key themes and debates raised in Chapters 1 and 2 around the shifting political and policy terrains in which race and multiculture are embedded. The second part reviews the nature of the connections and relationalities between the different policy sites that Chapters 3 to 8 have examined in detail.

Reflecting back, thinking forward: the changing terrains of race and multiculture

In all of the previous chapters we have emphasised the necessity of history for framing the narratives of the policy agendas. Events and developments of the past are important in their own terms and they are crucial in enabling an understanding of the current political, social, cultural, economic and policy environments and discourses. The shifting boundaries of ethnic difference and cultural diversity are part of the debates that have taken place since the mid-1950s about the position of minority ethnic groups within the wider social relations of British society generally and the major English conurbations in particular. Such debates were shaped by multiple agendas and processes but they were also a product of the politicisation of questions about race around certain key arenas including the effective governance of multiculture, the maintenance of social order and the changing meanings of national identity and belonging. During the 1980s, for example, particular sites of public debate included such issues as the alienation of second generation young African-Caribbean men, policing of multicultural communities and concentrations of urban poverty in specific localities and communities (see Chapters 2 and 5). The focusing of attention on these issues was the outcome of the social and political transformations around questions about race and the formation of minority communities that took place during this period. They also reflected a refocusing on questions about the future of second and third generation children of migrants and their position in multicultural urban Britain.

These shifts were further accentuated by the question of urban unrest as a major social phenomenon, from the 1980s onwards. As Chapters 2 and 5 noted, the urban unrest that took place in 1980, 1981 and in 1985 became a particular focus of debate during the 1980s. And much of the public and media debate about the unrest in the 1980s was focused on questions about race and the role of the police, on criminality, and on the alienation of young black and other minority ethnic groups from the mainstream of British society. Lord Scarman's report on the Brixton riots of 1981 reflected in part this frame of analysis when he argued that the violence in Brixton was the result of a combination of factors including social exclusion, racism, racist policing and structural factors (Benyon 1984; Scarman 1981a; see also Chapters 1 and 2). Concerns about the future of the UK as a multicultural and increasingly diverse society were further accentuated in the late 1980s and 1990s by a number of developments that fed into both public and media discourses as well as the formation of policy agendas during this period. Although these are discussed in detail in Chapters 1 and 2 it is worth briefly reflecting on three of the key trends as they capture, and highlight, the changing spatial and social formations of race and multiculture in the last decade and the impact of these on policymaking and interventions, the themes at the heart of the book. These trends can be identified as: (i) new migration patterns and the re-emergence of new debates about immigration in the 1990s and 2000s; (ii) the emergence and politicisation of questions about ethnic segregation and community cohesion; (iii) the emergence of policy discourses about cultural difference, security and the threat of terrorism.

In the UK, as we have argued above and as Chapter 3 outlined in some detail, immigration has been intimately tied to questions about race since the beginning of the 20th century. Nevertheless, there was a perceived attempt during the 1970s and 1980s to halt primary migration and focus policies on the integration of minority communities already established in Britain. While political debates about immigration continued throughout this period it was to some extent presented as an issue that was under control. During the late 1990s and 2000s, however, this notion was questioned as new patterns of migration and refugee movement raised the profile of immigration within both political culture and civil society.

The tensions around the question of immigration became particularly evident during the period when New Labour was in power, from 1997 to 2010. As Chapter 2 notes, while the Blair administration promised radical action to promote greater equality of opportunity and an inclusive nation, it quickly became embroiled in the politics of controlling immigration and regulating the rights of asylum seekers once they had arrived in the UK. In practice, this policy paradox meant that over its 13 years in power the Labour Party was more preoccupied with questions about asylum and refuge rather than racial justice and the rights of minorities.

The second development that has shaped both thinking and policy in the past two decades is the issue of segregation and community cohesion and this is discussed in detail in Chapters 1 and 2. The disturbances led to the emergence of public worries about race and cultural difference that were expressed through various panicky pronouncements about the end of multi-culture, the death of multiculturalism and the prevalence of segregated communities. These responses marked a distinctive shift away from what can be seen as open and reflexive race thinking discussed above (see Chapter 1).

The third significant turning point in public debates, and addressed in detail in Chapters 1 and 5, can be traced to the aftermath of the 11 September 2001 terrorist attacks in the US. Taken together with the 2001 riots and the discourse around segregated communities, the events of 9/11 focused attention on the role of radical terrorist movements within migrant communities of Muslim origin. This was accentuated further by the terrorist attacks on the transport systems in London on 7 July 2005, as well as a number of either averted or failed terrorist attacks during the past decade. The issue of emerging forms of political mobilisation among radical Muslim organisations and movements had been widely discussed in relation to the Rushdie Affair in the early 1990s, with a particular focus on forms of fundamentalism and their associated religious and political ideologies (Asad 1990; Malik 2009). The impact of 2001 and 2005, however, pushed the issue much higher in the political agenda and it became a recurrent theme in popular media discourses about Muslim communities. The attacks in London in July 2005 also came to symbolise the material reality of the potential threat posed by radical political Islamists from 'within' British society.

In this context it is not surprising that the notion of Britain as a society being shaped by diversity has become both a contested issue as well as something that is taken for granted. In the aftermath of the 7/7, for example, there was intense debate about society and cultural difference. Some, including David Miliband, the then Minister of State for Communities and Local Government, talked of building community in a diverse society (Miliband 2006). In contrast, a growing number of commentators argued that there was a need to question the very idea of multiculturalism and to emphasise the need for common values, social responsibility and civic participation. This shift in policy agendas has been reinforced in the current climate by the growing concern that multiculture and cultural difference has been partly responsible for undermining the cohesiveness of social and national identities in British society (Husband and Alam 2011).

The cohesion agenda, along with the anxieties about how to effectively manage cultural difference, has continued to dominate policy thinking and circulate in the wider public sphere of race and multiculture debates in the 2000s. For example, it is worth noting that the Commission on Integration and Cohesion (2007) made a total of 57 recommendations across a range of areas for refining and extending the cohesion and integration agenda (see Chapter 2 for a fuller discussion). In the period since the publication of *Our Shared Future* we have seen, if anything, a strengthening of the shift towards cohesion, an emphasis on shared identities and integration. The policy focus on cohesion and integration can be understood, as we have argued in Chapters 1 and 2, as reflective of new migration patterns, new geographies of multiculture, super-diverse formations of multiculture including social, economic, generational differences within and between minority ethnic populations and communities. In short, while the UK, and England in particular, has become more multicultural and complex, political and policy discourses have increasingly been framed by the containment, management and securitisation of cultural difference. So while rights and cultural difference are to be respected the overwhelming emphasis is placed on responsibility, participation, social mobility, common values and social interaction.

A clear example of the influence of this shift can be found in the policies and agendas developed by the coalition government of David Cameron since 2010 (see for example Department for Communities and Local Government 2012; Chapter 2). Interestingly enough Cameron defines multiculturalism largely in a positive manner

> Multiculturalism, the notion that this country would be enriched by allowing each community to maintain and develop its own culture, lifestyle and value system, was founded on tolerance and fair play. (*The Times*, 7 February 2011)

While defining himself as in favour of this notion of multiculturalism he does not see it as succeeding in practice

> It has sadly, failed. Instead of new stream enriching the lifeblood of this country, all too often separate cultures have remained separate. Communities have become ghettos, mental and physical. (*The Times*, 7 February 2011).

In opposition to this failing multiculturalism he argued that 'we need less of the passive tolerance and much more active, muscular liberalism'. And while cohesion is still very much part of the current policy language it is increasingly used in conjunction with the return of the older term/concept of 'integration'. For example, in this same speech Cameron declared that the PVE as a counter-terrorism strategy (see Chapters 2 and 5) would be revised so as to make sure funding within the programme only went to those groups who encouraged integration and believed in universal human rights. The coalition government's remobilisation of integration alongside cohesion seems to reflect a desire to put a coalition marker on current government approaches to cultural difference but is an incremental rather than a radical policy shift. The palimpsest tendency of policymaking around race and cultural difference (see Chapter 2) is present in the current mobilisation of integration. With its resonances of the early assimilation strategies of the 1960s the coalition government's focus on integration continues the cohesion agenda's defensive demand on, and identification of, minority ethnic groups as responsible for social and cultural interaction and integration into an imagined majority culture.

Over the past two decades controversies about the rights to citizenship of migrants and refugees have provided us with an insight into some of the real political tensions about how we can define the boundaries of citizenship and belong in contemporary societies. The growing public interest about the role of fundamentalism among sections of the Muslim communities in a number of countries has given new life to debates about the issue of cultural differences and processes of integration. It is interesting to note in this regard that justifiable concerns about the rights of women are being exploited both to attack some minorities and to undermine a commitment to multiculturalism. By highlighting some of the most obvious limitations of multiculturalism and anti-racism in shaping policy change in this field, such controversies have done much to bring about a more critical debate about the role and impact of policies which are premised on notions such as multiculturalism (see Chapter 2). They have also highlighted the ever-changing terms of political and policy agendas about these issues and the fact that there is little agreement about what kind of strategies for change should be pursued.

The preoccupation in much of the literature in this field with issues of identity and the assertion of the relevance and importance of understanding the role of new ethnicities has not resolved the fundamental question of how to balance the quest for ever-more specific identities with the need to allow for broader and less-fixed cultural identities. Indeed, if anything, this quest for a politics of identity has helped to highlight one of the key dilemmas of liberal political thought. Yet what is quite clear is that the quest for more specific as opposed to universal identities is becoming more pronounced in the present political environment. The search for cohesive national and ethnic identities has become a prominent, if not dominant, feature of political debate within both majority and minority communities in a range of societies in the early 21st century.

In the present environment, as we have shown in such key areas as housing and employment, there is a clear possibility that new patterns of exclusion and segregation based not on – or at least not only on – ethnicity but on access to social goods (see below and Chapters 4, 6, 7 and 8 on housing, education, employment, health for example) and migration status (Chapter 3) could establish themselves and limit everyday interaction between socially and ethnically defined groups. Some of the experiences in Britain, alongside other European countries, echo the trends of the United States where the initiatives set in motion during the 1960s to reform race relations have had, at best, a partial impact on established patterns of racial inequality and have not stopped social divisions and entrenched differentiation (Brown et al. 2003; Smelser, Wilson and Mitchell 2001). Within the context of the UK, and other Northern European countries such as France and Denmark, there is, as we have argued throughout this book, the danger of institutionalising new forms of social, economic and cultural exclusion. This is not to say that such a development is at all inevitable, and there is evidence that minority communities themselves have been able to mobilise in various ways to challenge these trends and use political and civil society institutions to claim rights and strengthen their position both politically and in a wider context (Chimienti 2011; McNevin 2011).

In this shifting environment multiculture, belonging and exclusion are experienced in very complex ways in the communities formed as a result of changing patterns of migration and racialisation. Transnational economic, social and political relations have helped to create a multiplicity of migrant networks and communities that transcend received national boundaries. In this evolving environment the categories such as migrants and refugees are no longer an adequate way to describe the realities of movement and settlement in many parts of the globe. In many ways the idea of diaspora as an unending sojourn across different lands better captures the reality of transnational networks and communities than the language of immigration and assimilation. Multiple, circular and return migrations, rather than a single great journey from one sedentary space to another, have helped to transform transnational spaces by creating new forms of cultural and political identity. Such shifts are differentially experienced within communities and families that live their lives within a transnational context (Levitt 2009; Portes, Escobar and Arana 2008). Research on transnational families has also helped to highlight the complex forms of cultural and social interaction that can evolve within these transnational networks (Goulbourne et al. 2010; Zontini 2010).

The limits and legacies of old categories such as migrant and refugee were also raised in Chapter 1 when we addressed the question of the validity of using the category of race at the same time as recognising its fictive and social status. We noted that this same paradox has been at the centre of the post-race debates that have been a feature of some of the most recent theorising around race in the 2000s. The increasingly complex sets of migrations, belongings, mixings, ethnic identifications, settlements, globalisations and sets of events – terrorisms, the election of a black president in the United States, the emergence of anti-Muslim attitudes– which chapters in this book have all engaged with and highlight both the redundancy of race and its persistent force (Law 2010). While acknowledging the tension inherent in continuing to focus on what Gilroy (2000) describes as the absurd concept of race we suggested that the social dynamic of race, increasingly entangled with ethnicity, was necessary given that it persistently delivers exclusionary identifications, processes and outcomes. These have been particularly apparent and visible in the materiality of the policy fields that Chapters 3 to 8 have scrutinised. In each of these fields race is present as a 'not real' but 'real' category and as a constitutive marker of social division and inequality. In his examination of the linkages between constructions of race, the racialisation of social relations, anti-racism and the end of race Goldberg (2008: 1) worried as to what gets 'buried' and more, what gets 'buried alive'? He goes on to ask 'what residues of racist arrangement and subordination in social, economic, cultural, psychological, legal and political – linger unaddressed and repressed?' In this context it seems to us that it is important to connect the debates about the need to jettison the language and category of race (Miles and Brown 2003), with the debates about planetary humanism and transnational belongings (Gilroy 2000), with the debates about recognising the extent to which race is still an 'ordering mechanism' (Goldberg 2008: 2) in political and policy worlds and in the materiality of everyday lives. In many ways this book has attempted this combined project and has sought to inhabit a space in which race is both acknowledged as a fiction and as having a profound effect on social relations, as well as giving rise to profoundly unequal, damaging and exclusionary outcomes. We have suggested that the policy landscape particularly illuminates these strange tensions and, in the final stages of this book, it is this that we want to return to.

Intersections and multidimensionality: the double helix in the race, multiculture and policy relationship

As is evident from our discussions above (and in Chapter 1) we have sought in this book to look at multiculture and the social world and policies that make and shape this through a lens that looks 'beyond race'. By this we mean that we have argued that race and ethnicity are not the only causal factors in explaining and generating patterns of social inequality and exclusion. Social and economic status, locality and geography, education status, migration and residency status, religion, gender and age all intersect and interact with race and ethnicity. These are not even and symmetrical intersections and interactions; they are partial, unpredictable, contingent and evolving. However, there is always a relationship and a connection between one or more of these categories, between and within different ethnic groupings. We have repeatedly seen in the areas of health, housing, education, employment, migration and policing some of the ways in which there have been significant differences in the experiences and outcomes between and within diverse ethnic populations. As we saw in each of the policy arenas covered by Chapters 3 to 8 that social and economic factors can explain some of these distinctions but by no means completely or in straightforward ways. While also not foundational, social class and economic factors do need to be accommodated in explanations of current formations of multiculture and the inequalities in social resources and outcomes of particular populations. For example, while school trajectories tend to be better for better-off pupils the upward trend of educational achievement for Bengali pupils – amongst the most socially and economically deprived population group – has to be accounted for as do the significantly higher rates of fixed and permanent school exclusions of African-Caribbean boys, despite their average social and economic position. We have also argued that social and economic factors are themselves constituted in multidimensional ways and will be shaped by education status, locality, religion, age and gender.

Social and economic environments can be critical in explaining ethnic tensions and conflicts (see Chapter 5) but they can also be more marginal. For example, Cohesion for Integration and Cohesion Commission's (2007) *Our Shared Future* report found that even in the most deprived areas ethnic tensions were not necessarily apparent if the deprivation was not interpreted as being caused by cultural diversity. This was a finding echoed in the London Borough of Hackney's (2010) Cohesion Review which noted significant community resilience despite high levels of diversity, of social and economic deprivation and polarisation in the borough, tensions between super-diverse ethnic populations were very limited reflected in there being little to no support for the far right. These narratives of successful social cohesion in contexts of social and economic deprivation and significant ethnic diversity should not obscure the tensions that can and do erupt around cultural difference and competition over social goods (Valentine 2008), but they do disrupt any easy and linear equation between poverty, exclusion and ethnic conflict.

What this complex relationship also involves are the importance of place and geography and the identity and histories of locations in the processes of exclusion, racism and ethnic tensions. This has been a theme that has been threaded through the chapters of this book – not only that more places are becoming multicultural but also that those places that were already multicultural are now becoming even more so. In these dispersals and intensifications of multicultural settlement, places are being transformed and are incorporating newly diverse associations. This process is a highly dynamic one as we saw in Chapter 4 when we examined housing and looked in particular at the residential geographies of new migrants and at the affluent suburbanisation of established BME populations. What these new social and spatial formations of multiculture have demanded and generated are, as explored in each of the various policy sites in Chapters 3 to 8, various policy responses in which it is possible to identify both more nuanced interventions and understandings of diversity and difference *and* more punitive and exclusionary interventions. This contradictory policy narrative has been told in each of the chapters in Part II. For example, in Chapter 6 we noted some of the more progressive developments in health policy around sickle cell, haemoglobinopathies and Type 2 diabetes but these have taken place alongside the development of increasing restrictions on migrants' access to HIV related treatment and healthcare. Similarly, as Chapter 5 argued, despite the official recognition of institutional racism within policing processes and practices and the apparent willingness of forces such as the Metropolitan Police to address these, the ethnic breakdown of arrest and stop-and-search figures continue to be significant and of increasingly disproportionate rates for African-Caribbean men and some South Asian groups (Ministry of Justice 2010).

As well as detailing the ongoing contradictions between policies within the same policy field (and the lacuna that can feature between equality and multicultural policymaking and policy practices), what all the chapters in Part II consistently demonstrate is the strikingly high level of policy activity surrounding race and multiculture and social goods and resources. In other words, as we argued in Chapter 2, this is an intensely 'busy' and highly mediated policy space and, as this book had demonstrated, this level of policy activity and media engagement has shown no sign of reduction in the first decades of the 21st century. This is indicative of the highly political and turbulent nature of race and multiculture debates and their relationship to social goods and resources.

What is apparent in the various configurations of the race-multiculture-policy relationship are the ways in which social policy does not simply react and respond to the social world but also animates and drives it. In short, social policy interventions contribute to the ways in which the social world is publically described and perceived and materially experienced. It is in this context that it has been important to stress that policy does not just get 'done to' people but that groupings and collectivities are involved in, and impact on, policymaking and delivery. Some of this 'from below' policy shaping is driven through the aspirations, ambitions, creativities and social capacities within BME and migrant populations and some of it is driven and shaped by the differential needs, experiences and concerns of BME families, communities and populations in relation to health, housing, education, migration, employment and criminal justice. In the policy areas presented in Part II of this book it is possible to identify examples of sustained family and/ or community organised policy pressure that have led to policy development and intervention. This has amplified the ways in which it is possible to identify a constant crossing of the boundaries of the key policy fields that Chapters 3 to 8 each cover. From the perspective we have outlined in this book it is clear that migration, education, housing, health, employment and policing are not discrete and self-contained but influence and impact on each other. The relationality between social outcomes and race, ethnicity, class, religion, location, migration status, education status, age and gender has already been emphasised but it is also important to highlight the relationality of the policy fields themselves. We have argued that there are lines of connection between these policy fields. On the one hand, these can be interrupted and broken and are never completely closed but on the other, these connectivities can be entrenched. We have seen in the discussions across the chapters in this book that there are differential and continuing patterns between where populations live, the schools and universities they attend, the jobs they secure, the health problems and care they access and the nature of the criminal justice system they come into contact with. As well as the issues and concerns within individualised policy fields it is the connected collective outcomes and 'chains of jeopardy' that can operate to bind and then suture some BME and migrant populations into highly differential social worlds.

That said, our final concluding reminder is that the content of this book has sought to highlight the impossibility and inaccuracy of telling 'one story' about race and multiculture and social policy. In contemporary, super-diverse environments the increasing differences between black, minority ethnic and migrant populations and within majority ethnic populations demand a highly nuanced and sophisticated policy approach. Such an approach is all the more necessary if we are to move between acknowledging, prioritising and countering racism and ethnic inequalities and being able to reflect on the ways in which race and multiculture intersect with other lines of social division. In other words, in certain contexts and at certain moments, race and ethnicity will be *the* critical categories for understanding social relations and social practices and yet, in many others, race and ethnicity are likely to be much more relationally constituted. The ability to decipher and decode race and ethnicity in this way is perhaps the core challenge we face as the complexities of multiculture at the beginning of the 21st century are acknowledged and recognised.

Bibliography

Ahmad, W.I.U. (ed.) (1993) *'Race' and Health in Contemporary Britain*, Hemel Hempstead: Open University Press.

Ahmad, W.I.U. and Bradby, H. (2007) 'Locating Ethnicity and Health: Exploring Concepts and Contexts', *Sociology of Health & Illness*, 29, 6: 795–810.

Ahmed, S., Saleem, M., Modell, B. and Petrou, M. (2002) 'Screening Extended Families for Genetic Haemoglobin Disorders in Pakistan' *New England Journal of Medicine, 347: 1162–1168*

Aldridge, H., Parekh, A., MacInnes, T. and Kenway, P. (2011) *Monitoring Poverty and Social Exclusion 2011*, York: Joseph Rowntree Foundation.

Alexander, C.E. (2004) 'Imagining the Asian Gang: Ethnicity, Masculinity and Youth After "The Riots"', *Critical Social Policy*, 24, 4: 526–549.

Alexis, O. and Vydelingum, V. (2007) 'Experiences in the UK National Health Service: The Overseas Nurses' Workforce', *Health Policy*, 90: 320–328.

Allen, C. (2008) *Housing Market Renewal and Social Class*, London: Routledge.

Allen, C. (2011) 'Opposing Islamification or Promoting Islamophobia? Understanding the English Defence League', *Patterns of Prejudice*, 45, 4: 279–294.

Amin, A. (2002) 'Ethnicity and the Multicultural City', *Environment and Planning A*, 34, 6: 959–980.

Anionwu, E. (1993) 'Sickle Cell and Thalasaemia: Community Experiences and Official Responses', in Ahmad, W. (ed.) *'Race' and Health in Contemporary Britain*, Buckingham: Open University Press.

Anionwu, E. and Atkin, K. (2001) *The Politics of Sickle Cell and Thalassaemia*, Buckingham: Open University Press.

Arango, J. (2000) 'Explaining Migration: A Critical Review', *International Social Science Journal*, 65, 2: 283–296.

Archer, L., Hollingworth, S., Maylor, U., Sheibani, A. and Kowarzik, U. (2005) *Barriers to Employment for Refugees and Asylum Seekers in London*, London Institute for Policy Studies in Education, London Metropolitan University.

Asad, T. (1990) 'Multiculturalism and British Identity in the Wake of the Rushdie Affair', *Politics & Society*, 18, 4: 455–480.

Aspinall, P.J. (2009) 'The Future of Ethnicity Classifications', *Journal of Ethnic and Migration Studies*, 35, 9: 1417–1435.

Astin, F. and Atkin, K. (2010) *Ethnicity and Coronary Heart Disease: Making Sense of Risk and Improving Care*, London: Race for Health, Race Equality Foundation, pp. 1–7.

Audit Commission (2006) *Housing Market Renewal Annual Review 2005/06*, London: Audit Commission.

Back, L. (1996) *New Ethnicities and Urban Culture: Racisms and Multiculture in Young Lives* London: UCL Press.

Bagguley, P. and Hussain, Y. (2007) *The Role of Higher Education in Providing Opportunities for South Asian Women*, New York: Joseph Rowntre Foundation.

Balajaran, R. and Soni Raleigh, V. (1995) *Ethnicity and Health in England*, London: HMSO.

Ball, S.J. (2003) *Class Strategies and the Education Market: The Middle Class and Social Advantage*, London: Routledge Falmer.

Ball, S.J., Reay, D. and David, M. (2002) '"Ethnic Choosing": Minority Ethnic Students, Social Class and Higher Education Choice', *Race, Ethnicity and Education*, 5, 4: 333–357.

Ball, W. and Troyna, B. (1989) 'The Dawn of a New ERA? The Education Reform Act, "Race" and LEAs', *Educational Management Administration & Leadership*, 17, 1: 23–31.

Ballard, R. and Ballard, C. (1977) 'The Sikhs: The Development of South Asian Settlements in Britain', in Watson, J. (ed.) *Between Two Cultures: Migrants and Minorities in Britain*, Oxford: Blackwell.

Banton, M. (1973) *Police-Community Relations*, London: Collins.

Barot, M. and Jussab, K. (2012) 'Policing and fairness', in Sveinsson, K.P. (ed.) *Criminal Justice v. Racial Justice: Overrepresentation in the Criminal Justice System*, London Runnymede Trust.

Bauman, Z. (2011) 'Interview: Zygmunt Bauman on the UK Riots', *Social Europe Journal*, http://www.social-europe.eu/2011/08/interview-zygmunt-bauman-on-the-uk-riots/.

Beider, H. (2009) 'Guest Introduction: Rethinking Race and Housing', *Housing Studies*, 24, 4: 405–415.

Benezeval, M., Judge, K. and Whitehead, M. (eds) (1995) *Tackling Inequalities in Health: An Agenda for Action*, London: King's Fund.

Bennetto, J. (2009) *Police and Racism: What Has Been Achieved 10 Years after the Stephen Lawrence Inquiry Report?* London: Equality and Human Rights Commission.

Benyon, J. (ed.) (1984) *Scarman and After: Essays Reflecting on Lord Scarman's Report, the Riots, and their Aftermath*, First Edition, Oxford: Pergamon Press.

Benyon, J. and Solomos, J. (eds) (1987) *The Roots of Urban Unrest*, Oxford: Pergamon Press.

Benyon, J. and Solomos, J. (1988) 'The Simmering Cities-Urban Unrest During the Thatcher Years', *Parliamentary Affairs*, 41, 3: 402–422.

Bergesen, A. (1982) 'Race Riots of 1967: An Analysis of Police Violence in Detroit and Newark', *Journal of Black Studies*, 12, 3: 261–274.

Bernasconi, R. and Lott, T. (eds) (2000) *The Idea of Race*, Indianapolis: Hackett.

Berthoud, R. (1999) *Young Caribbean Men in the Labour Market: A Comparison with Other Ethnic Groups*, York: Joseph Rowntree Foundation.

Berthoud, R. (2000) 'Ethnic Employment Penalties in Britain', *Journal of Ethnic and Migration Studies*, 26, 3: 389–416.

Berthoud, R. and Blekesaune, M. (2007) *Persistent Employment Disadvantage*, London: Department for Work and Pensions.

Bhattacharyya, G., Ison, L. and Blair, M. (2003) *Minority Ethnic Attainment and Participation in Education and Training: The Evidence*, London: Department for Education and Skills.

Bird, J. (1996) *Black Students and Higher Education: Rhetorics and Realities*, Buckingham: Open University Press.

Birmingham City Council (2011) 'Ethnicity in Birmingham: Demographic Briefing 2011/02', http://www.birmingham.gov.uk.

Bjorgo, T. and Witte, R. (eds) (1993) *Racist Violence in Europe*, Basingstoke: Macmillan Press.

Bloch, A. (2000a) 'A New Era or More of the Same? Asylum Policy in the UK', *Journal of Refugee Studies*, 13, 1: 29–42.

Bloch, A. (2000b) 'Refugee Settlement in Britain: The Impact of Policy on Participation', *Journal of Ethnic and Migration Studies*, 26, 1: 75–88.

Bloch, A. (2002a) *The Migration and Settlement of Refugees in Britain*, Basingstoke: Palgrave Macmillan.

Bloch, A. (2002b) *Refugees, Opportunities and Barriers in Training and Employment*, Leeds: Department for Work and Pensions.

Bloch, A. (2004) *Making it Work: Refugee Employment in the UK*, London: Institute of Public Policy Research.

Bloch, A. (2008) 'Refugees in the UK Labour Market: The Contention Between Economic Integration and Policy-Led Labour Market Restriction', *Journal of Social Policy*, 37, 1: 21–36.

Bloch, A. (2010) 'The Social and Economic Lives of Zimbabweans in Britain: Realities and Longer Term Aspirations', in Crush, J. and Tervera, D. (eds) *Zimbabweans Exodus: Crisis, Migration, Survival*, Kingston and Cape Town: Southern Africa Migration Programme.

Bloch, A. (2012) 'Migration and Asylum' in Alcock, P., May, M. and Wright, S. (eds) *The Student's Companion to Social Policy*, Oxford: Wiley-Blackwell.

Bloch, A. and Schuster, L. (2005) 'At the Extremes of Exclusion: Deportation, Detention and Dispersal', *Ethnic and Racial Studies*, 28, 3: 491–512.

Bloch, A., Sigona, N. and Zetter, R. (2009) *No Right to Dream: The Social and Economic Lives of Young Undocumented Migrants in Britain*, London: Paul Hamlyn Foundation.

Blunkett, D. (2002) 'Integration with Diversity: Globalisation and the Renewal of Democracy and Civil Society', in Griffith, P. and Leonard, M. (eds) *Reclaiming Britishness*, London: The Foreign Policy Centre.

Bochel, C. and Bochel, H.M. (2004) *The UK Social Policy Process*, Basingstoke: Palgrave Macmillan.

Boddy, M. and Fudge, C. (eds) (1984) *Local Socialism? Labour Councils and New Left Alternatives*, London: Macmillan.

Bolton, P. and Gillies, C. (2009) *Faith Schools: Admissions and Performance*, London: London House of Commons Standard Note.

Bonnett, A. (2000) *Anti-racism*, London: Routledge.

Boswell, C. (2001) *Spreading the Costs of Asylum Seekers: A Critical Assessment of Dispersal Policies in Germany and the UK*, London: Anglo-German Foundation.

Bowling, B. (1998) *Violent Racism: Victimization, Policing and Social Context*, Oxford: Clarendon Press.

Bowling, B. and Phillips, C. (2002) *Racism, Crime and Justice*, London: Longman.

Brah, A. (1996) *Cartographies of Diaspora: Contesting Identities*, London: Routledge.

Broecke, S. and Nicholls, T. (2007) *Ethnicity and Degree Attainment*, London: Department for Education and Skills.

Brown, C. (1984) *Black and White Britain: The Third PSI Survey*, London: Heinemann.

Brown, M.K., Carnoy, M., Currie, E., Duster, T., Oppenheimer, D.B., Shultz, M.M. and Wellman, D. (2003) *Whitewashing Race: The Myth of a Color-Blind Society*, Berkeley: University of California Press.

Bundey, S., Alam, H. and Kaur, A. (1991) 'Why Do UK-born Pakistani Babies have High Perinatal and Neonatal Mortality Rates?' *Paediatric and Perinatal Epidemology*, 5: 101–114.

Burch, M. and Wood, B. (1990) *Public Policy in Britain*, Oxford: Blackwell.

Burgess, S. and Wilson, D. (2005) 'Ethnic Segregation in England's Schools', *Transactions of the Institute of British Geographers*, 30, 1: 20–36.

Burnley Task Force (2001) *Report*, Burnley: Task Force.

Butler, P. (2001) 'Key Points of the Race Relations Amendment Act Implementation Report', *The Guardian*, 22 February 2011.

Butler, T. and Hamnett, C. (2011) *Ethnicity, Class and Aspiration: Understanding London's New East End*, Bristol: Policy Press.

Butler, T. and Lees, L. (2006) Super-gentrification in Barnsbury, London: globalization and gentrifying global elites at the neighbourhood level, *Transactions of the Institute of British Geographers*, 31, 4: 467–487

Butler, T. and Robson, G. (2003a) *London Calling: The Middle Classes and the Remaking of Inner London*, Oxford: Berg.

Butler, T. and Robson, G. (2003b) 'Plotting the Middle Classes: Gentrification and Circuits of Education in London', *Housing Studies*, 18, 1: 5–28.

Byrne, B. (2006) *White Lives: The Interplay of 'Race', Class and Gender in Everyday Life*, London: Routledge.

Cabinet Office (2003) *Ethnic Minorities and the Labour Market: Final Report*, London: Cabinet Office.

Cameron, D. (2011) 'PMs Speech to Munich Security Conference', *The Guardian*, 5 February 2011.

Cantle, T. (2001) *Community Cohesion: A Report on the Independent Review*, London: Home Office.

Cantle, T. (2008) *Community Cohesion: A New Framework for Race and Diversity*, Revised and updated Edition Basingstoke Palgrave Macmillan.

Carby, H.V. (1982) 'Schooling in Babylon' in Studies', in Centre for Contemporary Cultural Studies *The Empire Strikes Back: Race and Racism in 70s Britain*, London: Hutchinson.

Care Quality Commission (2009) *Count Me in 2009. Results of the 2009 National Census of Inpatients in Mental Health and Learning Disability Services in England and Wales*, London: Care Quality Control.

Care Quality Commission (2010) *Count Me in 2010. Results of the 2009 National Census of Inpatients in Mental Health and Learning Disability Services in England and Wales*, London: Care Quality Control.

Carling, A. (2008) 'The Curious Case of the Mis-claimed Myth Claims: Ethnic Segregation, Polarisation and the Future of Bradford', *Urban Studies*, 45, 3: 553–589.

Cashmore, E. and Troyna, B. (eds) (1982) *Black Youth in Crisis*, London: Allen & Unwin.

Castles, S. (2000) 'International Migration at the Beginning of the Twenty-First Century: Global Trends and Issues', *International Social Science Journal*, LII, 165: 269–281.

Castles, S. (2004) 'Why Migration Policies Fail', *Ethnic and Racial Studies*, 27, 2: 205–227.

Castles, S. and Miller, M.J. (2009) *The Age of Migration: International Population Movements in the Modern World*, Fourth Edition Basingstoke: Palgrave Macmillan.

Cathcart, B. (1999) *The Case of Stephen Lawrence*, London: Viking.

Chan, P.C.W. (2006) 'The Protection of Refugees and Internally Displaced Persons: "Non-Refoulement" Under Customary International Law?' *International Journal of Human Rights*, 10, 3: 231–239.

Cheong, P.H., Edwards, R., Goulbourne, H. and Solomos, J. (2007) 'Immigration, Social Cohesion and Social Capital: A Critical Review', *Critical Social Policy*, 27, 1: 24–49.

Children's Society (2012) *Highlighting the Gap Between Asylum Support and Mainstream Benefits*, London: The Children's Society.

Chimienti, M. (2011) 'Mobilization of Irregular Migrants in Europe: A Comparative Analysis', *Ethnic and Racial Studies*, 34, 8: 1338–1356.

Clark, K. and Drinkwater, S. (2007) *Ethnic Minorities in the Labour Market: Dynamics and Diversity*, York: Joseph Rowntree Foundation.

Clarke, J., Critcher, C., Jefferson, T. and Lambert, J.R. (1974) 'The Selection of Evidence and the Avoidance of Racialism: A Critique of the Parliamentaty Select Committee on Race Relations and Immigration', *New Community*, III, 3: 172–192.

Clayton, J. (2009) 'Thinking Spatially: Towards an Everyday Understanding of Inter-ethnic Relations', *Social and Cultural Geography*, 10, 4: 481–498.

Coard, B. (1971) *How the West Indian Child is Made Educationally Subnormal in the British School System: The Scandal of the Black Child in Schools in Britain*, London: New Beacon for the Caribbean Education and Community Workers' Association.

Cohen, R. (1994) *Frontiers of Identity: The British and the Others*, London: Longman.

Cole, J. and Flint, J. (2006) *Demolition, Relocation and Affordable Rehousing: Lessons from the Housing Renewal Pathfinder Programme*, York: Joseph Rowntree Foundation.

Collins, J. (2010) 'Sydney's Cronulla Riots: The Context and Implications', in Noble, G. (ed.) *Lines in the Sand: The Cronulla Riots, Multiculturalism and National Belonging*, Sydney: Sydney Institute of Criminology.

Collins, R. (2008) *Violence: A Micro-Sociological Theory*, Princeton: Princeton University Press.

Commission for Racial Equality (1984) *Annual Report 1983*, London: Commission for Racial Equality.

Commission for Racial Equality (1985) *Annual Report 1984*, London: Commission for Racial Equality.

Commission for Racial Equality (2006) *Employment and Ethnicity, Fact File 1*, London: Commission for Racial Equality.

Commission on Integration and Cohesion (2007) *Our Shared Future*, London: Commission on Integration and Cohesion.

Commission on Integration and Cohesion (2007a) *Our Interim Statement*, London: Commission on Integration and Cohesion

Community Links and the Refugee Council (2011) *Understanding the Informal Economic Activity of Refugees in London*, London: Community Links and Refugee Council.

Connell, J. (2010) *Migration and the Globalisation of Health Care: The Health Worker Exodus*, Cheltenham: Edward Elgar.

Connor, H., Tyers, C., Davis, S., Tackey, N.D. and Modood, T. (2003) *Minority Ethnic Students in Higher Education: Interim Report*, London: Department for Education and Skills.

Connor, H., Tyers, C., Modood, T. and Hillage, J. (2004) *Why the Difference? A Closer Look at Higher Education Minority Ethnic Students and Graduates*, London: Department for Education and Skills.

Cope, R. (1989) 'The Compulsory Detention of Afro-Caribbeans Under the Mental Health Act', *New Community*, 15, 3: 343–56.

Corden, A. and Sainsbury, R. (2006) 'Exploring "Quality": Research Participants' Perspectives on Verbatim Quotations', *International Journal of Social Research Methodology*, 9, 2: 97–110.

Cottle, S. (2004) *The Racist Murder of Stephen Lawrence: Media Performance and Public Transformation*, Westport, Conn.: Praeger.

Critcher, C., Parker, M. and Sondhi, R. (1975) *Race in the Provincial Press: A Case Study of Five West Midlands Newspapers*, Birmingham: University of Birmingham.

Cuthill, V. (2010) *Global Welcome? Migrant Workers, Service Cultures and Tourist Places*, Paper presented to the ESRC Mobilities, Migrations, Service Work and Place End of Project Workshop, Lancaster University.

Dabydeen, D. (1985) *Hogarth's Blacks: Images of Blacks in Eighteenth Century English Art*, Kingston-upon-Thames: Dangaroo.

Dale, A., Fieldhouse, E., Shaheen, N. and Kalra, V.S. (2002) 'The Labour Market Prospects for Pakistani and Bangladeshi Women', *Work, Employment and Society*, 16, 1: 5–25.

Daniel, W.W. (1968) *Racial Discrimination in Britain*, London: Penguin.

Darr, A. and Modell, B. (1988) 'The Frequency of Consanguineous Marriage among British Pakistanis', *Journal of Medical Genetics*, 25: 186–190.

Davey Smith, G., Barlety, M. and Blane, D. (1990) 'The Black Report on Socio-economic Inequalities in Health 10 Years On', *British Medical Journal*, 1, 301: 373–377.

Denham, J. (2001) *Building Cohesive Communities: A Report of the Ministerial Group on Public Order and Community Cohesion*, London: Home Office.

Department for Children, Schools and Families (2007) *Guidance on the Duty to Promote Community Cohesion*, London: Department for Children, Schools and Families.

Department for Communities and Local Government (2008) *Preventing Violent Extremism: Next Steps for Communities*, London: Department for Communities and Local Government.

Department for Communities and Local Government (2010) *English Housing Survey Household Report 2008–09*, London: Department for Communities and Local Government.

Department for Communities and Local Government (2012) *Creating the Conditions for Integration*, London: Department for Communities and Local Government.

Department for Education (2010a) *Statistical First Release GCSE and Equivalent Attainment by Pupil Characteristics in England 2009/10*, London: Department for Education.

Department for Education (2010b) *Statistical First Release Permanent and Fixed Period Exclusions in Schools in England 2009/10*, London: Department for Education.

Department for Education (2010c) *Voluntary and Faith Schools* London: Department for Education.

Department for Education (2012) *Academies Annual Report 2010/11*, London: Department for Education.

Department of Education and Science (2005) *Ethnicity and Education: The Evidence on Minority Ethnic Pupils*, London: Department of Education and Science.

Department of Health (2003) *Inside Out: Improving Mental Health Services for Black and Minority Ethnic Communities in England*, London: Department of Health.

Department of Health (2005) *Delivering Race Equality in Mental Health Care: An Action Plan for Reform Inside and Outside Services and the Government's Response to the Independent Inquiry on the Death of David Bennett*, London: Department of Health.

Department of Health (2009) *Delivering Race Equality in Mental Health Care: A Review*, London: Department of Health.

Diabetes in the UK (2010) *Key Statistics on Diabetes Report*, London: Diabetes in the UK

Dodds, C., Hickson, F., Weatherburn, P., Reid, D., Hammond, G., Jessop, C. and Adegbite, G. (2008) *BASS Line Survey: Assessing the Sexual and HIV Prevention Needs of African People in England*, London: Sigma Research.

Doyal, L., Hunt, G. and Mellor, J. (1981) 'Your Life in their Hands: Migrant Workers in the National Health Service', *Critical Social Policy*, 1, 2: 54–71.

Doyle, L. (2009) *'I Hate Being Idle': Wasted Skills and Enforced Dependence among Zimbabwean Asylum Seekers in the UK*, London: Refugee Council and Zimbabwean Association.

Drake, R.F. (2001) *The Principles of Social Policy*, Basingstoke: Palgrave.

Dwyer, C. and Bressey, C. (eds) (2008) *New Geographies of Race and Racism*, Aldershot: Ashgate.

Dwyer, C. and Parutis, V. (2012) 'Faith in the System'? State Funded Faith Schools and Contested Geographies of Identity, Integration and Citizenship', *Transactions of the Institute of British Geographers*, doi:10.1111/j.1475-5661.2012.00518.

Dyer, S., McDowell, L. and Batnitzky, A. (2008) 'Emotional Labour/Body Work: The Caring Labours of Migrants in the UK's National Health Service', *Geoforum*, 39: 2030–2038.

Dyson, S.M. (2005) *Ethnicity and Antenatal Screening for Sickle Cell and Thalassaemia*, Oxford: Elsevier/Churchill Livingstone.

Editorial (2011) 'Tackle the Enemy Within' *The Sun*, 8 August 2011.

Equalities and Human Rights Commission (2012) *Equality Act*, London: Equalities and Human Rights Commission.

Equality Challenge Unit (2010) *Equality in Higher Education: Statistical Report 2010*, London: Equality Challenge Unit.

Erel, U. (2011) 'Complex Belongings: Racialization and Migration in a Small English City', *Ethnic and Racial Studies*, 34, 12: 2048–2068.

Esmail, A. and Etherington, S. (1997) 'Asian Doctors are Still Discriminated Against', *British Medical Journal*, 314: 618.

Esping-Andersen, G. (1990) *The Three Worlds of Welfare Capitalism*, Cambridge: Polity.

Ettlinger, N. (2009) 'Surmounting City Silences: Knowledge Creation and the Design of Urban Democracy in the Everyday Economy', *International Journal of Urban and Regional Studies*, 33, 1: 217–30.

Fenton, S. (2003) *Ethnicity*, Cambridge: Polity.

Fielding, A., Charlton, C., Kounali, D. and Leckie, G. (2008) *Degree Attainment, Ethnicity and Gender: Interactions and the Modification of Effects – A Quantitative Analysis*, York: Higher Education Academy.

Finney, N. and Simpson, L. (2009) *'Sleepwalking to Segregation?' Challenging Myths about Race and Migration*, Bristol: Policy Press.

Flynn, D. (2005) 'New Borders, New Management: The Dilemmas of Modern Immigration Policies', *Ethnic and Racial Studies*, 28, 3: 463–490.

Fogelson, R.M. (1971) *Violence and Protest: A Study of Riots and Ghettos*, New York: Anchor Books.

Forrest, R. and Kearns, A. (2000) *Social Cohesion, Social Capital and the Neighbourhood*, ESRC Cities Programme Neighbourhoods Colloquium, Liverpool.

Forrest, R. and Kearns, A. (2001) 'Social Cohesion, Social Capital and the Neighbourhood', *Urban Studies*, 38, 12: 2125–2143.

Fortier, A.M. (2007) *Multicultural Horizons: Diversity and the Limits of the Civil Nation*, London: Routledge.

Fryer, P. (1984) *Staying Power: The History of Black People in Britain*, London: Pluto Press.

Gaffney, J. (1987) *Interpretations of Violence: The Handsworth Riots of 1985*, Coventry: Centre for Research in Ethnic Relations.

Gartner, L.P. (1973) *The Jewish Immigrant in England 1870–1914*, London: Simon Publications.

Gidley, B. (2013) 'Landscapes of Belonging, Portraits of Life: Researching Everyday Multiculture in an Inner City Estate', *Identities*.

Gifford, L. (1986) *The Broadwater Farm Inquiry*, London: Karia Press.

Gilbert, A. and Koser, K. (2006) 'Coming to the UK: What Do Asylum Seekers Know about the UK before Arrival?' *Journal of Ethnic and Migration Studies*, 32, 7: 1209–1225.

Gillborn, D. (2008) *Racism and Education: Coincidence or Conspiracy?* London: Routledge.

Gillborn, D. and Gipps, C. (1996) *Recent Research on the Achievements of Ethnic Minority Pupils*, London: Her Majesty's Stationery Office.

Gillborn, D. and Rollock, N. (2009) 'Education', in Bloch, A. and Solomos, J. (eds) *Race and Ethnicity in the 21st Century*, Basingstoke: Palgrave Macmillan.

Gilman, S.L. (1985) *Difference and Pathology: Stereotypes of Sexuality, Race and Madness*, Ithaca: Cornell University Press.

Gilroy, P. (1987) *There Ain't No Black in the Union Jack: The Cultural Politics of Race and Nation*, London: Hutchinson.

Gilroy, P. (1990) 'The End of Anti-Racism', in Ball, W. and Solomos, J. (eds) *Race and Local Politics*, Basingstoke: Macmillan.

Gilroy, P. (2000) *Between Camps: Nations, Cultures and the Allure of Race*, London: Allen Lane.

Gilroy, P. (2004) *After Empire: Melancholia or Convivial Culture?* London: Routledge.

Gish, O. (1971) *Doctor Migration and World Health*, London: Bell.

Goldberg, D.T. (2002) *The Racial State*, Oxford: Blackwell.

Goldberg, D.T. (2008) *The Threat of Race: Reflections on Racial Neoliberalism*, Malden, MA: Wiley-Blackwell.

Goldberg, D.T. (2010) 'Call and Response', *Patterns of Prejudice*, 44, 1: 89–106.

Gordon, P. (1987) 'Inquiring into the "Riots": A Review of Reports on the 1985 Urban Disorders', *Sage Race Relations Abstracts*, 12, 3: 4–22.

Goulbourne, H. (1998) *Race Relations in Britain since 1945*, Basingstoke: Palgrave Macmillan.

Goulbourne, H., Reynolds, T., Solomos, J. and Zontini, E. (2010) *Transnational Families: Ethnicities, Identities and Social Capital*, London: Routledge.

Gray, R., Headley, J., Kurinczuk, J., Brocklehurst, P. and Hollowell, J. (2009) *Inequalities in Infant Mortality Project Briefing Paper 3. Towards an Understanding of Variations in Infant Mortality Rates Between Different Ethnic Groups in England and Wales*, Oxford: National Perinatal Epidemiology Unit.

Hall, S. (1967) *The Young Englanders*, London: National Committee for Commonwealth Immigrants.

Hall, S. (2000) 'Conclusion: The Multi-cultural Question', in Hesse, B. (ed.) *Un/settled Multiculturalisms: Diasporas, Entanglements, Transruptions*, London: Zed Books.

Hall, S. (2012) *City, Street and the Citizen: The Measure of the Ordinary*, London: Routledge.

Hall, S., Critcher, C., Jefferson, T., Clarke, J. and Roberts, B. (1978) *Policing the Crisis: Mugging, the State and Law and Order*, Basingstoke: Macmillan.

Hansen, R. (2007) 'Diversity, Integration and the Turn from Multiculturalism in the United Kingdom', in Banting, K., Courchene, T.J. and Seidle, F.L. (eds) *Belonging? Diversity, Recognition and Shared Citizenship in Canada*, Montreal: Institute for Research on Public Policy.

Harries, B., Richardson, L. and Soteri-Proctor, A. (2008) *Housing Aspirations for a New Generation: Perspectives from White and South Asian British Women*, Coventry: Chartered Institute of Housing.

Harris, F.R. and Wilkins, R.W. (1988) *Quiet Riots: Race and Poverty in the United States*, New York: Pantheon Books.

Harrison, M. (1995) *Housing, 'Race', Social Policy and Empowerment*, Aldershot: Avebury.

Hayes, D. (2002) 'From Aliens to Asylum Seekers: A History of Immigration Controls and Welfare in Britain', in Cohen, S., Humphries, B. and Mynott, E. (eds) *From Immigration Controls to Welfare Controls*, London: Routledge.

Health Protection Agency (2008) *HIV in the UK 2008 Report*, London: Health Protection Agency.

Heath, A. and Cheung, S. (eds) (2007) *Unequal Chances: Ethnic Minorities in Western Labour Markets*, Oxford: Oxford University Press.

Heath, A. and Cheung, S.Y. (2006) *Ethnic Penalties in the Labour Market: Employers and Discrimination*, London: Department for Work and Pensions.

Henderson, J. and Karn, V. (1987) *Race, Class and State Housing: Inequality and the Allocation of Public Housing in Britain*, Gower: Aldershot.

Henry, L. (2007) 'Institutionalised Disadvantage: Older Ghanian Nurses' and Midwives' Reflections on Career Progression and Stagnation in the NHS', *Journal of Clinical Nursing*, 16: 2196–2203.

Hesse, B., Rai, D.K., Bennett, C. and McGilchrist, P. (1992) *Beneath the Surface: Racial Harassment*, Aldershot: Avebury.

Hewitt, R. (2005) *White Backlash and the Politics of Multiculturalism*, Cambridge: Cambridge University Press.

Hickling, F. (1991) 'Psychiatric Hospital Admission Rates in Jamaica', *British Journal of Psychiatry*, 159: 817–821.

Hickman, M.J., Cowley, H. and Mai, N. (2008) *Immigration and Social Cohesion in the UK: The Rythms and Realities of Everyday Life*, York: Joseph Rowntree Foundation.

Hilditch, M. (2006) 'Regulator Slams Pathfinder for Failing its Communities', *Inside Housing,*, http://www.insidehousing.co.uk 15 December 2006.

Ho, S.Y. and Henderson, J. (1999) 'Locality and the Variability of Ethnic Employment in Britain', *Journal of Ethnic and Migration Studies*, 25, 2: 323–33.

Hobbiss, A. (2006) *Background Literature on the Public Health Aspects of Infant Mortality*, Bradford: Bradford NHS PCT.

Holland, K. and Hogg, C. (2001) *Cultural Awareness in Nursing and Health Care*, London: Arnold.

Hollingworth, S. and Williams, K. (2010) 'Social Mixing or Social Reproduction?: The White Middle Classes in London Comprehensive Schools', *Space and Polity*, 14, 1: 47–64.

Holmes, C. (1988) *John Bull's Island: Immigration and British Society 1871–1971*, Basingstoke: Macmillan.

Holmes, C. (1991) *A Tolerant Country: Immigrants Refugees and Minorities in Britain*, London: Faber.

Home Office (2000) *Asylum Statistics, United Kingdom, 1999*, London: Home Office.

Home Office (2001) *Building Cohesive Communities: A Report of the Ministerial Group on Public Order and Community Cohesion*, London: Home Office.

Home Office (2005) *Integration Matters: A National Strategy for Refugee Integration*, London: Home Office.

Home Office (2011) *Prevent Strategy*, London: Home Office.

House of Commons (1995) *Hansard*, London: House of Commons.

House of Commons Communities and Local Government Committee (2010) *Preventing Violent Extremism, Sixth Report of Session 2009–10*, London: House of Commons.

House of Commons Home Affairs Committee (2011) *New Landscapes of Policing*, London: The Stationery Office.

Hudson, M., Phillips, J., Ray, K. and Barnes, H. (2007) *Social Cohesion in Diverse Communities*, York: Joseph Rowntree Foundation.

Humphry, D. and John, G. (1972) *Police Power and Black People*, London: Panther.

Hurstfield, J., Pearson, R., Hooker, H., Ritchie, H. and Sinclair, A. (2004) *Employing Refugees: Some Organisations' Experiences*, Brighton: Institute for Employment Studies.

Husband, C. and Alam, Y. (2011) *Social Cohesion and Counter-Terrorism*, Bristol: Policy Press.

Hussain, Y. and Bagguley, P. (2005) 'Citizenship, Ethnicity and Identity: British Pakistanis after the 2001 "Riots"', *Sociology*, 39, 3: 407–25.

Huysmans, J. (2009) 'Conclusion: Insecurity and the Everyday', in Noxolo, P. and Huysmans, J. (eds) *Community, Citizenship and the 'War on Terror': Security and Insecurity*, Basingstoke: Macmillan.

Hynes, P. and Sales, R. (2010) 'New Communities: Asylum Seekers and Dispersal', in Bloch, A. and Solomos, J. (eds) *Race and Ethnicity in the 21st Century*, Basingstoke: Palgrave Macmillan.

Illich, I. (1975) *Medical Nemesis*, London: Calder and Boyars.

Jacobs, S., Owen, J., Sergeant, P. and Schostak, J. (2007) *Ethnicity and Gender in Degree Attainment: An Extensive Survey of Views and Activities in English HEIs*, York: Higher Education Academy.

Jenkins, R. (2008) *Rethinking Ethnicity*, Second Edition, Thousand Oaks: Sage.

Jesson, D. (2009) *Strong Schools for Strong Communities: Reviewing the Impact of Church of England Schools in Promoting Community Cohesion*, London: Church of England Archbishops Education Division.

John, G. (1970) *Race in the Inner City: A Report from Handsworth*, London: Runnymede Trust.

John, G. and Humphry, D. (1972) *Because They're Black*, Harmondsworth: Penguin.

John, P., Margetts, H., Rowland, D. and Weir, S. (2006) *The BNP: The Roots of its Appeal*, Essex: Democratic Audit and Human Rights Centre.

Johnson, M., Biggerstaff, D., Clay, D., Collins, G., Gumbar, A., Hamilton, M., Jones, K. and Szczepura, A. (2004) *'Racial' and Ethnic Inequalities in Health: A Critical Review of the Evidence*, Draft report to the Home Office, Coventry: Centre for Evidence in Ethnicity Health and Diversity.

Johnson, M.R.D. (2006) 'Ethnicity' in Killoran, A., Swann, C. and Kelly, M. (eds) *Public Health Evidence: Tackling Health Inequalities*, Oxford: Oxford University Press.

Johnston, R., Poulsen, M. and Forrest, J. (2010) 'Moving on from Indices, Refocusing on Mix: On Measuring and Understanding Ethnic Patterns of Residential Segregation', *Journal of Ethnic and Migration Studies*, 36, 4: 697–706.

Jones, A. (2009) *Monitoring the Ethnicity of Housing Service Users: Forty Years of Progress?* London: Race Equality Foundation Briefing Paper.

Jones, C. (1977) *Immigration and Social Policy in Britain*, London: Tavistock.

Jones, M. and Tracy, I. (2010) *Ethnic Minority Customers' Experiences of Claiming Disability Benefits*, London: Department for Work and Pensions.

Joshua, H. and Wallace, T. (1983) *To Ride the Storm: The 1980 Bristol 'Riot' and the State*, London: Heinemann.

Kangasniemi, M., Winters, L. and Commander, S. (2007) 'Is the Mmedical Brain Drain Beneficial? Evidence from Overseas Doctors in the UK', *Social Science and Medicine*, 65: 915–923.

Karlsen, S. (2004) '"Black Like Beckham?" Moving Beyond Definitions of Ethnicity Based on Skin Colour and Ancestry', *Ethnicity & Health*, 9, 2: 107–137.

Karlsen, S. and Nazroo, J.Y. (2002) 'Agency and Structure: The Impact of Ethnic Identity and Racism on the Health of Ethnic Minority People', *Sociology of Health & Illness*, 24, 1: 1–20.

Karlsen, S., Nazroo, J.Y., McKensie, K., Bhui, K. and Weich, S. (2005) 'Racism, Psychosis and Common Mental Disorder among Ethnic Minority Groups in England' *Psychological Medicine*, 35: 1795–1803

Kay, D. and Miles, R. (1988) 'Refugees or Migrant Workers? The Case of the European Volunteer Workers in Britain', *Journal of Refugee Studies*, 1, 3/4: 214–236.

Kay, D. and Miles, R. (1992) *Refugees or Migrant Workers?: European Volunteer Workers in Britain, 1946–1951*, London: Routledge.

Keenan, J. (2008) *Sickle Cell and Thalassaemia in Sheffield: Final Report*, Sheffield: Department of Geography, University of Sheffield.

Keith, M. (1993) *Race, Riots and Policing: Lore and Disorder in Multi-racist Society*, London: UCL Press.

Keith, M. (2008) 'Public Sociology? Between Herioc Immersion and Critical Distance: Personal Reflections on Academic Engagement with Political Life', *Critical Social Policy*, 28, 3: 320–334.

Kesten, J. (2011) *Multiculture and Cohesion in New City Spaces*, Unpublished PhD Thesis, Milton Keynes: Open University.

Kesten, J., Cochrane, A., Mohan, G. and Neal, S. (2011) 'Multiculture and Community in New City Spaces', *Journal of Intercultural Studies*, 32, 2: 133–150.

Kettle, M. and Hodges, L. (1982) *Uprising!* London: Pan.

Kirk, R. (2004) *Skills Audit for Refugees*, London: Home Office.

Kirkwood, A. (2005) *Department for Work and Pensions: Delivery of Services to Ethnic Minority Clients Fourth Report of Session 2004–05*, London: House of Commons Work and Pensions Committee.

Kivisto, P. (2010) 'Multiculturalism and Racial Democracy: State Policies and Social Practices', in Hill Collins, P. and Solomos, J. (eds) *The Sage Handbook of Race and Ethnic Studies*, London: Sage.

Knopf, T.A. (1975) *Rumors, Race and Riots*, Brunswick, N.J.: Transaction Publishers.

Kudenko, I. and Phillips, D. (2009) 'The Model of Integration? Social and Spatial Transformations in the Leeds Jewish Community', *Journal of Ethnic and Migration Studies*, 35, 9: 533–49.

Kundnani, A. (2001) *From Oldham to Bradford: The Violence of the Violated*, London: Institute of Race Relations.

Kushner, T. and Knox, K. (1999) *Refugees in an Age of Genocide*, London: Frank Cass.

Kyriakides, C. and Virdee, S. (2003) 'Migrant Labour, Racism and the British National Health Service', *Ethnicity and Health*, 8, 4: 283–305.

Lambert, J.R. (1970a) *Crime, Police and Race Relations: A Study in Birmingham*, Oxford: Oxford University Press.

Lambert, J.R. (1970b) 'Race Relations: The Role of the Police', in Zubaida, S. (ed.) *Race and Racialism*, London: Tavistock.

Lancee, B. (2011) 'The Economic Returns of Bonding and Bridging Social Capital for Immigrant Men in Germany', *Ethnic and Racial Studies*, 36, 4: 664–684.

Lansley, S., Goss, S. and Wolmar, C. (1989) *Councils in Conflict: The Rise and Fall of the Municipal Left*, Basingstoke: Macmillan.

Law, I. (1996) *Racism, Ethnicity and Social Policy*, London: Prentice Hall.

Law, I. (2010) *Racism and Ethnicity: Global Debates, Dilemmas, Directions*, Harlow: Longman.

Law, I., Phillips, D. and Turney, L. (2004) *Institutional Racism in Higher Education*, Stoke on Trent: Trentham.

Layton-Henry, Z. (1992) *The Politics of Immigration: Immigration, 'Race' and 'Race' Relations in Post-war Britain*, Oxford: Blackwell.

Leese, M., Thornicroft, G., Shaw, J., Thomas, S., Mohan, R., Harty, M. and Dolan, M. (2006) 'Ethnic Differences among Patients in High Security Psychiatric Hospitals in England', *British Journal of Psychiatry*, 188: 380–385.

Lentin, A. and Titley, G. (2011) *The Crises of Multiculturalism: Racism in a Neoliberral Age*, London: Zed Books.

Levitt, P. (2009) 'Roots and Routes: Understanding the Lives of the Second Generation Transnationally', *Journal of Ethnic and Migration Studies*, 35, 7: 1225–1242.

Lindblom, C.E. and Woodhouse, E.J. (1993) *The Policy-Making Process*, Third Edition, Englewood Cliffs, N.J.: Prentice Hall.

Lister, R. (1998) 'From Equality to Social Exclusion: New Labour and the Welfare State', *Critical Social Policy*, 18, 2: 215–225.

Littlewood, R. and Lipsedge, M. (1997) *Aliens and Alienists: Ethnic Minorities and Psychiatry*, Third Edition, London: Routledge.

Local Authorities Coordinators of Regulatory Services (2007) 'Migrant Workers Present Housing Challenge for Councils' *Press release*, http://tinyurl.com/3warkg.

London Borough of Hackney (2010) *Community Cohesion Review*, London: Hackney Council.

London Deanery (2008) *Cultural Competency Evidence*, http://londondeanery.ac.uk/cultural competence/pdf 1-10.

Loveland, I. (1993) ' Racial Segregation in State Schools: The Parent's Right to Choose?' *Journal of Law and Society*, 20, 3: 263–323.

Macdonald, I.A., Bhavnani, R., Khan, L. and John, G. (1989) *Murder in the Playground: the Report of the Macdonald Inquiry into Racism and Racial Violence in Manchester Schools*, London: Longsight.

Macpherson, W. (1999a) *The Stephen Lawrence Inquiry*, London: Stationery Office.

Macpherson, W. (1999b) *The Stephen Lawrence Inquiry: Report of an Inquiry by Sir William Macpherson of Cluny*, London: Stationery Office.

Malik, K. (2008) *Strange Fruit: Why Both Sides are Wrong in the Race Debate*, Oxford: Oneworld.

Malik, K. (2009) *From Fatwa to Jihad: The Rushdie Affair and its Legacy*, London: Atlantic Books.

Marmot, M., Allen, J., Goldblatt, P., Boyce, T., McNeish, D., Grady, M. and Geddes, I. (2010) *Fair Society, Healthy Lives*, London: Strategic review of health inequalities in England post-2010, The Marmot Review.

Marx, G.T. (1970) 'Issueless Riots', *Annals of the American Academy of Political and Social Science*, 391: 21–33.

McCrone, P., Dhanasiri, S., Patel, A., Knapp, P. and Lawton-Smith, S. (2008) *Paying the Price: The Cost of Mental Health Care in England to 2026*, London: The Kings Fund.

McCulloch, N. (2011) 'The Erosion of Morality is Behind This', *The Sunday Telegraph*, 14 August 2011.

McDowell, L. (2008) 'On the Significance of Being White: European Migrant Workers in the British Economy in the 1940s and 2000s', in Dwyer, C. and Bressey, C. (eds) *New Geographies of Race and Racism*, Aldershot: Ashgate.

McGarrigle, J. and Kearns, A. (2009) 'Living Apart? Place, Identity and South Asian Residential Choice', *Housing Studies*, 24, 4: 451–475.

McGhee, D. (2008) *The End of Multiculturalism? Terrorism, Integration and Human Rights*, Maidenhead: Open University Press.

McKay, S. (2009) 'Looking for Work: Exploring the Job Search Methods of Recent Refugees and Migrants', in McKay, S. (ed.) *Refugees, Recent Migrants and Employment: Challenging Barriers and Exploring Pathways*, New York and London: Routledge.

McKenzie, K. and Bhui, K. (2007) 'Institutional Racism in Mental Health Care', *British Medical Journal*, 334: 649–650.

McLaughlin, E. (2007) *The New Policing*, London: Sage.

McLaughlin, E. (2010) 'Community Cohesion and National Security: Rethinking Policing and Race', in Bloch, A. and Solomos, J. (eds) *Race and Ethnicity in the 21st Century*, Basingstoke: Palgrave Macmillan.

McLaughlin, E. and Murji, K. (1999) 'After the Stephen Lawrence Report', *Critical Social Policy*, 19, 3: 371–385.

McLaughlin, E. and Neal, S. (2004) 'Misrepresenting the Multicultural Nation', *Policy Studies*, 25, 3: 155–174.

McLaughlin, E. and Neal, S. (2007) 'Who Can Speak to Race and Nation? Intellectuals, Public Policy Formation and the Future of Multi-ethnic Britain Commission', *Cultural Studies*, 21: 910–930.

McNevin, A. (2011) *Contesting Citizenship: Irregular Migrants and New Frontiers of the Political*, New York: Columbia University Press.

Meer, N. (2010) *Citizenship, Identity and the Politics of Multiculturalism: The Rise of Muslim Consciousness*, Basingstoke: Palgrave Macmillan.

Mercer, K. (1986) 'Racism and Transcultural Psychiatry', in Miller, P. and Rose, N. (eds) *The Power of Psychiatry*, Cambridge: Polity.

Merrick, J. (2011) 'Starkey Raving Bonkers!' *The Independent on Sunday*, 14 August 2011.

Metcalf, H., Modood, T. and Virdee, S. (1997) *Asian Self-Employment: The Interaction of Culture and Economics*, London: Policy Studies Institute.

Migration Observatory (2012a) *Migrants in the UK: An Overview*, Migration Observatory: University of Oxford.

Migration Observatory (2012b) *UK Public Opinion Toward Immigration: Overall Attitudes and Level of Concern*, Migration Observatory: University of Oxford.

Miles, R. and Brown, M. (2003) *Racism*, Second Edition, London: Routledge.

Miles, R. and Solomos, J. (1987) 'Migration and the State in Britain: An Historical Overview', in Husband, C. (ed.) *'Race' in Britain: Continuity and Change*, London: Hutchinson.

Miliband, D. (2006) *Building Community in a Diverse Society*, Scarman Memorial Lecture, January 2006, London: Scarman Trust.

Milton Keynes Intelligence Observatory (2010) *Schools Census 2010*, Milton Keynes: Milton Keynes Council.

MIND (2011) *A Collective Failure for Race Equality in Mental Health*: http://www.mind.org.uk/blog/4839

Ministry of Justice (2010) *Statistics on Race and the Criminal Justice System 2008/09*, London: Ministry of Justice.

Mirza, M., Senthkumaran, A. and Ja ' far, Z. (2007) *Living Apart Together: British Muslims and the Paradox of Multiculturalism*, London: Policy Exchange.

Modood, T., Berthoud, R., Lakey, J., Nazroo, J.Y., Smith, P., Virdee, S. and Beishon, S. (1997) *Ethnic Minorities in Britain: Diversity and Disadvantage*, London: Policy Studies Institute.

Mooney, G. and Neal, S. (eds) (2009) *Community: Welfare, Crime and Society*, Maidenhead: McGraw Hill.

Moore, K. (2008) 'Class Formations: Competing Forms of Black Middle Class Identity', *Ethnicities*, 8, 4: 492–517.

Morissens, A. and Sainsbury, D. (2005) 'Migrants' Social Rights, Ethnicity and Welfare Regimes', *Journal of Social Policy*, 34, 4: 637–660.

Morris, L. (2007) 'New Labour's Community of Rights: Welfare, Immigration and Asylum', *Journal of Social Policy*, 36, 1: 39–57.

Murji, K. and Neal, S. (2011) 'Riot: Race and Politics in the 2011 Disorders', *Sociological Research Online*, 16, 4: 24.

Mynott, E. (2002) 'From a Shambles to a New Apartheid: Local Authorities, Dispersal and the Struggle to Defend Asylum Seekers', in Cohen, S., Humphries, B. and Mynott, E. (eds) *From Immigration Controls to Welfare Controls*, London: Routledge.

National Aids Trust (2008) *The Myth of HIV Tourism*, London: National Aids Trust.

National Audit Office (2008) *Increasing Employment Rates for Ethnic Minorities*, London: National Audit Office and Department for Work and Pensions.

National Cancer Intelligence Network and Cancer Research UK (2009) *Cancer Incidence and Survival by Major Ethnic Group, England 2002–2006*,London: Cancer Research UK with London School of Hygiene and Tropical Medicine.

National Health Service (2005) *Health Survey for England 2004: The Health of Minority Groups – The Headline Tables*, London: NHS Health and Social Care Information Centre.

Nayak, A. (2006) 'After Race: Ethnography, Race and Post-race Theory', *Ethnic and Racial Studies*, 29, 3: 411–430.

Nayak, A. (2008) 'Young Peoples' Geographies of Racism and Anti-racism: The Case of the North-East of England', in Dwyer, C. and Bressey, C. (eds) *The New Geographies of Race and Racism*, Aldershot: Ashgate.

Nazroo, J.Y. (1997) *The Health of Britain's Ethnic Minorities: Findings from a National Survey*, London: Policy Studies Institute.

Nazroo, J.Y. (2001) *Ethnicity, Health and Class*, London: Policy Studies Institute.

Nazroo, J.Y. (2010) 'Health and Health Care', in Bloch, A. and Solomos, J. (eds) *Race and Ethnicity in the 21st Century*, Basingstoke: Palgrave Macmillan.

Neal, S. (1998a) 'Embodying Black Madness, Embodying White Feminity: Populist (Re)presentations and Public Policy', *Sociological Research Online*, 3, 4.

Neal, S. (1998b) *The Making of Equal Opportunities Policies in Universities*, Buckingham: Open University Press.

Neal, S. (2003) 'The Scarman Report, the Macpherson Report and the Media: How Newspapers Respond to Race-centred Social Policy Interventions', *Journal of Social Policy*, 32, 1: 55–74.

Neal, S. (2009) *Rural Identities: Ethnicity and Community in the Contemporary English Countryside*, Aldershot: Ashgate.

Neal, S., Bennett, K., Cochrane, A. and Mohan, G. (2013) 'Living Multiculture: Understanding the New Social and Spatial Relations of Ethnicity and Multiculture in England', *Environment and Planning C, Policy and Governance*.

Nee, V. and Sanders, J. (2001) 'Understanding the Diversity of Immigrant Incorporation: A Forms-of-Capital Model', *Ethnic and Racial Studies*, 24, 3: 386–411.

Newburn, T. (2011) *Reading the Riots*, London: London School of Economics.

Noble, G. (2010) '"Where the Bloody Hell are We?" Multicultural Manners in a World of Hyperdiversity', in Noble, G. (ed.) *Lines in the Sand: The Cronulla Riots, Multiculturalism and National Belonging*, Sydney: Sydney Institute of Criminology.

Office for National Statistics (2006) *Focus on Ethnicity: Employment Patterns*, London: Office for National Statistics.

Office of Deputy Prime Minister (2006) *The State of English Cities: Urban Research Summary 21*, London: Office of the Deputy Prime Minister.

Office of National Statistics (2011) *Populations Estimates for Ethnic Group (experimental) Mid-2009*, London: Office of National Statistics.

Office for National Statistics (2012) *Ethnicity and National Identity in England and Wales 2011*, London: Office of National Statistics.

Oldham Independent Review (2001) *One Oldham, One Future*, Oldham: Oldham Independent Review.

Olzak, S. and Shanahan, S. (1996) 'Deprivation and Race Riots: An Extension of Spilerman's Analysis', *Social Forces*, 74, 3: 931–961.

Ouseley, H. (2001) *Community Pride, Not Prejudice: Making Diversity Work in Bradford*, Bradford: Bradford Vision.

Owen, D., Reza, B., Green, A., Maguire, M. and Pitcher, J. (2000) 'Patterns of Labour Market Participation in Ethnic Minority Groups', *Labour Market Trends*, November, 505–510.

Owuor, J. (2009) *HIV Prevention Among Black Africans in England: A Complex Challenge*, London: Race Equality Foundation.

Panayi, P. (1993) 'Refugees in Twentieth Century Britain: A Brief History', in Robinson, V. (ed.) *The International Refugee Crisis: British and Canadian Responses*, Basingstoke: Macmillan.

Panayi, P. (1994) *Immigration, Race and Ethnicity in Britain:1815–1945*, Manchester: Manchester University Press.

Panayi, P. (2010) *An Immigration History of Britain: Multicultural Racism since 1800*, London: Longman.

Papadopoulos, I. (2006) 'The Papadopolos, Tilki and Taylor Model for Developing Cultural Competence', in Papadopoulos, I. (ed.) *Transcultural Health and Social Care: Developing Culturally Competent Practitioners*, Oxford: Elsevier.

Parekh, B. (2000) *The Future of Multi-Ethnic Britain: Report of the Commission on the Future of Multi-Ethnic Britain*, London: Profile Books.

Parsons, C. (2008) 'Race Relations Legislation, Ethnicity and Disproportionality in School Exclusions in England', *Cambridge Journal of Education*, 38, 3: 401–419.

Parsons, C., Godfrey, R., Annan, G., Cornwall, J., Dussart, M., Hepburn, S., Howlett, K. and Wennerstrom, J. (2005) *Minority Ethnic Exclusions and the Race Relations (Amendment) Act 2000*, London: DfES.

Paul, K. (1997) *Whitewashing Britain: Race and Citizenship in the Postwar Era*, Ithaca: Cornell University Press.

Peach, C. (1986) 'Patterns of Afro-Carribean Migration and Settlement in Britain', in Brock, C. (ed.) *The Caribbean in Europe: Aspects of West Indian Experience in Britain, France and the Netherlands*, London: Frank Cass.

Peach, C. (2008) *Slippery Segregation: Discovering or Manufacturing Ghettoes?* University of Manchester: University of Manchester Institute for Social Change Working Paper.

Peach, C. (2009) 'Slippery Segregation: Discovering or Manufacturing Ghettos?' *Journal of Ethnic and Migration Studies*, 35, 9: 1381–1395.

Perry, J. (2005) 'Housing Refugees and People Seeking Asylum', in Harrison, M., Phillips, D., Chahal, K., Hunt, L. and Perry, J. (eds) *'Race', Housing and Community Cohesion*, Coventry: Chartered Institute of Housing.

Perry, J. (2008) *The Housing and Neighbourhood Impact of Britain's Changing Ethnic Mix: Reviewing the Evidence*, York: Joseph Rowntree Foundation.

Phillimore, J. (2011) 'Approaches to Health Provision in the Age of Super-Diversity: Accessing the NHS in Britain's Most Diverse City', *Critical Social Policy*, 31, 1: 5–29.

Phillips, D. (2006a) 'Moving Towards Integration: The Housing of Aylum Seekers and Refugees in Britain', *Housing Studies*, 21, 4: 539–553.

Phillips, D. (2006b) 'Parallel Pives? Challenging Discourses of British Muslim Self-segregation', *Environment and Planning D-Society & Space*, 24, 1: 25–40.

Phillips, D. (2010a) *Claiming Spaces and Negotiating Urban Citizenship: Accommodating New Migrants in the UK*, Paper presented to the Association of America Geographers Conference Washington D.C.

Phillips, D. (2010b) 'Minority Ethnic Segregation, Integration and Citizenship: A European Perspective', *Journal of Ethnic and Migration Studies*, 36, 2: 209–225.

Phillips, T. (2005a) *Britain: Pride in Diversity*, Manchester: Council for Community Relations, 22 September 2005.

Phillips, T. (2005b) *Highway Code for Multi-Ethnic Britain*, Speech to Conservative Party Conference Muslim Forum, 3 October 2005.

Phoenix, A. (2009) 'De-colonising Practices: Negotiating Narratives from Racialised and Gendered Experiences of Education', *Race, Ethnicity and Education*, 12, 1: 101–114.

Platt, L. (2007) *Poverty and Ethnicity in the UK*, York: Joseph Rowntree Foundation.

Popkin, S., Levy, D. and Buron, L. (2009) 'Has Hope VI Transformed Residents' Lives? New Evidence from the Hope VI Panel Study', *Housing Studies*, 24, 4: 477–502.

Portes, A., Escobar, C. and Arana, R. (2008) 'Bridging the Gap: Transnational and Ethnic Organizations in the Political Incorporation of Immigrants in the United States', *Ethnic and Racial Studies*, 31, 6: 1056–1090.

Poulsen, M. and Johnston, R. (2008) 'The "New Geography" of Ethnicity in England and Wales?' in Dwyer, C. and Bressey, C. (eds) *New Geographies of Race and Racism*, Aldershot: Ashgate.

Poynting, S., Noble, G. and Collins, J. (2004) *Bin Laden in the Suburbs, Criminalising the Arab Other*, Sydney: Institute of Criminology.

Proctor, S. and Smith, I. (1997) 'Factors associated with birth outcome in Bradford Pakistanis', in Clarke, A. and Parsons, E. (eds) *Culture, Kinship and Genes*, Basingstoke: Macmillan.

Purcell, K., Elias, P., Ellison, R., Atfield, G., Adam, D. and Livanos, I. (2008) *Applying for Higher Education – The Diversity of Career Choices, Plans and Expectations. Findings from the First Futuretrack Survey of the 'Class of 2006' Applications for Higher Education*, Coventry: IER/HECSU, University of Warwick.

Putnam, R.D. (2000) *Bowling Alone. The Collapse and Revival of American Community*, New York: Simon and Schuster.

Putnam, R.D. (2007) 'E Pluribus Unum: Diversity and Community in the Tewenty-first Century. The 2006 Johan Skytte Prize Lecture', *Scandinavian Political Studies*, 30, 5: 137–174.

Race for Opportunity (2009) *Race into Higher Education*. Business in the Community.

Raghuram, P. (2009) 'Caring about "Brain Drain" Migration in a Postcolonial World', *Geoforum*, 40: 25–33.

Ratcliffe, P. (2004) *'Race', Ethnicity, and Difference: Imagining the Inclusive Society*, Maidenhead: Open University Press.

Ratcliffe, P. (2009) 'Re-evaluating the Links Between "Race" and Residence', *Housing Studies*, 24, 4: 433–450.

Ratcliffe, P., Harrison, M., Hogg, R., Line, B., Phillips, D. and Tomlins, R. (2001) *Breaking Down Barriers: Improving Asian Access to Social Rented Housing*, London: Charted Institute of Housing.

Reay, D., David, M.E. and Ball, S.J. (2005) *Degrees of Choice: Class, Gender and Race in the Higher Education Choice Process*, Stoke on Trent: Trentham Books.

Reay, D., Hollingworth, S., Williams, K., Crozier, G., Jamieson, F., James, D. and Beedell, P. (2007) '"A Darker Shade of Pale?" Whiteness, the Middle Classes and Multi-ethnic Inner City Schooling' *Sociology*, 41, 6: 1041–1060.

Refugee Council (1999) 'Catch 22', *iNexile* 5 : 4–5.

Rendall, M. and Salt, J. (2005) 'The Foreign-Born Population', in Chappell, R. (ed.) *Focus on People and Migration*, Basingstoke: Palgrave Macmillan.

Rex, J. and Moore, R. (1967) *Race, Community and Conflict: A Study of Sparkbrook*, Oxford: Oxford University Press.

Rex, J. and Tomlinson, S. (1979) *Colonial Immigrants in a British City: A Class Analysis*, London: Routledge & Kegan Paul.

Rhodes, J. (2009a) 'The Political Breakthrough of the BNP: The Case of Burnley', *British Politics*, 4, 1: 22–46.

Rhodes, J. (2009b) 'Revisiting the 2001 Riots: New Labour,and the Rise of "Colour Blind Racism"', *Sociological Research Online*, 14, 5: 3.

Rhodes, J. (2011) '"It's Not Just Them, It's Whites as Well": Whiteness, Class and BNP Support', *Sociology*, 45, 1: 102–117.

Robinson, D., Coward, S., Forham, T., Green, S. and Reeve, K. (2004) *How Housing Management Can Contribute to Community Cohesion*, Coventry: Chartered Institute of Housing/Housing Corporation.

Robinson, D. and Reeve, K. (2006) *Neighbourhood Experiences of New Immigration: Reflections on the Evidence Base*, York: Joseph Rowntree Foundation.

Robinson, D., Reeve, K. and Casey, R. (2007) *The Housing Pathways of New Immigrants*, York: Joseph Rowntree Foundation.

Robinson, V. (1993) 'Marching into the Middle Classes? The Long-term Settlement of East African Asians in the UK', *Journal of Refugee Studies*, 6, 3: 230–247.

Robinson, V., Andersson, R. and Musterd, S. (2003) *Spreading the Burden: A Review of Policies to Disperse Asylum Seekers*, Bristol: Policy Press.

Robinson, V. and Carey, M. (2000) 'Peopling Skilled International Migration: Indian Doctors in the UK', *International Migration*, 38: 89–108.

Robinson, V. and Segrott, J. (2002) *Understanding the Decision Making of Asylum Seekers*, London: Home Office.

Rocheron, Y. (1988) 'The Asian Mother and Baby Campaign: The Construction of Ethnic Minorities' Health Needs', *Critical Social Policy*, 22: 4–23.

Rogaly, B. and Taylor, B. (2009) *Moving Histories of Class and Community: Identity, Place and Belonging in Contemporary England*, London: Palgrave Macmillan.

Rollock, N. (2009) *The Stephen Lawrence Inquiry 10 Years On: An Analysis of the Literature*, London: Runnymede Trust.

Rowe, M. (2004) *Policing, Race and Racism*, Cullompton: Willan.

Rowe, M. (ed.) (2007) *Policing Beyond Macpherson: Issues in Policing, Race and Society*, Cullopmton: Willan Publishing.

Runnymede Trust (2011) *Community Cohesion – Where Next for Schools? A Briefing for Teachers, NGOs and Policy-Makers*, London: Runnymede Trust.

Rutter, J. and Latorre, M. (2009) *Social Housing Allocation and Immigrant Communities*, London: Equalities and Human Rights Commission.

Sabater, A. (2008) *Ethnic Segregation Over Time and Cohorts in England and Wales, 1991–2001*, University of Manchester: Cathie Marsh Centre for Census and Survey Research, Working Paper 14.

Sales, R. (2002) 'The Deserving and the Undeserving? Refugees, Asylum Seekers and Welfare in Britain', *Critical Social Policy*, 22, 3: 456–478.

Sales, R. (2007) *Understanding Immigration and Refugee Policy: Contradictions and Continuities*, Bristol: The Policy Press.

Salway, S., Nazroo, J.Y., Mir, G., Craig, G., Johnson, M. and Gerrish, K. (2010) 'Fair Society, Healthy Lives: A Missed Opportunity to Address Ethnic Inequalities in Health', *BMJ Rapid Response*, 340 c684.

Sarre, P. (1986) 'Choice and Constraint in Ethnic Minority Housing: A Structurationist View', *Housing Studies*, 1, 2: 71–86.

Sarre, P., Phillips, D. and Skellington, R. (1989) *Ethnic Minority Housing: Explanation and Policy*, Aldershot: Avebury.

Sashidharan, S. (1993) 'Afro-Caribbeans and Schizophrenia: The Ethnic Vulnerability Hypothesis Re-examined', *International Review of Psychiatry*, 5: 129–144.

Sashidharan, S. and Francis, E. (1993) ' Epidemiology, Ethnicity and Schizophrenia', in Ahmad, W. (ed.) *'Race' and Health in Contemporary Britain*, Buckingham: Open University Press.

Scarman, L. (1981a) *The Brixton Disorders 10–12 April 1981. Report of an Inquiry by the Rt. Hon. The Lord Scarman OBE*, London: HMSO.

Scarman, L. (1981b) *The Brixton Disorders 10–12 April 1981. Report of an Inquiry by the Rt. Hon. The Lord Scarman OBE*, London: HMSO.

Scarman, L. (1985) 'Brixton and After', in Roach, J. and Thomaneck, J. (eds) *Police and Public Order in Europe*, London: Croom Helm.

Schuster, L. and Solomos, J. (2004) 'Race, Immigration and Asylum: New Labour's Agenda and its Consequences', *Ethnicities*, 4, 2: 267–300.

Scott, S. (2011) 'The Voices of Tottenham are Being Marginalised', *The Guardian*, 17 October 2011.

Select Committee on Race Relations and Immigration (1969) *The Problems of Coloured School Leavers*, London: HMSO.

Select Committee on Race Relations and Immigration (1972) *Police/Immigrant Relations*, London: HMSO.

Select Committee on Race Relations and Immigration (1977) *The West Indian Community*, London: HMSO.

Shah, B., Dwyer, C. and Modood, T. (2010) 'Explaining Educational Achievement and Career Aspirations among Young British Pakistanis: Mobilizing "Ethnic Capital?"' *Sociology*, 44, 6: 1109–1127.

Shelter (2008) 'Eastern European Migrant Workers and Housing: Policy Briefing'. http://www.shelter.org.uk/policybriefings.

Simpson, L., Husband, C. and Alam, Y. (2009) 'Comment: Recognising Complexity, Challenging Pessimism: The Case of Bradford's Urban Dynamics', *Urban Studies*, 46, 9: 1995–2001.

Simpson, L. and Peach, C. (2009) 'Measurement and Analysis of Segregation, Integration and Diversity: Editorial Introduction', *Journal of Ethnic and Migration Studies*, 35, 9: 1377–1380.

Simpson, L., Purdam, K., Tajar, A., Fieldhouse, E., Gavalas, V., Tranmer, M., Pritchard, J. and Dorling, D. (2006) *Ethnic Minority Populations and the Labour Market: An Analysis of the 1991 and 2001 Census*, London: Department of Work and Pensions.

Singh, S.P. and Burns, T. (2006) 'Race and Mental Illness: There is More to Race than Racism', *British Medical Journal*, 333: 648–651.

Smaje, C. (1995) *Health 'Race' and Ethnicity: Making Sense of the Evidence*, London: King's Fund Institute.

Smaje, C. (1996) 'The Ethnic Patterning of Health: New Directions for Theory and Research', *Sociology of Health & Illness*, 18, 2: 139–171.

Small, S. (1983) *Police and People in London. II A Group of Young Black People*, London: Policy Studies Institute.

Smelser, N.J., Wilson, W.J. and Mitchell, F. (eds) (2001) *America Becoming: Racial Trends and their Consequences, Volumes One and Two*, Washington D.C.: National Academy Press.

Smith, S.J. (1986) *Crime, Space, and Society*, Cambridge: Cambridge University Press.

Solomos, J. (1988) *Black Youth, Racism and the State: The Politics of Ideology and Policy*, Cambridge: Cambridge University Press.

Solomos, J. (1989) 'Equal Opportunities Policies and Racial Inequality: The Role of Public Policy', *Public Administration*, 67, 1: 79–93.

Solomos, J. (1999) 'Social Research and the Stephen Lawrence Inquiry', *Sociological Research Online*, <Go to ISI>://0000798474000054, 1, March.

Solomos, J. (2003) *Race and Racism in Britain*, Third Edition, Basingstoke: Palgrave Macmillan.

Solomos, J. (2011) 'Race, Rumours and Riots: Past, Present and Future', *Sociological Research Online*, 16, 4, http://www.socresonline.org.uk/16/4/20.html.

Somerville, W. (2007) *Immigration under New Labour*, Bristol: Policy Press.

Spencer, I.R.G. (1997) *British Immigration Policy Since 1939 : The Making of Multi-Racial Britain*, London: Routledge.

Spickard, P.R. (2007) *Almost all Aliens: Immigration, Race, and Colonialism in American History and Identity*, New York: Routledge.

Stewart, E. (2003) *A Bitter Pill to Swallow: Obstacles Facing Refugee and Overseas Doctors in the UK, New Issues in Refugee Research, Working Paper 96*, Geneva: UNHCR.

Stratton, A. (2011) 'UK Riots: Cameron and Miliband Go Head to Head in Riot Aftermath', *The Guardian*, 15 August 2011.

Sveinsson, K.P. (2012) *Criminal Justice v. Racial Justice: Overrepresentation in the Criminal Justice System*, London: Runnymede Trust.

Swann Report (1985) *Education for All: Report of the Committee of Inquiry into the Education of Children from Minority Ethnic Groups*, London: Her Majesty's Stationery Office.

Swanton, D. (2008) 'Everyday Multiculture and the Emergence of Race', in Dwyer, C. and Bressey, C. (eds) *The New Geographies of Race and Racism*, Aldershot: Ashgate.

Taylor, B. and Rogaly, B. (2004) *Migrant Working in West Norfolk*, University of Sussex: Sussex Centre for Migration Research.

Titmuss, R.M. (1974) *Social Policy: An Introduction*, London: George Allen & Unwin.

Tolley, J. and Rundle, J. (2006) *A Review of Black and Minority Ethnic Participation in Higher Education*, London: Aimhigher.

Townsend, P. and Davidson, N. (1982) *Inequalities in Health: The Black Report*, Harmondsworth: Penguin.

Troyna, B. and Carrington, B. (1990) *Education, Racism and Reform*, London: Routledge.

Troyna, B. and Williams, J. (1986) *Racism, Education, and the State*, London: Croom Helm.

Twomey, J. and Reynolds, M. (2011) 'New the Riots Spread as Twitter Thugs Fan Flames', *The Express*, 9 August 2011.

Tyler, K. (2006) 'Village People: Race, Class, Nation and the Community Spirit', in Neal, S. and Agyeman, J. (eds) *The New Countryside? Ethnicity, Nation and Exclusion in Contemporary Rural Britain*, Bristol: Policy Press.

Valentine, G. (2008) 'Living with Difference: Reflections on Geographies of Encounter', *Progress in Human Geography*, 32, 3: 323–337.

Vertovec, S. (2007) 'Super-Diversity and its Implications', *Ethnic and Racial Studies*, 30, 6: 1024–1054.

Vincent, C. (1992) 'Tolerating Intolerance? Parental Choice and Race Relations – The Cleveland Case', *Journal of Education Policy*, 7, 5: 429–443.

Vincent, C. and Ball, S.J. (2006) *Childcare, Choice and Class Practices*, London: Routledge Falmer.

Vincent, C. and Ball, S.J. (2007) '"Making Up" the Middle-Class Child: Families, Activities and Class Dispositions', *Sociology*, 41, 6: 1061–1077.

Vincent, C., Rollock, N., Ball, S.J. and Gillborn, D. (2011) *The Educational Strategies of the Black Middle Classes: Project Summary*, London: Institute of Education.

Virdee, S. (2010) 'The Continuing Significance of "Race": Racism, Contentious Antiracist Politics and Labour Markets in Contemporary Capitalism', in Bloch, A. and Solomos, J. (eds) *Race and Ethnicity in the 21st Century*, Basingstoke: Palgrave Macmillan.

Waddington, D., Jobard, F. and King, M. (eds) (2009) *Rioting in the UK and France: A Comparative Analysis*, Cullompton: Willan Publishing.

Ward, L. (1993) 'Race, Equality and Employment in the National Health Service' in W. Ahmed (ed.) *'Race' and Health in Contemporary Britain*, Hemel Hempstead: Open University Press

Warren, S. (2005) 'Resilience and Refusal: African-Caribbean Young Men's Agency, School Exclusions, and School-Based Mentoring Programmes', *Race, Ethnicity and Education*, 8, 3: 243–259.

Watt, P. (2009) 'Housing Stock Transfers, Regeneration and State-led Gentrification in London', *Urban Policy and Research*, 27, 3: 229–242.

Webster, C. (2012) 'Different Forms of Discrimination in the Criminal Justice System', in Sveinsson, K.P. (ed.) *Criminal Justice v. Racial Justice: Overrepresentation in the Criminal Justice System*, London: Runnymede Trust.

Weekes-Bernard, D. (2007) *School Choice and Ethnic Segregation: Education Decision-making among Black and Minority Ethnic Parents*, London: Runnymede Trust.

Wessendorf, S. (2012) *Commonplace Diversity and the 'Ethos of Mixing': Perceptions of Difference in a London Neighbourhood*, Oxford: COMPAS Working Paper.

Wilkinson, S.I. (2009) 'Riots', *Annual Review of Political Science*, 12, 1: 329–343.

Wills, J., Datta, K., Evans, Y., Herbert, J., May, J. and McIlwaine, C. (2010) *Global Cities at Work: New Migrant Divisions of Labour*, London: Pluto.

Wise, A. (2009) 'Everyday Multiculturalism: Transversal Crossings and Working Class Cosmopolitans', in Wise, A. and Velayutham, S. (eds) *Everyday Multiculturalism*, Basingstoke: Palgrave Macmillan.

Wohland, P., Rees, P., Norman, P., Boden, P. and Jasinka, M. (2010) *Ethnic Populations Projections for the UK and Local Areas 2001–2051*, Leeds: University of Leeds.

World Health Organisation (2010) *Health Systems Financing: The Path to Universal Coverage*, Geneva: World Health Organisation.

Xu, Y. (2007) 'Strangers in Strange Lands: A Metasynthesis of Lived Experiences of Immigrant Asian Nurses Working in Western Countries', *Advances in Nursing Science*, 30, 246–265.

Zetter, R. and Pearl, M. (2000) 'The Minority Within the Minority: Refugee Community-Based Organisations in the UK and the Impact of Restrictionism on Asylum Seekers', *Journal of Ethnic and Migration Studies*, 26, 4: 675–697.

Zontini, E. (2010) *Transnational Families, Migration, and Gender: Moroccan and Filipino Women in Bologna and Barcelona*, New York: Berghahn Books.

Index